Classroom

Other titles of interest...

Teaching Speaking and Listening in the Primary School 3e
Elizabeth Grugeon, Lyn Dawes, Carol Smith and Lorraine Hubbard
1-84312-255-3

Literacy through Creativity
Prue Goodwin
1-84312-087-9

Language Knowledge for Primary Teachers 3e
Angela Wilson
1-84312-318-5

Literacy Moves On
Using Popular Culture, New Technologies & Critical Literacy in the Primary Classroom
Janet Evans
1-84312-249-9

Teaching Literacy
Using Texts to Enhance Learning
David Wray
1-85346-717-0

Writing Under Control 2e
Judith Graham and Alison Kelly
1-84312-017-8

Reading Under Control 2e
Judith Graham and Alison Kelly
1-85346-646-8

The Literate Classroom

Second Edition

Edited by Prue Goodwin

 **David Fulton** Publishers

Acknowledgements

The illustrations within chapter 14 are reproduced by the kind permission of Crick Software (www.cricksoftware.com) and 2Simple Software (www.2simple.com).

This edition reprinted 2009 by Routledge
2 Park Square, Milton Park, Abingdon, Oxon OX14 4RN
Simultaneously published in the USA and Canada
By Routledge
270 Madison Avenue, New York, NY 10016

First published in Great Britain in 1999 by David Fulton Publishers.

British Library Cataloguing in Publication Data
A catalogue record for this book is available from the British Library.

ISBN 1 84312 318 5

Typeset by FiSH Books, London

Contents

About the contributors

Suzi Clipson-Boyles is an education adviser and author. She has written extensively about drama and delivers workshops nationally. She has been a headteacher in three schools and was previously a principal lecturer at Oxford Brookes University where she also led the team that developed the nationally-renowned Catch Up programme.

Geoff Fenwick taught in primary schools in the UK and East Africa for 15 years before becoming a lecturer in higher education, specialising in language and literature. He is currently honorary lecturer and associate member of Education Research Centre, Liverpool John Moores University. He has written a considerable number of books and papers on language education

Prue Goodwin taught in primary and middle schools for over 20 years and was an advisory teacher for language development before taking up a post at the University of Reading. Prue edited *The Literate Classroom* in 1999, a companion volume *The Articulate Classroom* in 2001 and *Literacy through Creativity* in 2004 (all published by David Fulton).

Teresa Grainger is a principal lecturer at Canterbury Christ Church University College. Although most of her time is spent in teacher education, she still teaches regularly in classrooms where her particular interests are in the language arts. Her published work includes *Practical Storytelling in the Primary Classroom* (Scholastic, 1997), *Resourcing Drama 5–8* and *Resourcing Drama 8–14* with Mark Cremin (NATE, 2000) and *Inclusive Educational Practice: Literacy* with Janet Tod (David Fulton 2000).

Judith Graham is officially retired but she still works occasionally at Roehampton University, and the Faculty of Education in Cambridge. Her interests are in all areas of literacy and children's literature. She is the author of *Pictures on the Page* and *Cracking Good Books* (NATE 1990 and 1997) and co-editor (with Alison Kelly) of *Reading Under Control* and *Writing Under Control* (David Fulton 2000 and 2003, second editions). Her most recent publication (with Fiona Collins) is *Historical Fiction: Capturing the Past* (David Fulton 2001).

Nigel Hall is Professor of Literacy Education at the Institute of Education, Manchester Metropolitan University. He is a co-founder and joint-editor of the *Journal of Early Childhood Literacy*, and is on the editorial board of *Reading Research Quarterly*. He has interests in young children's developing knowledge of language and literacy, particularly with respect to punctuation, play and literacy, and writing and has published extensively in all the above areas. Nigel is also Director of the Punctuation Project, which seeks to understand how children make sense of punctuation and how teachers might best teach it.

George Hunt has taught in several London primary schools and has worked on literacy programmes in Dominica, Mongolia and South Africa. He is currently a Lecturer in Language in Education at the University of Edinburgh. His publications include *Inspirations for Grammar* (Scholastic 1994) and *Curriculum Bank: Reading at Key Stage 2* (Scholastic 1995).

Gillian Lathey is Reader in Children's Literature at Roehampton University and Deputy Director of the National Centre for Research in Children's Literature. She was for many years an infant teacher in north London, and combines interests in children, childhood and literature by teaching an MA in children's literature, supervising doctoral students in children's literature, and researching the practices and history of translating for children. She also administers the biennial Marsh Award for children's literature in translation.

Liz Laycock has been involved in primary education for several decades as a classroom teacher, an advisory teacher and in higher education and ITE. She was Programme Convener for the Primary PGCE and Director of Programmes in the Faculty of Education at Roehampton University. She is a contributor to *Reading under Control, Writing under Control, Literacy through Creativity, Historical Fiction for Children* and *Education in the United Kingdom* all published by David Fulton.

Maureen Lewis has worked as a teacher, university lecturer, education researcher and as a regional director for the National Literacy Strategy and Primary National Strategy. She has published extensively including classroom materials and books such as *Extending Literacy* (Routledge), *Writing Frames* and *Writing across the Curriculum* (Reading and Language Information Centre) and *Literacy in the Secondary School* (David Fulton).

Michael Lockwood taught in schools for eight years before becoming a Lecturer in English and Education at the University of Reading. His publications include *Opportunities for English in the Primary School* (Trentham 1996), *Practical Ways to Teach Standard English and Language Study, Poetry in and out of the Literacy Hour* and *Drama in and out of the Literacy Hour* (all three published by the Reading and Language Information Centre, The University of Reading).

Tony Martin is head of the Education Development Unit at St Martin's College from where he works with teachers and schools on inservice projects and courses in different parts of the country. Tony is a past president of the United Kingdom Reading Association (now the United Kingdom Literacy Association, UKLA) and has published a number of books on the teaching of English/literacy. The most recent is *The Really Useful Literacy Book* (with Chira Lovat and Glynis Purnell), Routledge-Falmer 2004.

Catriona Nicholson was, for many years, a teacher in primary and special schools before becoming a Lecturer in English and Children's Literature at Reading University. She has been a co-director of CIRCL (Reading) and was a tutor on the MA course in children's literature. Recent publications include contributions to *A Necessary Fantasy: The Heroic Figure in Children's Popular Culture* (Garland 2000), *The Cambridge Guide to Children's Books in English* (CUP 2001), *Literacy Through Creativity* (David Fulton 2004), and *Children in War* (DSM Technical Publications 2004) with Michael Lockwood.

Olivia O'Sullivan is currently Assistant Director of the Centre for Literacy in Primary Education. She coordinates ICT training and initiatives at CLPE and has led substantial literacy projects and courses. She is co-author with Anne Thomas of *Understanding Spelling*, the result of a three-year research project, and has contributed to a range of CLPE publications including *The Reading Book* and *Whole-to-part Phonics*. She has recently directed a research project looking at raising boys' achievement in literacy which resulted in the book *Boys on the Margin* (CLPE 2004).

Margaret Perkins has worked in initial teacher training for many years in different institutions. She previously taught across the primary age range, although she is predominantly an early years teacher. Her research has been principally into teachers as readers and the teaching of reading. She has a keen interest in children's ideas about and response to popular culture.

Chris Powling was in education for 30 years as a class teacher, a head and a lecturer in English at King Alfred's University College, Winchester. He is author of many books for young readers and was editor of Books for Keeps for seven years. He is an enthusiastic participant in the writers-in-schools initiative and regularly undertakes INSET with primary teachers.

Ruth Wood worked as a primary school teacher for ten years prior to becoming a senior lecturer for Information and Communications Technology at Kingston University. She currently works in initial teacher training and the INSET CPD programme. She is interested in a wide range of aspects related to the integration of ICT within the educational context and has developed a particular interest in the design and development of multimedia talking books.

David Wray is Professor of Education at the University of Warwick. He was previously Reader in Literacy at the University of Exeter and the co-director of the Exeter Extending Literacy Project (EXEL) funded by the Nuffield Foundation. He has wide experience of working in primary schools and has published many books and articles related to literacy.

The literate classroom: an introduction

Prue Goodwin

This book is about teaching children to read and write. It contains a collection of chapters by authors, all of whom are experienced classroom practitioners, accomplished at literacy teaching and committed to supporting colleagues through the sharing of good practice. The book aims to highlight issues about literacy learning which are currently under debate and to give practical guidance on teaching. With 19 contributors, it is not surprising that there are different styles in the presentation of the research, opinions and case studies that illustrate the best ways to support children's developing literacy. Some chapters give straightforward descriptions of research projects, with their consequent impact on pedagogy, while others express strongly held views about classroom experience or offer suggestions of immediate practical value. All are deeply concerned to support teachers in offering their pupils the most effective literacy learning experiences possible.

Creating a literate community

Every school is a literate community and every classroom a special place with its own communal values: children's attitudes about reading and writing reflect those values. Where children believe themselves to be readers and writers they will read and write. Teachers should strive to provide a place where children experience what it is like to be literate; a community of readers and writers who – through purposeful discussion – spark ideas, support each other and celebrate the power and pleasure of literacy. Successful literacy learning takes place where there is purposeful talk about reading and writing. The teacher's role in providing opportunities for purposeful talk, interaction and collaboration is a focal point of this book.

⌣ than one sort of literacy

Multi modal

Although the chapters in this book concentrate principally on being able to read and write in a conventional sense, constructing meaning from the printed page has long been too limited a view of what literacy means. 'Children now have available to them many forms of text which include sound, voices, intonation, stance, gesture, movement, as well as print and image.' (Bearne 2003). Pupils are familiar with both creating and interpreting multimodal texts and we should remember that, even in the most traditional definition of reading, print will not appear exclusively on paper but will be presented on screens, on mobile phones and as part of a myriad of other media. Equally, writers produce a wide variety of texts using a range of tools. These days children are experienced with film, animation, video and computer texts in addition to more usual 'pen to paper' and word processing techniques.

Becoming a reader

There is more to being a reader than being able to read. Readers not only know how to read but about reading and about being a reader. They feel in control of their reading, confident about their preferred literary choices and aware of how their literacy can influence everyday situations. Teachers must provide the experiences and the learning environment to enable all children to achieve their potential as readers. It is essential to get the balance right when introducing children to the complex interweaving of skills, experiences and emotions involved in learning to read.

Experienced teachers know that no single teaching method nor set of books 'teach' reading. As the Bullock Report, *A Language for Life*, pointed out in 1975:

> There is no method, medium, approach, device or philosophy that holds the key to the process of learning to read. We believe that the knowledge does exist to imporove the teaching of reading, but that it does not lie in the triumphant discovery, or rediscovery, of a particular formula. Simple endorsements of one or another nostrum are of no service to the teaching of reading. A glance at the past reveals the truth of this. The main arguments about how reading should be taught have been repeated over and over again as the decades pass, but the problems remain. (p. 77)

Successful teachers of literacy engage their pupils in the pleasure of reading as much as in functional tasks, ensuring that learning to read never becomes a chore and that, every day, books are shared for sheer enjoyment. Reading aloud to children is essential: it engages imaginations and inspires youngsters to pick up books for themselves. What better way can there be to teach the purposes of literacy than to demonstrate how it provides us all with enlightenment, comfort and delight?

To ensure that children have a broad and balanced experience when learning to read, teachers should:

- Provide experiences that demonstrate and develop the processes of reading and the meaning making strategies for all the different sorts of reading (e.g. through shared or guided reading)
- Make strategic interventions in children's independent reading experiences when appropriate
- Read aloud daily from a range of texts, including non-fiction
- Demonstrate an enthusiasm for books as a source of pleasure and enlightenment
- Provide an environment where literacy is valued and celebrated.

Pupils should have regular opportunities to:

- Read alone and with friends
- Discuss books in group reading sessions
- Choose from a range of texts and time to develop selection skills
- Share reading experiences with each other through Booktalk (Chambers 1985) sessions
- Respond imaginatively to what they have read
- Have time with an adult to consider reading.

Children's first impressions of the status given to literacy will be based on the physical environment. First rate children's books should be at the heart of the resources collection, although other texts – journals, comics, letters, calendars, posters, labels and instructions – will all contribute to an authentically literate environment. The computer will play a leading role in literacy activities, especially reading for research. There should be displays of children's work celebrating success, demonstrating progress and emphasising the central role which reading and writing play in the general organisation of the classroom.

Becoming a writer

Writing is hard work. Learning to write involves everything necessary to express ideas in written form. This can be as practical as being proficient with a writing tool (be it a pencil or a word processor) or as abstract as transforming thought into accessible written language. The production of legible print, a knowledge of the conventions of written language (such as spelling and punctuation) and an ability to write cohesively are all important, but they only really matter if you have something to convey. Unfortunately, many writing lessons have led children to believe that they learn to write in order to be able to spell correctly or to produce neat handwriting. The following anonymous statements from a group of eleven-year-olds are taken from many examples of pupils' opinions about learning to write:

Child A: I feel nervous when somebody reads my writing, especially a teacher, because I am not very good at writing stories and poems. I think they might ask me to do it again. I am not sure why we write it. I think the handwriting is the most important and the quality and the quantity.

Child B: I think writing is for my education and for handwriting. Teachers are looking to see if they can read it and can enjoy it but we are different things so it is hard.

Child C: When I write I feel bored. Some teachers put a time limit on it, that makes you do mistakes and it makes you rush it. I think we write to improve our handwriting and to help us when we are older. Teachers look at the style and the spelling mistakes.

These pupils were from a school with high standards and conscientious, caring teachers. Yet the children had not really understood the point of learning to write. In the same collection, statements from younger children show that they, too, believe they learn to write so that they can spell correctly and do neat handwriting. If children are going to learn to be effective writers, they need the circumstances that promote thoughtful, imaginative writing. Such circumstances do not fit into neatly timetabled lessons. If we want children to understand what it is like to be a 'real' writer we must provide opportunities when they:

- Have time to think, talk and day dream
- Let their imaginations 'ramble' freely around ideas
- Feel in control of their ideas and how they express them.

These things don't happen automatically. Teachers must model how it's done by writing alongside their pupils, talking about their ideas as well as demonstrating how to express them in print. Imaginations need to be fed with a regular diet of stories, drama, pictures, poetry, music, problem solving, and so on. If the response to children's work relates to the quality of the ideas, young writers will not mistake composition with transcription. They will know that they spell in order to write, not write in order to spell. Children need experiences that enable them to understand:

- The processes of writing/composition
- The purposes of writing
- The crafting of writing
- The conventions of punctuation, spelling and textual organisation
- The significance of legible presentation.

Some of the aspects on the list above can fit into timed literacy sessions but there should always be flexibility in the timetable to allow for the process of composition to take place.

An integrated process

Ask any author how to become a better writer and you will regularly receive the answer, 'Read!'. The fundamental relationship between reading and writing, so clearly illustrated by the research of Barrs and Cork (2001) in *The Reader in the Writer*, means that the whole literacy learning process should be integrated and seamless. Reading will feed writing, writing will enhance reading and speaking and listening will underpin every experience of literacy.

Creativity in writing is regularly acknowledged – and should be re-emphasised as often as possible; however, reading is also a creative pursuit. Every time readers' minds take them beyond the literal, they are engaging their imaginations in the creation of meaning. Creative and innovative teaching will help children to become more proficient creators of meaning, whether interpreting what they have read or in constructing texts themselves. Teachers should see all creative activity as a means to support literacy learning and should offer opportunities to respond through the arts – dance, drama, art, music – and through creative thinking in problem solving. Offering a range of creative activities caters for the different learning styles in the classroom. A child who cannot say how they understand what they have read may well be able to draw a response. 'The engagement of all the senses in interpreting different parts of the story offers visual, auditory and kinaesthetic support to all the children – especially those for whom language and literacy are not easy' (Goodwin, 2004). A literate classroom will be one where literacy and creativity go hand-in-hand.

The structure of the book

This book is organised into four parts:

- Part I, Starting points for literacy
- Part II, Becoming readers
- Part III, Becoming writers
- Part IV, The world of literacy

Part I, Starting points for literacy, covers aspects of introducing literacy learning in nursery schools and at key stage 1. Margaret Perkins points out in Chapter 1 that, right from the start, children should become familiar with the full range of feelings, competencies and experiences that constitute being a reader. Perkins identifies the immense complexity of what it is to be a reader. When they are very young it is essential that children get a balanced experience of the joys as well as the linguistic functions of text. In Chapter 2, Liz Laycock gives a comprehensive description of shared reading and writing with a class of young learners. Laycock considers the importance of teacher modeling and how the skilled practitioner makes the experience rewarding and enjoyable. In Chapter 3, Judith Graham revisits the question of reading aloud to children to ask whether Mr Magnolia (Blake 1980) survived the recent functional uses of children's literature.

Part II, Becoming readers, looks at reading as it develops through the primary years. Tony Martin (Chapter 4) demonstrates how, as young readers develop, comprehension and response are totally intertwined. At this stage teachers need to offer children opportunities to respond to what they read in a variety of ways. Youngsters also need to develop an 'inner' life as readers – something that can only come about through independent sustained, silent reading (SSR) as discussed by Geoff Fenwick in Chapter 5. Gillian Lathey (Chapter 6) shows that there is an important place for supporting the wider curriculum through books in which complex and sometimes disturbing ideas are dealt with in an accessible way for young readers. The value of allowing children time to talk about books is evident from the depth of understanding shown by the children discussing Rose Blanche (McEwan and Innocenti 1985) described by Catriona Nicholson in Chapter 7.

Part III, Becoming writers, concentrates on children's experience of the process of writing, especially how teachers can support their growing independence. In Chapter 8, Teresa Grainger considers how to motivate youngsters to write. She points out how teachers must allow for the time, talk, imaginative activity and personal control over the writing that will enable children to feel like writers. More formally structured approaches to writing are provided in Chapters 9 and 10 where Maureen Lewis describes using stories to support the writing of fiction (Chapter 9). Lewis joins with David Wray to look at writing frames for writing non-fiction in Chapter 10. Spelling is the focus of Chapter 11, where Olivia O'Sullivan describes research into teaching spelling. She offers highly practical advice about supporting young spellers. Nigel Hall describes research into children's developing concepts of punctuation as they become more confident as writers (Chapter 12). He questions whether didactic approaches, implied by lists in government initiatives, actually enhance pupils' understanding of the function of punctuation.

Part IV, The world of literacy, introduces other issues and aspects of literacy which are relevant to all the foundation and primary years. George Hunt, in Chapter 3, looks at vocabulary development, working with words in a rewarding way that encourages an exploration of language. Ruth Wood considers the place of the computer in promoting children's confidence and skill with proof-reading their work (Chapter 14). Liz Laycock gives guidance and advice about working with pupils with English as an additional language (Chapter 15). Suzi Clipson-Boyles describes the importance of drama in supporting literacy learning in Chapter 16. A comprehensive list of drama activities demonstrates the many ways in which imagined experience can support children's comprehension and creation of text. In Chapter 17, Michael Lockwood examines how explicit discussion about dialect and standard English can help develop pupils' knowledge about language. Chris Powling, using the first-hand experience of teacher Sean O'Flynn, explores the need for teachers to introduce children to a wide range of poetry (Chapter 18).

Into the classroom

Literacy is an integral part of all learning. It influences success in every other subject on the school curriculum and, when formal schooling ends, in society as a whole. It also provides a framework for thinking that allows children to consider the 'possible worlds' (Bruner 1986) beyond their immediate environment. A literate classroom is one which provides children with the experience of being literate in the company of fellow readers and writers. In an ideal world we would have class-rooms fully stocked with all the best resources for reading and writing. In reality, we can only be certain to provide the most important factor that creates a literate classroom – a literate teacher.

References

Barrs, M. and Cork, V. (2001) *The Reader in the Writer.* London: CLPE.

Bearne, E. (2003) in Styles, M. and Bearne, E. (eds) (2003) *Art, Narrative and Childhood.* Stoke on Trent: Trentham Books.

Blake, Q. (1980) *Mr Magnolia.* London: Jonathan Cape.

Bruner, J. S. (1986) *Actual Minds, Possible Worlds.* Cambridge, MA: Harvard University Press.

Chambers, A. (1985) *Booktalk.* London: The Bodley Head.

DfES (1975)*A Language for Life* (The Bullock Report), London: HMSO.

DfES (2003) *Excellence and Enjoyment.* London: DfES.

Goodwin, P. (ed.) (2004) *Literacy through Creativity.* London: David Fulton.

McEwan, I. and Innocenti, R. (1985) *Rose Blanche.* London: Jonathan Cape.

PART

I

Starting points for literacy

Making space for reading: teaching reading in the early years

Margaret Perkins

Introduction

At the start of each new academic year, teachers consider their classrooms and look at their teaching plans in the light of what they want their pupils to experience and achieve. The teaching of reading is an area where they are not short of advice; the foundation stage curriculum, the National Curriculum and the National Literacy Strategy framework are just the beginning of a plethora of documentation offering advice and 'guidance'. It can be confusing and one is tempted to ask 'Where do I begin?' in deciding how to teach reading.

Perhaps a useful starting point is to reflect on what we actually want the children to be able to do – how do we define reading? The National Literacy Strategy is simple in its aspirations; 'Literate primary pupils should...be interested in books, read with enjoyment and evaluate and justify their preferences' (DfES 2001: 3). So reading is everything – but yet it is even more. When I read I enter into the worlds and minds of others – I know what it feels like to be in a certain place, in a certain situation, facing a certain dilemma. When I read my feelings are engaged; I sympathise and empathise with the characters I am reading about and often my emotions are as raw as theirs. When I read I learn things; I gain new information; my bank of knowledge is enlarged. When I read I hear others' opinions and I evaluate them against my own viewpoint and against what I know of the writer. When I read I argue with the ideas on the page; I interpret them in the light of my own experiences, I absorb them or I reject them; I create worlds and ideas which grow from what I have read. When I read I know what to do; I follow the instructions to make the IKEA bookcase, to cook that new recipe, to find an address. When I read I enjoy the delights of language, of laughing as the joke plays with the meanings of words, of struggling with hidden meanings as I complete the crossword, of revelling in the craft of the skilled wordsmith. When I read I curl up on the sofa enjoying the escape from the bustle of life, but then I want to talk, 'Have you read this? What do you think? Did you know that...? What happens next?' Friends and family recommend books to me, colleagues show me where to find out certain information, the internet takes me on unending journeys of discovery. Reading is a part of me and my life – without reading my life would be poorer.

How do I begin to teach that? How can I hope to show children what reading offers them and what they can achieve through reading? It was Halliday who reminded us that effective and successful readers are those who understand the functions of reading; they know what reading can do and they want to exploit it to its fullest (Halliday 1978).

Starting points

As I contemplate my teaching programme, I need to remind myself that I am not starting from nothing. As teachers it is important to acknowledge and build on what children already know, understand and can do in relation to literacy. What experiences have three- to seven-year-olds had with regard to literacy? They are sure to be avid watchers of television – Cbeebies, CBBC and CITV are probably key features of their lives. They follow the antics of Arthur, Rotten Ralph and Ballamory. They begin to see that Rotten Ralph does not always say exactly what he means and that understanding comes by looking beyond the text. Of course, they cannot express that idea but their laughter at many of the antics suggests that they are reading the text of the programme inferentially. They also will have been to the cinema and seen *Shrek, Spiderman* or *The Incredibles*. They probably went with their families and afterwards discussed which bit they liked best and what they thought of the behaviour of the characters. They may travel in the back of the car and watch adults looking for roadsigns, trying to find where they are on the map and attempting to make sense of the directions. They watch adults connecting the DVD player, assembling a new bookcase and complaining that the instructions don't make any sense. They play games on the PlayStation 2 or Game Boy and read much more effectively than I can what is happening on the screen. They take advice from their older siblings who have probably downloaded cheats from the internet and can show them how to move on quickly to the next level. They may visit museums, stately homes or art galleries and follow a trail using a guide which asks them to find things out and record them. They may have visited the library and taken out lots of books so they can collect the stickers – they may even have looked at the books! They have done all these things and they have watched even more. They have experienced the power and invasiveness of the printed word in their lives and the lives of those around them.

In short, they have learnt that the written word moves – it changes, it can be played with, it is there to do what I want it to do. They have learnt that it informs, it tells you things. They have learnt that reading can be fun and can be done with lots of other people. Of course, not all children will have had all those experiences. Many children will have done things with print but not talked about it with a more experienced reader – for them their learning may be deeply embedded so that they do not realise what they know. For some their experiences of print will be very different from what I have described. We can be confident though that all children will have had experiences of print. We know from research going back over many years (Heath 1983; Minns 1997; Gregory 2000; Dyson 2001; Pahl 1999) that children come to school with understandings of how literacy works and what it can do. The danger is that we assume their understandings are the same as ours and even more dangerous is the assumption that we are right and they are wrong. As teachers, our starting point must be a recognition of the knowledge, skill and understanding with which children come to school and to use those as the starting point for our teaching and planning.

Making space

How do we do that? I would argue that we begin by making space for reading within our classroom and within our teaching programme. It is as we create time, experiences, opportunities, conversations and resources for reading and observe children within those spaces that we can identify their understanding. I watched Andy reading *The Guardian* in the role play area; I watched Jessica looking up a number in the phone book before she made a call; I watched Edward rejecting all the books in the book corner because 'I don't know how to read yet'; I watched Taylor who struggles with many books, devouring a challenging book about fishing because, 'I go fishing every week with my Dad'; I watched Lucy and Sophie talking and laughing together as they read a picture book; I watched Ryan's mum asking him if he had a new book to read and telling him to ask me for one; I watched Thomas laughing with joy as I read to the class. As I watched these children and their encounters with reading so I came to know what reading meant to them (and perhaps to their families) and what they were expecting reading in school to be. This enables me to plan so that I can extend their understanding of print and what it can do and enable them to become effective readers. I do this by making space within my classroom in many ways.

Space for texts

We live in a print rich environment and I want to reflect that within my classroom. I want the print in my classroom to serve all the different purposes that the children have seen and experienced it serving in their homes and communities. That means, among other things, that they will have access to a wide range of texts.

There will be conventional picture books, pop-up books and non-fiction books. There will be collections of books by the same author, collections of books on the same theme (joke books, school stories, stories that challenge convention, poetry), books that allow the more inexperienced reader to enjoy them independently because of the relationship between the words and the illustrations and/or the use of natural language that follows the rhythm of spoken English. In short, there will be lots and lots of books of all different sorts. I will create a space for these books within my classroom that allows them to show themselves off and which supports children in their reading. I will put similar books together. I will draw attention to related books. I will suggest what they might look for in the books and I will recommend ones I have enjoyed and suggest they do the same. This space for books will be like a treasure island inviting exploration and discovery.

However, a treasure island takes time to explore and so within my classroom I will provide time for the children to be there. They will be encouraged to browse and allowed to pick up a book, flick through it and take it away to read or reject it. I will encourage the children to make decisions about what they read and give them time to encounter a variety of texts. I will provide time for *general browsing*.

There will also be time for *focused browsing*. I want children to be able to use books for their own purposes and so there will be times when I will ask them to browse with a given aim in mind.

> 'Look at all these books about Preston Pig – how many different ways has he escaped from the wolf?'
> 'Can you find out where milk comes from?'
> 'What are the difference between these different versions of *The Three Little Pigs*?'
> 'Which of these stories about Alfie do you like best?'

It is clear that both during and/or after general and focused browsing must come *talk*. The children need to talk about their discoveries and to be encouraged to tell where and how they found this out, what their reasons are for thinking this and what the text tells them about that. An informed adult will build on their responses and by asking the right questions will encourage them to look and think further.

> 'Why do you think Alfie felt shy about going to the party?'
> 'Why do you think the wolf wanted the pigs to go and pick apples?'
> 'How does the milk get from the farmer to the shop?'
> 'Do you think Preston Pig knows the wolf is always chasing him?'

Reading is a social activity and talk is an essential element of the reading process. By talking with children about their reading we can encourage them to respond to what they have read. Chamber's (1993) model of the three sharings is useful in this context.

- Tell me the things you enjoyed and didn't enjoy about this book. What made you excited and what annoyed you? Tell me the good bits and the not so good bits. Did you like the same parts as I did? I wonder why not?

- Tell me what puzzles you about this book. What don't you understand? What doesn't make sense to you?

- Tell me the patterns you see in this book. What do you think it is about? What things go together? What is linked to what?

This model helps children to engage in depth with a text. *The Magic Bed* by John Burningham is a book which prompted long discussion with a group of children.

'I was really cross with Granny when she sold the bed.'
'I loved it when he chased the pirates away.'
'Who is Frank?'
'What is the magic word?'
'When he travelled on his magic bed he looked after lots of people.'
'He had lots of secrets from the grown-ups.'

By listening to children's comments and inviting them continually to refer back to the book to support what they are saying the adult is teaching the children to read intelligently. This sort of talk can happen during shared or guided reading, when working at text level. A group could also browse during independent time or discuss a book with another adult at that time. The adult needs only to have read the book and to know the framework of three sharings. As children and adult respond together the children are equal contributors to the discussion.

When planning my teaching programme I will also include space for me to *read aloud* to the children. I will do this as often as I can and whenever I can. Reading to children is an important time for establishing group cohesion but it is also a vital reading lesson. I will choose to read texts that the children cannot read for themselves; I will introduce them to new texts and new authors; I will use this opportunity to extend their repertoire and teach them more about being a reader. What do I want them to learn from these lessons?

- I want them to hear what fluent phrased expressive reading sounds like. They will have a model of 'good' reading on which they can base their own reading. This means that I must be sure that I read the book well, that I know it and have prepared this reading lesson as much as any other. I will also put in my classroom a listening corner with tapes of lots of people reading different books. They will hear different voices reading in a variety of accents and even languages.

- I want them to be introduced to a large range of different authors and books. I want the children to be enthused and want to read these books for themselves.

Children's literature will be the bedrock of my reading curriculum. There is a huge disparate range of published books and I want children to be the sort of readers who can discriminate and choose quality texts. However, literature is not the only sort of text we read and in my classroom I want to make space for many *different types of texts*.

There will be audio texts – both commercial and home-made – which will enable children to hear different readings and different voices.

There will be comics, magazines, newspapers, posters, mail – examples of the texts that surround us all in day-to-day life. My role play area, in whatever form it takes at this particular moment, will contain props which allow the children's play to reflect the literate behaviours which naturally occur within that context. So a home corner will have phone books and message pads, cookery books, notice boards with memos and calendars, newspapers, letters and junk mail, and so on. Talk about these props and how they are used will inform and guide the children's play.

There will be electronic texts of all types – talking books, web pages from the internet, e-mails and text messages, adventure games, etc. Talk around these will focus on how we read different texts in different ways and how our reading depends on our purpose.

The classroom will be full of print and the whole room will be like a text in itself. Labels will show me where things are kept. Instructions will tell me how to use apparatus. Notices will inform me about what is happening and what I need to be doing. Memos will remind me what I must not forget. Other notices will invite me to think about displays and to make some kind of response to it. In British primary schools we are rightly very concerned about the quality of our display. We value children's work by mounting it and ensuring that it is set off to its best advantage. Our classrooms are a plethora of beautifully mounted and colourful displays. It is not quite the same in French primary schools. They place equal value on display but for them it often appears to be a reflection of 'work in process' rather than a celebration of what has been done. They will collect thoughts about a topic, list a word family, plan a science investigation. Ideas will be written on a flip chart or on a sheet of paper and pinned on the wall. They will be reflected on and discussed and on subsequent days taken down and maybe added to or changed. Display in these classrooms is a real lesson in the functions of print and of how a reader and writer can change and adapt what is written. It is likely that, as with most things, the best practice lies somewhere between the two. We do not want our displays to be so beautiful that it seems as though once written the print is sacrosanct and cannot be changed but equally we want our display to reflect the high value we give to the children's work. As a teacher, I will think carefully about each element of display I have in my classroom to make sure that the lessons it teaches about literacy are appropriate for the class at this time.

Space to be independent

A high priority in the teaching of reading is to enable children to be independent and so in my teaching programme I will ensure that I plan to give them the skills they need to be independent readers. How will I do this?

Much of what has been discussed so far has been concerned with teaching children about the behaviours which effective readers adopt and giving them the expectations of what reading can offer. Understanding this is a big part towards becoming an effective and independent reader. There are some aspects, however, which require explicit teaching and it is essential that space for this teaching is a priority in my planning.

The independent reader is one who has strategies for tackling the unknown and my teaching of reading will make those strategies explicit to the children. This will be done during shared reading when I will model and demonstrate the reading process to the children. Much of reading is invisible to the observer and in shared reading I am making what normally goes on inside my head visible and explicit. The children had read *This is the Bear and the Scary Night*. (Hayes and Craig 1991). They had talked about the story, relating it to their own experiences of feeling scared and being lost. They empathised with the bear and also with the desperate feelings when a favourite toy is lost. They came back to the text the following day and this time, because the story was known to them, they were more able to focus on the words. The children read along with the teacher and emphasis was put on the rhyming words; those words were repeated together with an emphasis on the rhyme. On the next page the children again joined in with the reading but this time when they came to the final word it was covered up with a post-it. The children guessed what the word was – some had remembered it from the day before and some worked it out from the rhyming word. The teacher asked them how they could be sure what it was. 'If it is "soon" what letter would we see at the beginning? Let's see if you're right.' The teacher slowly peeled away the post-it to reveal an 's'. 'Hurray, we were right! But there is more. If "soon" rhymes with "moon" what do you think the rest of the word would look like? Let's look. It's "-oon". See how it is the same as "moon" but with a different beginning letter.'

There are times when the phonic strategy is not the most useful one and then I will encourage the children to choose another strategy. They might:

■ Leave the word out and read on

■ Go back to the beginning of the sentence and re-run

■ Look at the picture

■ Think about what they know about the story

■ Look for words they do know inside the new one, e.g. 'sun' inside 'sunshine'.

In guided reading I will focus the children's attention on one particular strategy, choosing carefully the text they are reading to ensure it is appropriate. I can then remind the children of what to do when they come to an unknown word, demonstrating the strategy with other words so that when they read independently they will have that strategy in the forefront of their minds.

There is no doubt that for beginner readers the main element of learning to read is the process of making sense of written language as a symbol. If children are to become independent readers, they need to know how that symbolic system works and they need to be able to use and manipulate the 'code'.

Essentially written language is a relationship between sound and symbol but unfortunately it is not a simple relationship. We have about 44 phonemes (or sounds) in the English language which are represented in print by 26 letters. How much easier life would be if it were a one-to-one correspondence!

The first thing that children need to be able to do is to hear and discriminate between the sounds and it is important that this is done before any reference to how they are represented in print. Our starting point therefore is work on 'phonological awareness'. The Primary National Strategy publication *Playing with Sounds* (DfES 2004) gives many ideas for doing just that and is an excellent resource. It contains examples of both child-initiated learning and play and planned teacher-directed activities. Classroom experiences related to phonological awareness will involve a lot of drama, movement, singing, clapping, listening and music. All these activities become reading lessons as the children learn to hear, identify and discriminate between different sounds.

Space needs to be given for this phonological awareness to be firmly established before explicit teaching about how sounds are represented in print is given. An independent effective reader is in control of written language and that is the purpose of our teaching. There are many resources available which give ideas for classroom activities (for example in *Progression in Phonics* (DfES 2000), *Jolly Phonics* (Lloyd 1992)) but I do not want to list activities here. Rather I want to recall some key principles of phonic teaching:

- The purpose of phonic teaching is to enable independent access to the meaning of the text and that must remain at the forefront of our thinking and planning. Phonics can be fun when we play with language and use texts like the Dr Seuss books, nursery rhymes, or the brilliant *Tanka Tanka Skunk* by Steve Webb.

- Sounds are represented by the symbols; the letters do not 'say' anything themselves. Children can become very confused by our careless use of language and we must be careful that we do not try to over-simplify and so be less accurate.

- There are no rules in phonics. There are more common ways of representing sounds but often well known words do not conform to usual patterns. Think of the phoneme /ie/. It can be represented in many different ways: light, tie, eye, kite, I, climb, height, fly. Which is the most common? Which is the most unusual? Collecting words and sorting them is a powerful way of helping children to understand how the English language uses symbols to represent sound.

- Children need to understand that there are some differences which matter and some which don't. In their previous experience a chair has always been a chair whichever way it is facing and which ever way up it is. Letters do not work like that. Playing with letters is a way of becoming familiar with their forms – magnetic letters, letters made from sandpaper, fur fabric, satin, wood, letters written on a partner's back, letter shapes I can make with my body, letters drawn in wet sand, in rice, in sawdust, letters painted in water on the playground, grown in cress on blotting paper, made out of playdough. It is important to give children every possible opportunity of becoming familiar with the shapes of letters.

- Listening to sounds and playing with them does not stop when we move to more focused phonic teaching. This can still be text based. There are many wonderful texts which play with language; jokes and poetry are a useful way of accessing this.

Conclusion

Reading is a complex and rich activity. It demands much of readers and yet offers huge rewards. The teaching of reading is similarly a complex and rich process. We are being reminded again (Ofsted 2004) that children's enjoyment of texts and experiences of reading for pleasure are the key to successful reading and so it follows that effective teaching of reading focuses on the texts with which children can and want to engage. Our teaching needs to give children the strategies to enable them to access these texts independently and that is what teaching at sentence and word level does. The searchlights model (National Literacy Strategy 2001) shows how the different strategies interrelate in helping us to read successfully. Our teaching of reading must explicitly show the relationship between these strategies and demonstrate how they are used together as a support and check. However, all this must be done in a context in which children can experience the purposes and functions of reading and the pleasures which reading can offer.

Reading is an extremely complex and diverse process and yet it is one which is rewarding and exciting. In my classroom I want the teaching of reading programmes to reflect that complexity, diversity, reward and excitement. To do that I need to make space: physical space for the wide variety of different types of texts, temporal space for reading and talking about reading, cultural space to recognise and exploit the different interpretations of reading and text that children hold; social space to allow interaction and talk between adults and children and children and children; conceptual space to recognise and accept uncertainties and questions and to use them as starting points for exploring texts. Above all, I need to allow children the space to enjoy reading and to share their personal responses to the variety of texts they encounter both in and out of the classroom. For therein lies the door to the magic that is reading.

References

Burningham, J. (2003) *The Magic Bed*. London: Red Fox.

Chambers, A. (1993) *Tell Me: Children, Reading and Talk*. Stroud: Thimble Press.

DfES (2000) *Progression in Phonics*. London: DfES.

DfES (2001) *The National Literacy Strategy: Framework for Teaching*. London: DfES.

DfES (2004) *Playing with Sounds: A Supplement to Progression in Phonics*. London: DfES.

Dyson, A. H. (2001) 'Where are the childhoods in childhood literacy? An exploration in outer school space.' *Journal of Early Childhood Literacy*, **1**(1), pp. 9–39.

Gregory, E. (2000) *City Literacies*. London: Routledge.

Halliday, M. A. K. (1978) *Language as Social Semiotic: The Social Interpretation of Language and Meaning*. London: Edward Arnold.

Hayes, S. and Craig, H. (1991) *This is the Bear and the Scary Night*. London: Walker Books.

Heath, S. B. (1983) *Ways with Words: Language, Life and Work in Communities and Classrooms*. Cambridge: Cambridge University Press.

Lloyd, S. (1992) *The Jolly Phonics Handbook*. Jolly Learning Company.

Minns, H. (1997) *Read It to Me Now! Learning at Home and School*. Buckingham: Open University Press.

Ofsted (2004) *Reading for Purpose and Pleasure: An Evaluation of the Teaching of Reading in Primary Schools*. London: Ofsted Publications.

Pahl, K. (1999) *Transformations: Making Meaning in Nursery Education*. London: Routledge.

Webb, S. (2003) *Tanka Tanka Skunk*. London: Random House.

Shared reading and shared writing at key stage 1

Liz Laycock

Introduction

It is now more than 25 years since Don Holdaway published *The Foundations of Literacy* (1979) which introduced the idea of shared reading to thousands of teachers. Drawing on what was then new research about literacy learning before school, especially Clay (1972) and Clark (1976), Holdaway proposed a pedagogy which attempted to replicate some of the factors which seemed to promote literacy development in the home environment, in the 'bedtime story routine'. One of the reasons for the success of this reading was the books which were used. As Holdaway says, 'The language of the books used by parents, even with infants below the age of two, is remarkably rich in comparison with the caption books and early readers used in the first year at school'. Parents read to their children and the children engage in this activity, for the sheer pleasure and satisfaction of sharing the books.

Holdaway also recognised the collaborative nature of adult–child reading experiences in pre-school settings, as well as the 'visual intimacy with the print'. If these were factors in the successful learning about reading that children had engaged in at home, he suggested, we should attempt to recreate a similar non-competitive, collaborative learning context in school. His proposals for the use of enlarged texts for 'shared book experience' with large numbers of children took account of these insights. The teachers with whom he worked decided that there should be 'lots of books' – 'simple stories that the children will readily understand'. They produced enlarged versions of both the favourite stories and the rhymes, songs and poems used in the classroom. From the beginning it was apparent that the children were fully engaged and that, in subsequent readings, they began to join in with repeated parts of the text.

The publication of Holdaway's book in England introduced British teachers to 'shared reading' and, once they had begun to use this teaching context, teachers wanted to use the most popular picture books in the large format. These were not often available so they continued to produce their own. The class-made versions of stories often involved the children, which made teachers increasingly aware of the potential of this collaborative writing as a teaching context. Thus, many teachers and their classes began to compose, through 'shared writing', new texts which, in turn, became reading material for 'shared reading'. In both activities there was a focus on a meaningful text as a context for teaching the skills of reading and writing. There was also a healthy collaboration in this learning enterprise, between adults and children, and among the children.

Children's participation in both shared reading and shared writing involves them in activities which they could not do alone, but from which they can learn a great deal, with the support of others. Thus, these learning contexts fit with what we understand about effective learning from developmental psychologists such as Vygotsky (1978) and Bruner in Wood et al. (1976). Vygotsky showed that essential elements in learning are social and collaborative, where learners are enabled to attempt things which are beyond their current developmental stage. He believed that activity within this 'zone of proximal development', which the child could not do independently, was when real learning takes place; 'what the child can do in co-operation today, he can do alone tomorrow?' Bruner (in Wood et al. 1976) talks of 'scaffolding' the child's learning, providing support until the child can act independently in a particular area. In shared reading and writing, children are supported as they take on more and more of the tasks for themselves.

Others, (see, for example, Smith (1984: 150)), have pointed to the importance of 'demonstrations' which teach children about what readers and writers have to do. In learning to be literate, children need to know not just how, but why, particular kinds of reading and writing are done. Smith says that 'each demonstration shows an aspect of the power of written language' and that reading and writing need to be purposeful. There are differences between demonstrations and formal decontextualised instruction; 'demonstrations provide opportunities for learners to engage in the purpose of the activity, to share an intention with the demonstrator, whether to construct a story or to discover what someone else is thinking or planning'. In shared reading and writing activities the teacher can be explicit about the purpose of the writing as well as about the conventions of how meanings are communicated or transferred to the page. These activities thus provide contexts for appropriate demonstration. The guidance given in the National Literacy Strategy documentation *Developing Early Writing* (DfEE 2001) refers constantly to teacher demonstration, but these are heavily teacher directed.

Shared reading in practice

With the inclusion of shared reading in the literacy hour framework, it is important to understand the potential of this teaching context. It has been stated that the

Literacy Strategy is a 'framework for teaching' but we need to use it to create a framework for learning. The first priority must be the selection of texts. Because of the literacy hour, there are now hundreds of texts to choose from. Some of these are the high-quality children's literature which Holdaway felt should be used, while others are merely 'big' versions of rather uninspiring books. You will need to consider whether the enlarged texts that you use have sufficient depth to be worth sustained study and analysis. You will also need to select a book which is matched to your teaching and learning intentions for a particular session. If, for example, you wish to focus on encouraging readers to use their knowledge of what has gone before to predict what might happen next, the book must be sufficiently predictable to enable readers to use the language and/or story structure to do this; if you wish to focus on an aspect of punctuation, you will need to make sure there are examples of what you intend to teach in the text.

What happens in shared reading?

The book will need to have print large enough to be seen clearly by the children sitting furthest away; this may seem an obvious point, but some commercially published big books have print which is difficult to decipher at a distance. The book will need to go on a stand or easel which will give adequate support for the big pages. As you will want to point to words as you read, it helps to use a pointer so that you do not unintentionally obscure parts of the text.

The first time that you read a new book, it should be read right through so that the children are given a sense of the whole story. If children ask questions or make comments, you should respond to these, but without destroying the flow of the reading. In the transcript below, of an actual shared reading session with a year 1 class, the teacher makes a few teaching points at the beginning but does not interrupt the reading, in this first session, with too many questions. While reading *Hot Hippo* (Hadithi and Kennaway 1992), the teacher points to the text.

Teacher:	We're going to look at *Hot Hippo* together. (Teacher points to title.) It's by the same person as *Lazy Lion* I read yesterday (pointing to author's and illustrator's names, Mwenye Hadithi and Adrienne Kennaway).
Child A:	They're both in hot countries.
Teacher:	What do you notice about 'lazy lion' and 'hot hippo'?
Child L:	They're both the same letters.
Teacher:	That's right, 'lazy' and 'lion' begin with the same letter, 'L' and 'hot' and 'hippo' both begin with 'H'. (In both examples, the teacher uses the letter name, followed by the single phoneme. She turns the page and reads aloud, pointing word by word to the text on pp. 1 and 2.) 'Hippo was hot.' (pp. 3 and 4) 'He sat on the river

	bank and gazed at the little fishes swimming in the water.' (pp. 5 and 6, and points to the hippo in the picture) What's he thinking?
Child B:	He's thinking he'd like a drink!
Teacher:	(points to 'think' bubbles) What are these? What does it mean? (Many hands are up to answer.)
Child C:	He's thinking.
Teacher:	(reads) 'If only I could live in the water, he thought, how wonderful life would be.' (Turns to pp. 7 and 8) What are the other animals?
All:	Giraffes.
Teacher:	(reads) 'So he walked and he ran and he strolled and he hopped and he lumbered along until he came to the mountain where Ngai lived.' (Turns to pp. 9 and 10, picture shows god-like form in the rock.)
Child B:	He's got no body.
Teacher:	(reads) 'Ngai was the god of Everything and Everywhere.' (turns to pp. 11 and 12, looking at the big picture) What can we see?
Children:	Elephant, lion, giraffe, shark, horse, crocodile, ...
Teacher:	(reads) 'Ngai told the animals to live on the land and the fishes to live in the sea. (Turns to pp. 13 and 14 to a new picture.) 'Ngai told the birds to fly in the air and the ants to live under the ground.' (Turns pp. 15 and 16 to a new picture.) 'Ngai had told Hippo he was to live on the land and eat grass.'
Child B:	Why's the god got ...?
Child D:	Why's he made of stone?
Teacher:	(reading pp. 17 and 18) ' "Please, O great Ngai, god of Everything and Everywhere, I would so much like to live in the rivers and streams," begged Hippo hopefully. "I would still eat grass." (pp. 19 and 20) "I would show you," promised Hippo. "I will let you look in my mouth whenever you like, to see that I am not eating your little fishes." ' (Children become really involved, concentrating.)
Child E:	He ain't eating it ...
Teacher:	(reading pp. 21 and 22) ' "But you must come out of the water at night and eat grass, so that even in the dark I can tell you are not eating my little fishes. Agreed?" "Agreed!" sang Hippo happily.'
Child B:	When it's dark sometimes in Africa you don't get hot.
Teacher:	(reading pp. 23 and 24) 'And he ran all the way home until he got to the river, where he jumped in with a mighty SPLASH!' (Turning to next page (pp. 25 and 26)). – Oh, look what happened ...
Child H:	He sank.

Teacher:	(reads) 'And he sank like a stone because he couldn't swim.' (pp. 27 and 28) 'But he could hold his breath and run along the bottom which he does to this very day. And he stirs up the bottom by wagging his little tail so that Ngai can see he has not hidden any fish-bones.'
Child B:	And he's too heavy. Can hippos breathe under water?
Teacher:	(reading) '…opens his huge mouth ever so wide.'
Several children:	(echoing) Opens his mouth wide! (…and opening their mouths!)

After a first reading you could initiate a discussion about the story, to allow the children to share their responses, to ask questions and to talk about the illustration. In the case of *Hot Hippo*, the teacher focused the children's attention on the illustrations because they reflect the heat of the Kenyan setting very effectively and create the context for the events. There were several points where the teacher could have picked up on the children's comments and questions: why the god, Ngai, has no body; why he is made of stone. Then there are the comments about the hippo 'not eating it' , the comment about it not being hot in Africa when it is dark, and the question about whether hippos can breathe under water. However, as this was a first reading, the teacher opted to keep the flow of the story going because the children were concentrating and totally involved; the comments that they made reflect this involvement. Had the comments been picked up on, the class could have been side-tracked into discussion which would have disrupted the flow. When the text was read again, the teacher was able to focus on the children's comments and questions and could allow them to explore more fully the issues that had occurred to them as they listened the first time. The teacher then moved into looking at particular words and at the punctuation (especially the use of inverted commas for speech).

In classes of young children, the focus of these reading demonstrations will need to be on what a reader has to do to read the text. The teacher will need to demonstrate all the cues that the reader needs to use and will talk about the conventions of print (that the print carries the same unvarying message, that the left-hand page is read before the right-hand page, where to start reading, left to right directionality in English, word boundaries, one-to-one correspondence and letter–sound correspondence). It is necessary to show that you can go back and reread if the reading does not make sense, and that a reader can predict what might come next by drawing on knowledge of what has gone before and on knowledge of how words fit together in English. This can be done simply by covering up words or phrases with masking devices (Holdaway 1979: Chapter 4) and asking children what would make sense. The teacher can demonstrate how to check guesses by looking at the letters at the beginnings or endings of words and show children how to make use of their graphophonic knowledge to work out unknown words. The focus of the teaching will vary according to the observed learning needs of the particular group. It is important, however, that there is a clear focus which avoids cramming everything into every shared reading session.

Shared writing in practice

Shared writing can be carried out by pairs or groups of children working without an adult or by groups of any number, working with an adult. Each context will be appropriate for different writing purposes but, in this chapter, the focus is on large groups of children (part of the class or the whole class) working with a teacher.

While shared reading provides opportunities to investigate existing texts, shared writing offers the opportunity to construct texts collaboratively and, at the same time, a context for teaching about the writing process. As Smith (1981: 86) says; 'Especially when writing is being learned, there is often a great need for, and advantage in, people working together on a letter, a poem or a story. The ability to write alone comes with experience and is not always easy or necessary.'

The texts created in shared writing could often not be achieved by individual children writing alone; the collaborative undertaking creates a 'zone of proximal development' (Vygotsky 1978), as in shared reading, in which more can be achieved with the support of others. The children who perhaps benefit most from this collaborative context are those who are at the earliest stages of becoming literate and those who find reading and writing alone difficult and demanding. Again it was Smith (1982: 21) who highlighted the challenge presented to writers of balancing the two strands of writing, the compositional aspects (namely getting the ideas, deciding what to say and selecting words and the grammar appropriate to the kind of writing), and the transcriptional aspects (namely the physical effort of writing, the spelling and the punctuation). He argued that 'composition and transcription can interfere with each other. The more attention you give to one, the more the other is likely to suffer.' In a shared writing context, the teacher can initially take on the transcriptional task, while children focus on what they wish to communicate in the writing. In undertaking the actual writing down of ideas, the teacher can talk about what he or she is doing, focusing on the structure of the text, the spelling or the punctuation, thus teaching about these things in a meaningful way.

Shared writing can be a valuable context for first attempts at a new genre. The shared writing session may be the culmination of a series of activities leading into writing. For example, the class may have read and analysed published examples of particular kinds of text – letters, poems or recipes, as well as stories – and the teacher may have talked about their characteristics and demonstrated how authors have structured these texts. An example of this is a collaboratively written recipe which was produced in a year 1 class. The children had begun by reading a version of the traditional story, *The Gingerbread Man*, as an enlarged text in shared reading.

After they had become very familiar with the text, which included considerable detail of how the gingerbread boy had been made, the teacher brought in recipes for gingerbread biscuits. The text of these recipes was enlarged and made into recipe cards, which were also used in shared reading. The teacher pointed out the similarities in the written forms of the different recipes and demonstrated the importance of ensuring that the list of ingredients was complete and that instructions were given in the correct order. The children then worked in groups, actually following a recipe and making their own gingerbread men, for class consumption. Two different recipes were used and the children were invited to evaluate which they preferred. It was only after all this preamble and preparation that the whole class came together to write their recipe in a shared writing session.

In another year 1 class, shared reading and shared writing were used as a vehicle to draw children's attention to rhyming words. The teacher's intention was 'to develop their ability to detect rhymes, to think of their own rhyming pairs of words and to look at common spelling patterns in order to foster the use of analogy'. She began by enlarging for shared reading, a short poem, 'Imagine' by Roland Egan:

> Imagine a snail
> As big as a whale,
> Imagine a lark
> As big as a shark,
> Imagine a bee
> As big as a tree.
> Imagine a toad
> As long as a road,
> Imagine a hare
> As big as a chair,
> Imagine a goat
> As long as a boat,
> And a flea the same size as me.

The children read this together and there was much discussion of spelling patterns and words which had the same sounds with different spellings. The class then moved on to write their own rhyming couplets for an 'Imagine' book which included the following couplets;

> Imagine eight men
> On a hen,
> Imagine a goat
> Eating a coat,
> Imagine a ghost
> Eating some toast,
> Imagine a snail
> As big as a bale,

> Imagine a flea
> As big as a bee,
> Imagine, I said,
> That I was a bed

The book was read frequently by groups and individuals, providing constant reinforcement of rhyme and spelling patterns.

What happens in shared writing?

It is possible to create all but the most personal kinds of text through shared writing. As with all writing, there needs to be a clearly defined and understood purpose for the activity and an understanding of the genre that is being attempted. The children need to know that they are going to write a list (for example, of questions to ask a visitor), a letter (for example, to an author or to parents), an account (for example, of a class visit), instructions (for example, how to make gingerbread men), a story or a poem.

The teacher will need a flip chart or several large sheets of paper attached to an easel, placed where all members of the group can see the text as it is written down. It is sometimes helpful to use different coloured pens for the writing – one for text, one for redrafting and/or editing, and one for punctuation – but this is not essential. The implementation of the National Literacy Strategy (DfEE 1998) has brought about an increase in the use of overhead projectors and shared writing can be done very effectively on acetates. Equally, in well-resourced schools, a word processor linked to a large screen or an interactive whiteboard can be used! The resources used will vary, but the intention, of making the composition and writing down of a text visible to all involved, will remain the same.

For teachers and children new to shared writing, a good starting point might be the retelling of a familiar story, perhaps from the viewpoint of one of the characters. When individual children offer suggestions about who the characters are or what will take place, it will often happen that others will not like an idea. This is when there can be useful discussion in which children must articulate their reasons why an event should or should not be incorporated. Sometimes the teacher will feel that a suggestion is not appropriate and will need to prompt children to reconsider an idea, using open questions, relating the idea to what has already been composed, generally thinking aloud. The interventions should not be designed to push children in a particular direction but should always be encouraging them to reflect on the writing process. Moira McKenzie (1985), who was a great advocate of shared writing, said; 'Shared writing obviously requires sensitive, skilled teachers, who listen carefully and who, without forcing ideas, can help children bring together their thinking and their language into a unified text.'

Once a consensus has been reached and while the text is being written down, the teacher can focus on whatever transcriptional details are relevant and appropriate to the needs of the children in the group. The focus might be on the use of full stops, capital letters or demarcation of speech. Sometimes it will be appropriate to invite children to offer the initial letter at the beginning of a word or even to tell the teacher how a word is spelt; the teaching focus might be a particular pattern of letters or unusual spellings.

As the writing proceeds the text is read and reread and children will often notice for themselves that the meaning is unclear or can be expressed more effectively. This is when the teacher scribe can demonstrate how writers can cross out, change the order of words, add or remove words or whole sentences, or find a better word or phrase. Through taking part in such redrafting, children can see that writers can and do change their minds and that the writing does not have to be 'right' first time. The completed text will need to be proofread and edited so that a further demonstration of this stage in the writing process is given and editing decisions are made explicit.

In the process of composing a text together, the group is being taught about and is involved in reflecting on the structure of the text; the beginning or opening; the sequencing of events; the characterisation, the setting and resolution if it is a story; the conclusion. Some of this terminology can be used purposefully with the children in discussing the writing as it proceeds. Equally, the whole process is an exercise in comprehension in which children actively work at comprehending and certainly strengthen their grasp of the structure of a narrative (or whichever other kind of text is being written).

A shared writing session is an excellent teaching context for every aspect of writing. In making explicit the processes that a writer must go through in constructing a text, the teacher models what writers actually have to do. She is also in a very good position to listen to the children as they compose the text; because they are working together children have, to some extent, to 'think aloud' and this can be very revealing. Misconceptions and misunderstandings become visible and assessments can be made which inform future planning.

Figure 2.1 attempts to bring together the various strands which make shared writing a productive teaching context. This model is rather different from that offered in *Developing Early Writing* (DfEE 2001) which proposes a three stage process: teacher demonstration; teacher scribing; supported composition. The emphasis at all stages is on the mechanics of writing, focusing on transforming speech into sentences, selecting vocabulary, choosing a range of connectives to sequence and structure the text and using style and voice appropriate to the style of the text, rather than on the collaborative creation of a piece of writing, led by the children. Whilst a shared writing session may include all of these aspects of writing, it should also consist of much more, and it should not always have this three stage structure. It is a far more flexible context than this model suggests, providing scope for imagination, personal interpretation and creativity if it is not over-directed by the teacher.

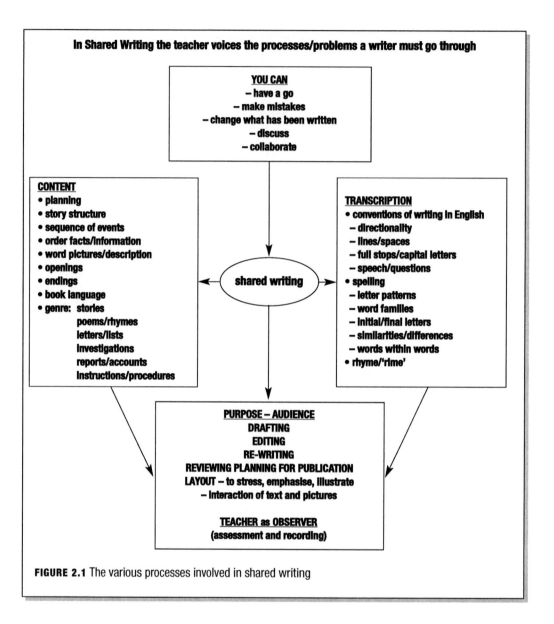

In Shared Writing the teacher voices the processes/problems a writer must go through

YOU CAN
– have a go
– make mistakes
– change what has been written
– discuss
– collaborate

CONTENT
- planning
- story structure
- sequence of events
- order facts/information
- word pictures/description
- openings
- endings
- book language
- genre: stories
      poems/rhymes
      letters/lists
      investigations
      reports/accounts
      instructions/procedures

shared writing

TRANSCRIPTION
- conventions of writing in English
  – directionality
  – lines/spaces
  – full stops/capital letters
  – speech/questions
- spelling
  – letter patterns
  – word families
  – initial/final letters
  – similarities/differences
  – words within words
- rhyme/'rime'

PURPOSE – AUDIENCE
DRAFTING
EDITING
RE-WRITING
REVIEWING PLANNING FOR PUBLICATION
LAYOUT – to stress, emphasise, illustrate
– interaction of text and pictures

TEACHER as OBSERVER
(assessment and recording)

FIGURE 2.1 The various processes involved in shared writing

For example, a group of year 2 children, inspired by shared readings of *Not now Bernard* (David McKee) and following lengthy discussion about what preoccupied and busy parents said to them, composed their own story, *Wait a Minute, Andrew*, modelled closely on *Not now Bernard*. In their story, the presence of a clumsy elephant who had placed Andrew on the roof, went un-noticed by busy parents when it took Andrew's place in the house. The children were immensely proud of their creation and the book quickly became favourite reading in this class and the parallel class, who, in turn, composed a further story called *Hang on, Rosie*, involving a girl and a dragon! In both cases, the ideas and the language of the text were the children's own; the teacher's interventions were largely limited to transcriptional details of spelling and punctuation, especially the use of inverted commas.

Conclusion

Shared reading and writing are sometimes criticised because not all children in a large group can or will participate actively. Clearly the teacher will need to be alert to the individual needs of children. The more reticent can often be drawn in by a carefully directed question or an invitation to comment on a suggestion for the text. Teachers will need to be particularly aware of pupils with English as an additional language to ensure they understand what is being said and can make sense of the demonstrations. That said, shared reading and writing are very good contexts for teaching about literacy in English, because so much has to be made explicit. The supportive participation in reading aloud in unison, which happens often in shared reading, and the memorable repetitive language patterns much used in children's books are immensely supportive to those children new to English. Even when children are not contributing verbally, they can be participating and be fully involved just by listening. Certainly all children are keen to return to the texts that they have read or have composed together to read independently and individually.

Shared reading and writing are important components of a programme for teaching reading and writing. Once children have read texts together or collaborated in writing a text, their confidence in tackling these independently is much increased. The modelling of the reading and writing processes in these contexts offers children strategies for working independently.

Acknowledgements

I am grateful to Alison Browning for permission to use the 'Imagine' examples and to Harriet Edwards for allowing me to observe her reading of *Hot Hippo*.

References

Clay, M. M. (1972) *Reading: the Patterning of Complex Behaviour*. Auckland: Heinemann Educational Books.

Clark, M. M. (1976) *Young Fluent Readers: What Can They Teach Us?* London: Heinemann Educational Books.

DfEE (1998) *The National Literacy Strategy: Framework for Teaching*. London: DfEE.

DfEE (2001) *The National Literacy Strategy: Developing Early Writing*. London: DfEE.

Hadithi, M. and Kennaway, A. (1992) *Hot Hippo*. London: Hodder Headline.

Holdaway, D. (1979) *The Foundations of Literacy*. Sydney: Ashton Scholastic.

McKee, D. (1987) *Not Now Bernard*. London: Beaver Books (Hutchinson).

McKenzie, M. (1985) 'Shared writing', in *Language Matters*, 1 and 2. London: Centre for Language in Primary Education.

Smith, F. (1981) 'Myths of writing' in *Language Arts*, **58**, 7. Urbana: National Council of English Teachers. In Smith, F. (1983) *Essays into Literacy*. London: Heinemann, pp. 81–8.

Smith, F. (1982) *Writing and the Writer*. London: Heinemann Educational Books.

Smith, F. (1984) 'The creative achievement of literacy', in *Awakening to Literacy*. H. Goelman, A. Oberg, and F. Smith, (eds). London: Heinemann Educational Books, pp. 143–53.

Wood, D., Bruner, J. S. and Ross, G. (1976) 'The role of tutoring in problem solving', *Journal of Child Psychology and Psychiatry*, 17, 89–100.

Vygotsky, L. S. (1978) *Mind in Society*. Cambridge, MA: Harvard University Press.

Mr Magnolia met the literacy hour: did he survive?

Judith Graham

Introduction

In the chapter I wrote for the first edition of *The Literate Classroom* (Graham in Goodwin, 1999), I debated whether children's books would survive the 'stop and analyse' approaches advocated by the NLS (National Literacy Strategy). I came to the conclusion that, on the whole, certain books might just survive. I suggested that books that involved a focus on language for its own sake (such as Quentin Blake's *Mr Magnolia* which has a joyous text woven round two dozen or so rhymes for the word 'boot') might not be too adversely affected but I voiced concern for books where more serious involvement with the story develops. Well, the years have passed and my sad conclusion is that the literacy hour was about many things but it was not about enjoying a story and thus it was not about making readers. Not even *Mr Magnolia* survives the dissecting that the literacy hour subjects him to and there is no great likelihood that children will remember their experience of the book with any pleasure. The only way that the integrity of books is respected in the class-room is if the teacher retains story-time, that is, a period when children are taken, without let or hindrance, by a fluent reader (or story-teller), into the secondary world of the book.

Many voices have been raised in alarm at the situation in schools at the moment. In April 2003, the Progress in International Reading Literacy Study (PIRLS) reported results from 35 countries. It confirmed that pupils in England read well compared to those in other countries, but found that their enjoyment of reading is poor by comparison. In the light of these findings, NFER decided to obtain more information on this important question by re-running a reading survey question-naire that was originally administered in 1998. The questionnaire was completed in June 2003 by year 4 and year 6 children in 74 schools.

The findings confirmed that children's enjoyment of reading had significantly declined since 1998. Although there is still a substantial majority of children who like to read stories, the percentage declined from 77 to 71 amongst the younger age group and from 77 to 65 amongst eleven-year-olds. There was also a decline in enjoyment of reading poems and information books, in both age groups. Children were less likely to enjoy going to the library, and more likely to prefer watching television to reading, than they were in 1998. Boys are less enthusiastic readers than girls and this survey showed that the decline in enjoyment over five years is more pronounced amongst boys than girls. The most stark pattern is found in the year 6 sample. Among eleven-year-olds, 15 per cent fewer boys say that they enjoy reading stories now than in 1998 (down from 70 to 55) whereas with girls there is a 10 per cent decline, from 85 to 75.

NFER's Principal Researcher, Dr Marian Sainsbury, who conducted both surveys, writes:

> Perhaps the most interesting findings from this study are the changes since 1998. The children who were surveyed in 2003 were the first to have received five years of teaching according to the National Literacy Strategy – all of their school careers in the case of the Year 4 pupils, and most of it for those in Year 6. The 1998 survey was carried out during the term before the strategy was introduced nationally.
>
> We know from national results and international studies that primary school children in England are good at reading, and their increased levels of confidence and independence are probably a direct reflection of this.
>
> On the other hand, enjoyment levels have declined. We have no direct evidence from this survey of the reasons for the change, and they may relate to broader shifts in children's interests over the last five years. But it is possible that this is also related to the drive to improve standards. Children are learning skills using reading material that has usually been chosen by the teacher rather than the children themselves. There may have been less emphasis on the sheer pleasure to be gained from books.
>
> (Sainsbury 2003).

(I do wonder if the decline in children's reading would have been even more dramatic if J. K. Rowling, Jacqueline Wilson and Philip Pullman had not been writing in this period.) NFER plan to repeat this survey every two years from now on, to track any changes in the future.

Dr Gemma Moss, at the Institute of Education, London, has also been researching how the NLS has changed practice in schools. She has found that before the strategy was introduced, a third of literacy time was used for comfortable, quiet reading where children could choose their own books. In most cases this has now disappeared – classrooms even look different.

> Reading used to look like fun, but now you won't find many beanbags. (The NLS) makes a difference as to how children think about reading; it makes the skills much more visible, but it also makes it clearer that reading is schoolwork.
>
> (Moss 1999)

A powerful voice that is heard frequently on these issues is that of Philip Pullman. He argues that we are creating a generation that 'hates reading and feels nothing but hostility for literature'. Here he is writing in *The Guardian*.

I recently read through the sections on reading in key stages 1 to 3 of the national literacy strategy, and I was very struck by something about the verbs. I wrote them all down. They included 'reinforce', 'predict', 'check', 'discuss', 'identify', 'categorise', 'evaluate', 'distinguish', 'summarise', 'infer', 'analyse', 'locate' ... and so on: 71 different verbs, by my count, for the activities that come under the heading of 'reading'. And the word 'enjoy' didn't appear once.

If we forget the true purpose of something, it becomes empty, a mere meaningless ritual. The purpose of what I do as a writer is to delight. I hope that the children who read me will do so because they enjoy it.

But this is what happens in schools now: a teacher wrote to me recently and complained that she'd been doing a book of mine called *The Firework Maker's Daughter* with her pupils, and she said she was finding the greatest difficulty preventing them from reading ahead to find out what was going to happen next. They had to stop, just when they got interested, and start predicting, or analysing, or evaluating, or something. They wanted to enjoy it, but she didn't feel she could let them.

I think she was paying me a compliment (see what exciting books you write), but her anxiety not to let a single verb in the literacy strategy go unticked, not a single box unfilled-in, was plain, and very dispiriting.

(Tuesday September 30, 2003 *The Guardian*)

Five children's authors, including Philip Pullman, write essays on the National Literacy Strategy in *Meetings with the Minister*. The authors argue that the use of extracts from 'texts' to teach everything from grammar to citizenship has made reading for pleasure a thing of the past. There is no longer time in the curriculum for reading aloud to the class, for silent reading or time for extended writing. Chris Powling succinctly states:

No child ever lost themselves in a *text*. It takes a book to do that.

and later,

An analytical and vigorously tested drills-and-skills approach has come to predominate in primary classrooms at the expense of enjoyment and the making of meaning.

(Powling in Ashley *et al.*, 1995)

Primary teachers are uncomfortably aware of the bind they are in. I asked some of them, 'How much do you read to your class just for the pleasure of reading?' By far the most frequent response was that there was now very little time to read aloud for more than a minute or two at a time and these moments were always 'snatched time'. Typical responses were:

'Literacy hours give children tasters of a wide variation of genres but they don't give them the experience of getting stuck in to a story. Reading aloud was supposed to give the children experience of intonation, expression and pace. Now they are just expected to acquire it from a few guided reads, not always the same genre, and only at the level they can read at.'

'This seems to be something that has been pushed to the side with the Literacy Strategy, reading a book for the pleasure of reading. I try and read to my year 1 class at least three times a week outside of the literacy hour. Even if it's only for 10 minutes before lunch/home. I've really tried to do this with my Y1 class but it's so HARD!!'

'Since we started getting free fruit! They eat and drink their milk and I read. And then in any odd moments I read to them.'

'Reading to the class is encouraged at my school, but getting the time to do it with my P6/7 is hard!'

'Whenever there's an odd minute or two. Sometimes we manage a page, sometimes a chapter, but the children love it!'

'I read while children are getting changed after PE and with one particularly boisterous bunch of year 5s the only way to get a peaceful art lesson is to read while they draw or paint!!'

What is poignant about these replies, is the recognition that the practice is so important. This comes out particularly in a comment such as:

I read to a year 1 class two or three times a day last week and it was incredibly noticeable that a couple of the boys (it was top-heavy with boys) who had most trouble sitting still in discussions and who were academically rather poor really came alive, and not only joined in discussion of the book, but dominated it.

Only the most confident can reply as these two teachers do:

I can't imagine a day in an infants' class without a story. What's the point of all that guff about predicting/beginning, middle and end/characters, etc. if it doesn't come from hearing stories and thereby developing an understanding of them? People talk about the uselessness of out-of-context drybones grammar exercises. The same applies to stories only much more so. Indeed, I would rather teach a child about predicting plots by watching *Coronation Street* with them every weekday for a month than by doing some of the rubbishy stuff produced by publishers hot on the literacy hour gravy train. I still can't forgive the idiot who expected me to 'teach' traditional stories to seven-year-olds by studying *Goldilocks* for six weeks. For heaven's sake, how pointless and boring can you get? No – I could have read them dozens of stories (and even told them a few as well) in the same amount of time. Yet here we have teachers (understandably) scared of getting into 'bad books' by telling stories to children.

My class are huge fans of me reading aloud to them. They are a mix of 2, 3 and 4. The results have been phenomenal! The amount of parents who have said to me that their son or daughter couldn't stand reading until they got to my class and then asked what I had done was great. We soon realised after chatting to the children it was my reading that had got them interested and yearning for more! Books I have read have been *Harry Potter*, *Charlie and the Chocolate Factory*, *Matilda* (which is a huge favourite) and *The Indian in the Cupboard*. I have also ensured that books we have begun in shared reading and perhaps ran out of time to finish are finished off by me. I read to them whenever we have a few minutes at the end of a lesson and I also timetable a slot before lunch every Monday. The kids just love it when I put on accents and become the characters for them. It gives me a break too as there are very few behaviour problems as the naughty ones just love to listen.

Of all the research that the anonymous compilers of the NLS might have consulted, the research on the value of reading aloud to children is the most copious, the most sustained over time, the most incontrovertible. William Teale writes:

> ...the belief that the practice of reading to young children is beneficial is accepted by researchers as well as by the educational community and, to a large degree, by the general public.
>
> (in Goelman, Oberg and Smith 1984)

Teale refers in his chapter to no fewer than 65 studies in which reading aloud to children is regarded as contributing directly to reading development. It is worth enjoying the words of Edmund Huey, one of the earliest writers to whom Teale refers:

> The child should long continue to hear far more reading than he does for himself. The ear not the eye is the nearest gateway to the child-soul, if not the man-soul ... There is no academy on earth that can compare with the practice (of reading good things aloud to children).
>
> (Huey 1908 [1968]: 334)

Nigel Hall looks at some of the same and several further studies and voices the same consensus:

> There is almost universal agreement that listening to stories is good for children who will be or are learning to read.
>
> (Hall 1987: 30)

Both Teale and Hall are particularly interested in parents reading to children but Stephen Krashen summarises a large body of research that indicates clearly that children read more when they listen to and discuss stories in school, and shows that even college students read more and 'better' books when they are read to.

> Gains were statistically significant after only 13 weeks of being read to for one hour a week.
>
> (Krashen 1993: 39)

If we move to individual experience and memories, the evidence is no less persuasive. Doris Lessing maintains:

> I was lucky that my parents read to my brother and me. I believe nothing has the impact of stories read or told. I remember the atmosphere of those evenings, and all the stories, some of them long-running domestic epics, made up by my mother, about the adventures of mice or our cats and dogs, or the little monkeys that lived around us in the bush and sometimes leapt around in the rafters under the thatch. Parents who read to their children or who make up stories are giving them the finest gift in the world.
>
> (Lessing in Fraser 1992: 44)

The poet Roger McGough is also under no illusion that his early listening experiences were of the essence:

> My mother...loved books and was a firm believer in the potency of words to charm, to heal and to educate. It was she who would put me on to a merry-go-round of nursery rhymes and simple prayers, then take me off, dizzy with words. Though books were scarce in those early years mother made sure I listened to a bedtime story every night.
>
> (McGough in Fraser 1992: 138)

Amongst recent writers who have passionately defended the role of reading aloud is the French writer Daniel Pennac whose hybrid of a book, *Reads Like a Novel* (1994), swept to best-sellerdom in its country of origin. In France, the sort of inquisitional teaching which the NLS espouses (though the NLS calls it 'interactive' rather than inquisitional) has been the model for older children for decades and is held responsible for the 57 per cent of the population thought to avoid reading after leaving school. Pennac persuades us of the importance both of home reading:

> We taught him everything about books during the period when he couldn't yet read. We opened him to the infinite diversity of things imaginary, initiated him into the joys of static travel, endowed him with ubiquity, delivered him from Chronos, plunged him into the fabulously populated solitude which is a reader's.
>
> (Pennac 1994: 9)

and of reading to school children:

> The voice of the teacher has certainly helped them to get back together with books. He has spared them the effort of deciphering, by drawing situations clearly, establishing settings, embodying characters, underlining themes, stressing nuances. He's acted like a photographic developer, bringing out the picture as clearly as possible.
>
> (Pennac 1994: 117)

That reading aloud to children is of major importance in the acquisition and maintenance of literacy should no longer need to be argued. It is everywhere we look, demonstrated by academics, teachers, writers, parents, researchers and ordinary readers. We are convinced of the importance of reading aloud because it so obviously models the activity: reveals to children what is between the covers of a book; convinces them that it is something they want; offers it to them repeatedly and then, as with so much learning, children begin to take over the task themselves and the parent or teacher can 'tiptoe away'. We should not need to revisit this scene but, extraordinarily, research and common sense appear to have been rejected by the NLS.

But wisdom and common sense have not deserted most teachers. At a workshop on the benefits of reading aloud, a group came up with the following ten reasons for 'teaching children the tune', a felicitous phrase that we owe to Margaret Meek and to Myra Barrs (Kimberley, Meek and Miller 1992: 20).

1 Reading aloud teaches children to want to read. It shows them their reading futures.

2 Children can listen to someone reading or telling a story for a long time. The words of a story weave a spell that they hesitate to interrupt. They get to hear a whole story and so have the satisfaction of hearing the story rounded off. The completeness and the pleasure of the experience means that they often request the same story again and again.

3 Through hearing a fluent reader reading aloud a child can hear the particular tune of continuous written prose. The language of books is not the same as in spoken conversation: new words, new rhythms, longer sentences, rhetorical effects such as repetition, alliteration, and so on. Access to all this must initially be through listening.

4 Children begin to appreciate that the words in the book stay the same so that they can have the story again and again. This stability, not so evident in spoken conversation, is very appealing.

5 Children can inspect and comment on the pictures of a picture book whilst the voice-over continues. If pictures extend or counterpoint the written text, children's contributions help them become equal constructors of meaning with all that that signifies for bonding with the book.

6 Children start to speak the text with the rhythm, pitch and intonation that they have heard. They imitate and play at being readers. In addition, they pick up whole phrase structures which they reproduce. (They do the same with what they have been exposed to several times on TV.) This 'reading-like behaviour' is part of the repertoire of early fluent readers.

7 The intonation patterns children pick up by listening to someone reading become internalised and support silent reading later on.

8 Learning how to write is certainly connected to the tunes in the head, accumulated from listening to fluent reading aloud.

9 A far greater repertoire of quality books can be acquired through listening than through early hesitant reading.

10 All the above may be equally true for non-narrative as for narrative. All the

'e is particularly true for EAL children and children with special educational needs.

If teachers know all this, then we have nothing to fear. They also know about the importance of telling as well as reading stories aloud to children; of giving children opportunities to browse; of children choosing books with and without guidance for private reading in and out of school. They particularly know about picture books and they know that at all stages the picture book can teach literary conventions, carry the culture, inform, build up knowledge of story grammar, delight, lay down images to live with, promote readerly satisfaction, be deliciously subversive and intensely affecting. They know that children start to write with commitment and sustain their writing at length and to completion when they are respected as authors and are not just practising techniques and focused worriedly on transcription. Any one of these items could be examined in the same way as I have approached the question of reading aloud. The NLS appeared to have forgotten all of this in its obsession with direct instruction.

Why should this be so? My only explanation is that in the excitement of new discoveries in the areas of phonics, grammar, narrative structure, genre and discourse analysis, the writers of the NLS convinced themselves that this new information must be essential for the task of learning to read and write. Because we have worked out the rules, they say to themselves, we can lay them down exactly and in great detail, then teachers can drill them into their pupils and then they will become a permanent part of children's competence.

But learning is not like that and language learning in particular is not like that. Transmission is not the name of the game, however informed the teacher. The question asked by many teachers 'How did anyone ever learn to read and write before they knew all of this?' is answered easily. Children learn to read and write, not when they dissect and analyse the processes prematurely, but when people around them indicate the benefits, joys, meaning and purposes of reading and writing and support the easy acquisition of them. Asking teachers to replace a natural and enjoyable process with something abstract, inappropriate and impossibly cumbersome is a mistake. We must hope that teachers continue to use their best instincts and professional judgement in these times of central control. *Mr Magnolia* must live.

References

Ashley, B., Fine, A., Gavin, J., Powling, C. and Pullman, P. (1995) *Meetings with the Minister*. Available for £4.95 from the National Centre for Language and Literacy, University of Reading, Bulmershe Court, Reading RG6 1HY.

Blake, Q. (1980) *Mr Magnolia*. London: Jonathan Cape.

DfEE (1998) *The National Literacy Strategy*. London: DfEE.

Fraser, A. (ed.) (1992) *The Pleasure of Reading*. London: Bloomsbury Publishing.

Goelman, H., Oberg, A. and Smith, F. (1984) *Awakening to Literacy*. New Hampshire: Heinemann Educational Books.

Goodwin, P. (ed.) (1999) *The Literate Classroom*. London: David Fulton.

Hall, N. (1987) *The Emergence of Literacy*. Sevenoaks: Edward Arnold.

Huey, E. (1968, first published in 1908) *The Psychology and Pedagogy of Reading*. Cambridge, MA: MIT Press.

Kimberley, K., Meek, M. and Miller, J. (1992) *New Readings: Contributions to an Understanding of Literacy*. London: A & C Black.

Krashen, S. (1993) *The Power Of Reading. Insights from the Research*. Colorado: Libraries Unlimited.

Moss, Gemma (1999) in a lecture delivered at United Kingdom Reading Association Conference at Chester.

Pennac, D. (1994) *Reads like a Novel*. London: Quartet Books.

Progress in International Reading Literacy Study (PIRLS) *PIRLS 2001 International Report: IEA's Study of Reading Literacy Achievement in Primary Schools*, Mullis, I.V.S., Martin, M.O., Gonzalez, E.J., and Kennedy, A.M. (2003), Chestnut Hill, MA: Boston College.

Pullman, P. (2003) *The Guardian*.

Sainsbury, M. (2003) *Children's Attitudes to Reading*. Slough: NFER.

PART

II

Becoming readers

Readers making meaning: responding to narrative

Tony Martin

Introduction

This chapter explores the potential of reader response approaches in the classroom for exploring narrative and teaching children about its characteristics. The ways in which readers and texts interact, with both sides contributing to the making of meaning, is explored. The problem of focusing exclusively on the text and its features, to the exclusion of the ways different child readers are responding to it, can result in children viewing narrative texts as things to be analysed. The exercise becomes one of answering 'text questions' correctly. Giving status initially to the responses of readers produces a much richer appreciation of narrative as through these responses the ways in which the text is constructed and written are exposed for consideration.

As schools engage with the idea of being creative with the literacy hour and viewing it as a 'springboard for teaching' rather than a 'set of constraints' (*Excellence and Enjoyment: A Strategy for Primary Schools*, DfES 2003) 'reader response' is a powerful idea to clarify thinking and guide planning. For all its successes, the National Literacy Strategy accorded 'response' (readers sharing their own responses to the texts they read) low status. While references to it do appear at different points in the 'termly objectives' (for example, text level work, year 6, term 1, 'to articulate personal responses to literature'), there is no explicit examination of the meaning of response or of ways of working in which children learn about texts through their responses to them. This has been further exacerbated by the so-called response question being the last question in the end of key stage 2 reading assessment – tagged on at the end of the 'important' comprehension questions. There is a danger in literacy hours of works of literature being viewed as text types to be analysed. The focus is on the text, with the different feelings, thoughts and ideas of the individual children making up the class barely getting a look in. Yet if the ultimate aim is to enable children to read and enjoy a range of texts (and I assume that *is* the ultimate aim), a key approach for teaching lies at the heart of reader response: begin with the reader's response and use that to explore the features of the text.

What is 'reader response'?

> The reader can begin to achieve a sound approach to literature only when he reflects upon his response to it, when he attempts to understand what in the work and in himself produced that reaction, and when he thoughtfully goes on to modify, reject or accept it.
>
> (Rosenblatt 1976)

The above quotation is nearly 30 years old. There are now many books, articles and research projects which have been published describing and discussing 'reader response' in terms of adult, adolescent and child readers. There has been work on novels, short stories, poetry and picture books, all of it making the same fundamental point. Response is *not* just about the personal responses of readers to what they read in the sense of likes and dislikes. In the classroom, questions concerning who enjoyed a story or a novel are just the starting point for response work. As the Rosenblatt quotation clearly states, it is the quality of how a reader 'reflects upon his response' which really counts.

Reader response is about reflection – thinking about what has been read. However, its starting point is not just the text (the story, novel, picture book or poem) but the way in which the reader responded to it and found it exciting or sad or funny or frightening. The interesting question then is 'Why did the text provoke the particular response?' and will involve two considerations simply represented by

reader – *interaction* – text

The interaction between reader and text is the response, and both sides of the process will contribute towards it. First, readers bring themselves to what they read; their personalities, beliefs, memories, relationships and indeed their whole lives will impact upon the reading. I am four years old listening to *Go To Sleep Little Bear* by Martin Waddell and staring wide eyed at Barbara Firth's illustrations. The reason is that I too am frightened of the dark and need a loved adult to reassure me. I am an adult reading a romantic novel and responding in terms of my own relationships – 'I've been there' or 'I wish...' As a private reader that sort of response may well be enough and much of it may not be articulated but in the classroom we can build on it to examine the second aspect of response; the ways in which texts work to produce their effects on readers. Four-year-olds can join in patterned repetitive texts and appreciate how they work. They can focus on particular words, phrases and sentences. Older children can search for words, phrases and sentences which made the text exciting or frightening or funny, mark them and discuss them, use them in their writing. Reading and listening to literature, whether by four-year-olds or adults, is about readers interacting with texts.

Response or comprehension: what's the difference?

Look back at the Rosenblatt quotation in terms of defining 'comprehension' of liter-ature. What we have is in fact a powerful definition of comprehension, which is generally discussed as an active process of readers engaging with what they read. However, there is a danger that it is viewed in the classroom as a passive process with questions focused purely on the text rather than building on how the reader responded. At its worst, it simply becomes a weekly test to answer questions on an extract in a course book. Here there is a confusion between an assessment tool and a teaching strategy. Presenting children with a passage and asking them questions will certainly tell us something about their ability as readers but it is not a teaching strategy. Oral and written response work aimed at children reflecting on what they have read is far more likely to produce 'thinking' readers who 'comprehend' what they read:

> As opposed to worksheets, which encourage 'right answer' responses and rarely expand thinking…the student is encouraged to interact with the text and use her own experi-ences and the book to interpret and construct meaning from what she reads. The student is always encouraged to go back to the text to support her response.
>
> (Routman 1991)

Examining the text to support and justify response means that we are a world away from simplistic notions of likes and dislikes. Of course, each reader will create their own meanings so that no two readers will read the same text in the same ways (and that is a challenging thought for any teacher) but 'to go back to the text to support…response' means the parts played by both the text and the reader are recognised and given status in the classroom. There is no difference between response and comprehension.

Response and the sharing of big books

Arthur Koestler (1964) wrote that 'literature begins with the telling of a tale' and so fiction begins with narrative books in the early years. Big books, around which the children sit so that they can see both pictures and print, are used in literacy hours. So, where does response fit in? I would argue that the real issue is the difference between the first reading of a text and the further readings which will take place. For the first reading the focus for narrative needs to be on book knowledge (titles, authors, illustrators, front covers and back covers) and response. The danger of rushing on immediately to draw attention to the print itself is just that – a rush. There are five ways in which we can highlight and give status to response at a first reading:

1   We look at the title and the picture on the cover and ask, 'What do you think this is going to be about?' This is answered on the basis of clues in the text (the cover). I like to put children into pairs so that the question is posed to a pair and they whisper their ideas to each other. Then we all hear some of them. This is wonderful in reception! (As an aside, all of the current promotion of 'whole class teaching' seems to be on posing questions which children have to answer alone. Has no one realised the potential of other strategies? Children in pairs or, as they get older, threes with the chance for discussion and an agreed answer?)

2   We read the text aloud with dramatic intonation. The aim is for our voice to bring the text to life and to show children how it ought to be read. We are almost defying them not to engage with the story.

3   We might stop at an opportune moment and ask 'What do you want to happen now?' In my experience this question is rarely asked, the emphasis being on what children 'think' will happen. What I *think* will happen is a text question. What I *want* to happen is a reader question. (Do not think that this only works for young children. It is exactly what we do as adults when faced with the dilemmas of characters in the novels we read. It is not the coolly rational 'I think that she will marry him' but the highly emotional 'Oh no, don't marry him!'.)

4   At the end of the story we share our enthusiasms. This can be done simply by getting children to talk about their favourite page (the teacher having discussed her favourite page first of course!). Some can come out and turn the pages of the book until they reach their favourite. This is much more effective for promoting discussion than rushing in immediately with a set of questions about the text which a child knows he or she might get wrong.

5   We end with silent reading. Grown-ups read silently, in their heads; so now the pages of the story are turned and each child gazes at them in silence. If they are unable to read the print they can use the pictures to tell the story in their heads.

Of course we need to teach the range of different skills and awareness that children need in order to learn to read, but a first reading should surely be on response and engagement.

How might this develop in key stage 1? One way is to use longer texts, the sort of 'novels' that we might read aloud to children, and help them to focus on a part of it in detail. Infant teacher, Margaret Munn, decided to use the opening page of *The Key* by Jan Mark as a focus for discussion with a group of year 2 children. She wrote:

> I read the opening to them and then attempted to keep pace in scribing their response as the ideas came tumbling out of them. The children used the writing and the pictures to weave their own stories about the text. Their ideas sparked off other ideas, they argued, went off at tangents...The scope of their imaginative creations seemed endless.

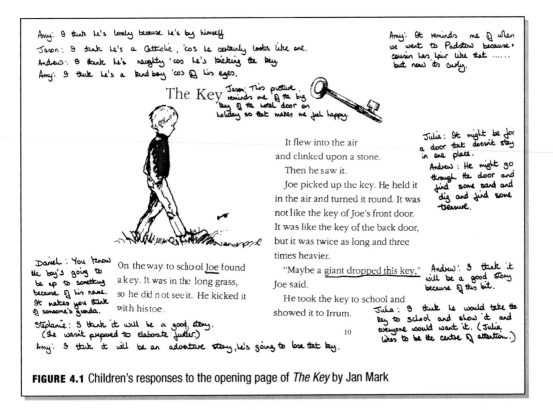

Amy: I think he's lonely because he's by himself
Jason: I think he's a Catholic, 'cos he certainly looks like one.
Andrew: I think he's naughty 'cos he's kicking the key.
Amy: I think he's a kind boy 'cos of his eyes.

Amy: It reminds me of when we went to Padstow because cousin has hair like that ...... but now it's curly.

The Key

Jason: This picture reminds me of the big key of the hotel door on holiday so that makes me feel happy.

It flew into the air
and clinked upon a stone.
　　Then he saw it.
　　Joe picked up the key. He held it
in the air and turned it round. It was
not like the key of Joe's front door.
It was like the key of the back door,
but it was twice as long and three
times heavier.

Julia: It might be for a door that doesn't stay in one place.
Andrew: He might go through the door and find some sand and dig and find some treasure.

Daniel: You know the boy's going to be up to something because of his name. It makes you think of someone's granda.
Stephanie: I think it will be a good story. (She wasn't prepared to elaborate further.)
Amy: I think it will be an adventure story, he's going to lose that key.

On the way to school Joe found
a key. It was in the long grass,
so he did not see it. He kicked it
with his toe.

"Maybe a giant dropped this key,"
Joe said.
　　He took the key to school and
showed it to Irrum.

Andrew: I think it will be a good story because of this bit.
Julia: I think he would take the key to school and show it and everyone would want it. (Julia likes to be the centre of attention.)

10

FIGURE 4.1 Children's responses to the opening page of *The Key* by Jan Mark

The children's responses (Figure 4.1) illustrate vividly the parts played by both readers and the text (as well as containing a wonderful response in Jason's first contribution 'I think he's a Catholic 'cos he certainly looks like one'!). In terms of what readers bring we have connections with the children's lives as both Jason and Amy are reminded about family holidays. For Daniel the name Joe makes him 'think of someone's granda'. In terms of picking up clues from the text, Amy thinks 'it will be an adventure story; he's going to lose that key', while Julia and Andrew are also making predictions. Andrew focuses even closer on one sentence which makes him think 'it will be a good story'. In these comments, no doubt triggered by careful questioning by the teacher, we begin to see how far true response work is from simple notions of likes and dislikes, and how closely it links with a view of comprehension as an active engagement with texts.

Fiction at key stage 2

At key stage 2, fiction will mean novels and short stories. A unit focusing on narrative ought to contain:

- At least one whole story, namely a short story (two would be better).

- Extracts chosen to illustrate particular aspects of narrative, for example, character descriptions, atmospheric settings, openings.
- Extracts from the novel currently being read to the class – so that the extract has a context: the children know the part of the novel from which the extract was taken.

In the classroom, approaches can be used to develop appreciation of what readers bring and how texts work in order to make children better readers in the sense of thinking about what they are reading and how they are reading it. Such work can be considered under five headings: range of reading; the teacher reading aloud; discussion of fiction; investigation of fiction; reading leading to writing.

A range of reading

Frank Smith (1978) wrote, 'Inexperienced readers must find all texts unconventional.' He was referring here to a key idea in developing children as readers, that of 'literary competence'. This means knowing 'how to read' a particular type of text, knowing how it will go and the conventions which are likely to operate. We develop this competence through reading. For example, if you are given a poem to read, your mind will automatically switch into poem mode. The voice in your head will be your poem voice. You will expect a certain type of text and poetic conventions. However, you can only do this because you have read poetry. Imagine that if you had never seen a poem. How well would you cope then? The same idea of 'literary competence' applies to fiction. As adults we are only faced with how much we know (or what we expect) when we open a novel with an unconventional opening; some of us will not want to read on; we feel lost and not sure what games the author is playing with us!

At key stage 2 there is a major distinction between experienced readers and inexperienced readers. The former, by year 6, will already have read widely. Faced with the next novel, short story or poem they can draw on their experience of all the previous ones. The latter group have not read widely. They have played safe or even been encouraged to do so by teachers who think that reading is only about getting the words right. Faced with a novel of some length the sheer number of pages puts them off. Faced with a subtle short story or poem they cannot 'comprehend' because they have not read enough of them to know how they work. It is interesting to consider how many year 6 children face the short story in the SAT as inexperienced readers of short stories.

We are able to choose between stories and novels in terms of the following:

- *Subject matter.* Different settings are used, historically, geographically and culturally, some of which children can identify with in terms of their own experience and some which take them into places and times and situations far removed from their own. Likewise the effect on the reader should vary so that children feel the power of fictional narrative – stories which make them laugh, cry and hold their breath, stories which shock and stories which delight. Some ought to have strong story lines so that the plot is the main attraction, but others will have less plot and instead focus on underlying themes as they explore character or situation.

■ *Style*. Some stories are written in the first person with a character narrator and others in the third person so that they can explore who is actually doing the telling. Some have a lot of dialogue, and others put the emphasis on description.

■ *Structure*. Some stories are based around one major idea. In others there may be a major plot and one or more subplots. Endings can tie up all the loose ends or may be left open so that readers are invited to speculate about what might happen.

Through being encouraged to read a range of fiction, children will develop the 'literary competence' necessary to appreciate the varied ways in which different stories and novels work.

Teacher reads aloud

This is a vital element in developing children as readers for two reasons. First, through reading aloud we model reading for children, demonstrating to them just how such a story ought to be read. We let them hear the 'voice' that they will need when they read themselves. This is vitally important for inexperienced readers, especially those who struggle with reading. In addition, they are able to respond to the power of a text without encountering the problems of having to decode it for themselves. Simply listening and responding to a dramatic voice telling a powerful story is a worthwhile experience in itself. While we ought to use texts of all types to focus children on sentence and word level matters, we must not forget the validity of literature for its own sake. It must not always be used for other purposes in the primary classroom. The second reason for reading aloud to children is that we can do so at a level beyond their own reading ability. We can choose challenging texts in terms of the three elements of range described above and through our reading – our use of varied intonation, rhythm and pace – enable them to appreciate a text they could not read for themselves. Teacher reading aloud is a precursor to teaching strategies such as guided reading.

Fiction can be discussed

Before any of us embark on a story or novel we have expectations and these can be explored in the classroom by children working in small groups. So, the story is called *Who's afraid?*, the author is Philippa Pearce (1977) and it is some six pages long – what are your expectations? There are three main categories of expectation provoked by the following:

- *The title*. 'This is a scary story perhaps, connections with "who's afraid of the big bad wolf?"'
- *The author*. 'I've already read other stories and novels by Philippa Pearce, so I think it will be about modern times and perhaps have lots to think about.'
- *The reader*. 'I think short stories are boring and so I won't enjoy it' or 'I love listening to short stories.'

Expectations can be gathered on a class list and then hidden until the story has been read, when they can be a fascinating focus for further discussion.

Some short stories are best read right through to the end in order for their power to affect children. If we constantly interrupt for discussion we can ruin the story. However, other stories and certainly novels can be discussed at different points in terms of aspects of response:

- Readers predict their way through narrative, thinking about both what will happen and what they want to happen.
- Readers turn texts into pictures so that they can imagine places, people and events. These pictures are always seen from a particular viewpoint so that we can discuss where children were looking from in a particular scene.
- Readers make connections between themselves and their own lives and those of characters – 'I've felt that' or 'I've been there'. Of course, we must not expect children to share what might be very personal connections, but the teacher should try and make some herself – 'I always feel sad at the end of "Who's afraid?" because I remember when my grandmother died.' Then children realise that this is on the reading agenda; this is a powerful reason why adults read. We have engaged in important reading teaching just through modelling our own response.
- Readers are affected by what they read, feeling sad, frightened, shocked or excited.

Each of these aspects of the reading process can be opened up through sensitive questioning and comment so that children are enabled to discuss how they read and what they read.

After reading, as we read the final sentence of a novel or short story, perhaps to the class or in a guided reading group, we have a choice of options:

- Ask some questions. Actually this can kill discussion rather than encourage it (and presumably discussion is what we are trying to encourage). The sort of question aimed at testing memory (what event was Joe attending in 'Who's afraid?') will involve some children but really miss the point. They immediately begin the process of reducing the reading of literature to memory tests. Indeed I would suggest that any questions involving right and wrong answers are not the best way to proceed at the end of a powerful read.

- It is far better to share our enthusiasm. We must not be afraid to allow a minute's silence at the end to let each reader feel and think. Then I, as the teacher, can say what I felt and thought: 'What an ending!', 'What a story!', 'I really liked the bit where...'. What we provide with such comments is a model of someone who genuinely enjoys reading and who also enjoys discussing it. Such an approach always leads to a much more enthusiastic discussion with children than we get with questions.

- Look back at the expectations that we listed before we began. How far were they met? Who was proved wrong? Who was surprised by any part of the story?

Of course, discussing fiction in a whole class setting often means the teacher discussing with a small number of pupils, while some of the others are on the edge of the discussion and others are thinking about something completely different. If the challenge is to include every child in the discussion, the range of speaking and listening strategies in 'speaking, listening learning' (National Primary Strategy 2003) can be used in powerful teaching sequences. Children can move from 'silent thinking' (for example, one minute to reflect), to discussing with a talk partner, to comparing with another pair (twos to fours), to sending an envoy to see how another group has got on, to reporting to the whole class.

Fiction can be investigated

Earlier I described the range of short stories in terms of subject matter, style and structure. These text features can be investigated by children through careful questioning. The aim is not to introduce some watered-down literary criticism exercise but to enable children to appreciate how stories and novels are crafted and the conventions which operate in them. So, the opening pages of a number of novels can be photocopied and compared. How are they similar? How are they different? Are there any clues in the text, for example, about what this novel might be about and what could happen? What sort of a novel will this be? Will it be a plot with a lot of incidents or more about characters and relationships?

The need for readers to orient themselves to what is going on at the beginning of a story is very important. Experienced readers learn to 'trust the author' and can tolerate a fair amount of uncertainty but we all know children who will not persevere with a novel – 'It's boring', 'Nothing's happened', 'Can I change it?' How many of these children are actually inexperienced readers who do not know 'how to read an opening', children who are unclear about the conventions and who actually lack the 'literary competence' to cope with a sustained read?

And then there is the range of drama strategies through which children can develop their understanding of the text. Characters can be hotseated and questioned. Scenes can be role played and freeze framed. The thoughts of characters can be tracked. Any story or novel contains opportunities for children to work in these ways, and through 'experiencing' the text (rather than just sitting being taught about it) they can deepen their response and appreciation of the way the text has been constructed and written.

Reading can lead to writing

The reading–writing connection can be harnessed powerfully when working on response in the classroom. Children can track their ever-changing and developing responses to a novel through keeping response journals. Instant responses can be captured using 'stickers' attached to each page, just for jotted thoughts and feelings on the aspects described above. These can be summarised at the end and used as the basis for discussion in small groups. Next, the text which has been read can lead to the creation of texts which the children write. In each case the aim is for the writing to reflect the reading and in some cases actually be modelled on the reading. So, one or more of the following possibilities could be chosen:

- They could write a sequel – 'Who's afraid 2', 'The return of Dicky Hutt'.
- They could omit the ending, write their own ending and then compare.
- They could write an alternative ending.
- They could write an imaginary journal kept by one of the characters through the action of the story.
- They could write a third person story in the first person, in 'Who's afraid?', we could write Joe's version or Dicky Hutt's version or Grandma's version.
- They could write letters between the characters after the story has finished.
- They could write poetry which reflects the underlying themes of the story.
- They could draw and annotate key scenes.

In examples such as a sequel or an ending, the modelling can be at the level of the plot, the themes and the style. For some children the plot might be enough but able, experienced readers can be helped to consider the way that the story has been written.

Writing is a powerful way for us to make sense of our thoughts and feelings. Through writing, whether it be a response journal or writing based on the text, children can reflect consciously on what they have read, how it affected them and ways in which the text was written to provoke particular responses. Such work can be a precursor to discussion as well as following it. Having written, children are better prepared to discuss what they have read.

We can never capture response in the sense of articulating exactly how we felt at particular moments in the reading of a story, novel or poem. The moment that we try to reflect and put it into words we realise how our language does not really enable us to say what we felt. Nevertheless, as adults we love discussing plays and films that we have seen and books that we have read. To produce children who not only can read but who also do read and enjoy discussing what they have read must surely be a key aim for the future of any national strategy.

References

DfEE (1998) *The National Literacy Strategy: Framework for Teaching*. London: DfEE.

DfES (2003) *Excellence and Enjoyment*. London: DfES.

Koestler, A. (1964) *The Act of Creation*. London: Hutchinson.

Pearce, P. (1977) 'Who's afraid?', in *The Shadow Cage*. London: Kestrel.

QCA and NLS (2003) *Speaking, Listening, Learning*. London: DfES.

Rosenblatt, L. (1976) *Literature and Exploration*, 3rd edn. New York: Noble and Noble.

Routman, R. (1991) *Invitations: Changing as Teachers and Learners K-12*. Portsmouth, New Hampshire: Heinemann Educational Books.

Smith, F. (1978) *Reading*. Cambridge: Cambridge University Press.

Reading silently

Geoff Fenwick

Introduction

This chapter intends to justify the use of silent reading in schools, to consider its organisation and to assess its standing at present, particularly in view of government initiatives on literacy teaching and subsequent revisions of the National Curriculum. In classrooms where pupils are developing their literacy, the use of silent reading should be taken for granted. As they grow older, silent reading becomes more frequent and, in most cases, more popular than reading aloud. What, then, is the problem? It rests with what might be termed 'the first S', namely the 'sustained' in sustained silent reading (SSR). Attitudes towards reading silently for considerable periods of time have fluctuated over many years. This is something which we need to consider particularly in view of its decline as a classroom activity since the late 1990s.

The trouble with silent reading

In a developed country almost everyone reads silently. It is, clearly, the form of reading most frequently used. Read a menu out to your friends and, if they have their own copies, you will probably be considered condescending or even boring. Read the paper aloud as you travel on public transport and you are likely to be thought an eccentric nuisance. Furthermore, reading silently is quick, convenient and almost impossible to avoid as we pick our way through the mass of environmental print which is such a feature of today's urban society. How could we do this if we were unable to read? It is worth considering, in a perverse way, just how ingenious illiterates must have to be, first to conceal their disability and second to come to terms with it in a society so saturated with the written word.

Yet there are suspicions about reading, especially if we do a lot of it. 'Bookish', 'deskbound', 'absent minded', 'impractical' and 'bookworm' are expressions which come to mind in this respect. They represent, to some extent, old prejudices and suspicions which contrast the theoretical with the practical, and the manual with the sedentary. They also represent social worries about being too clever. Claims by radicals such as Paulo Freire (1972) that literacy is the key to freedom for oppressed peoples did not go down well with authoritarian regimes. In more light-hearted vein, but not so much removed from opponents to Freire's ideas as they might at first appear, we have the thoughts of Miss Sarah Byng in one of Hilaire Belloc's (1930) celebrated cautionary tales. Sarah, having been tossed into a hedge by a furious bull because she could not read the warning notice, associated her plight with the latter and not the former. For Sarah, literature bred distress, as it still does to many people who, for one reason or another, find it unpleasant.

The development of silent reading

A primary teacher on being introduced to SSR some years ago remarked, 'This is just good old-fashioned silent reading modernised.' This definition seems to suit the activity nicely. To be sure, whole classes of children have in the past often read silently and for fairly lengthy periods. This at least is better than the arrangement whereby pupils have been asked to read silently after all other work has been completed. Such an arrangement ensures that many children, including some who need it most, will do little, if any, silent reading.

During the 1970s, reading experts in the USA began to scrutinise silent reading, especially in terms of how it should be conducted. This was important because hitherto the activity had seemed so straightforward that its value and implementation were taken for granted. Even today this assumption creates problems for teachers. Work in the USA in the 1970s established that silent reading could be carried out effectively as follows:

- when it is practised by a whole class;
- for a considerable period of time;
- in either silence or quietness;
- with little or no interruption;
- with no subsequent testing.

In justifying their programmes, US workers in the field made the point that reading, like most skills, requires practice and, to a certain extent, the more that it is practised, the greater the improvement will be. In this respect, reading might be likened to some more physical skills, for example, swimming, ice skating and marathon running. To become more proficient at these sports, intense practice is required. Once the skills are mastered, however, they must not be put to one side. The marathon runner, for example, will learn to run economically and with great sensitivity of pace. If he does not continue to practise running prodigious distances his performances will deteriorate rapidly. Similarly, reading needs to be practised to develop what might be termed 'reading stamina', namely the ability to read for substantial periods of time. Further justifications involved the conditions under which silent reading could be satisfactorily conducted, the economy of large groups of pupils taking part and the amount of time required. Initially some of the US experiments were perhaps too rigid in terms of the time allowed, 50 minutes being sometimes recommended. Today this would be regarded as too long and duration is now regarded as being age related. In addition, absolute silence and no changing of books were often expected.

As SSR became more frequently practised, its ground rules were not surprisingly adapted to suit individual schools and classes. The amount of time devoted to a session was more likely to be about 20 minutes. In addition, silence was often thought not to be necessary and the changing of books was often permitted during sessions which usually occurred several times a week. By 1980 Moore *et al.* (1980) were able to report that uninterrupted sustained silent reading (USSR) or SSR took place in many schools in USA and that both appeared to be successful in most cases although rigorous evaluation was somewhat sparse. The acronyms USSR and SSR by this time had become well known and were merely alternatives describing the same activity. Since then there have been frequent reports in US journals, notably *The Reading Teacher* and *The Journal of Reading*, of experiments in organisations ranging from the kindergarten to secondary schools. The great majority appear to have been successful although, admittedly, success rather than failure is always more likely to be reported. Two further important points have emerged from these reports. Some schools arranged SSR so that all classes participated at the same time. This has usually been termed 'whole-school reading' and seems particularly applicable to secondary schools where manipulation of the timetable is difficult. In addition, Perez (1986) provided evidence which showed that SSR was more likely to be effective when the teacher took part and read silently, acting as a model of good practice. So far we have examined events on the other side of the Atlantic. How has the activity developed in the UK?

Educationalists visiting USA and Canada in the mid-1980s reported enthusiastically on the merits of SSR. Their comments appeared in the educational press on a number of occasions. One such was Vera Southgate whose later research with colleagues (Southgate *et al.* 1981) claimed that too much time was devoted to hearing children read in British schools and not enough to silent reading. Her research backed up the findings of another study by Lunzer and Gardner (1979) who found that too much reading in secondary schools was of a 'short burst' variety; in other words it was not sustained. These researchers also found that many teachers worried about the consequences of visitors to the classroom observing SSR being practised and regarding it in a negative light.

It is not possible to say exactly when SSR was first adopted by British schools. Clearly, the work mentioned above made some impact. It was followed in the 1980s by descriptions of work which had actually taken place in the UK, (see, for example, Walker (1980) and Maybin (1983)), discussion of the activity (Campbell 1988) and a survey by Fenwick (1988) which included a number of accounts of good practice. Research on how SSR was conducted also provided helpful information. One of the most useful of these was the work of Wheldall and Entwistle (1988) which indicated quite clearly that the teacher as a role model was, as Perez (1986) had claimed earlier, an extremely important factor. Later work by Campbell and Scrivens (1995) showed that although the teacher as a role model was important, help given to individuals and groups of children during SSR could also be useful.

Justifying silent reading today

By 1990, it was widespread in both primary and secondary schools. The length of sessions varied according to age and, in primary schools at least, it occurred on average three times per week. Generally both teachers and pupils were enthusiastic about it, quietness rather than silence was usual and pupils were often encouraged to have several books available to avoid the disruption which was likely to happen when books were changed during sessions. In short, SSR seemed to be both a popular and a successful part of the reading programme. The following examples were taken during the 1990s from schools where the activity was practised successfully. They show that the way in which SSR is organised depends very much upon the age of the pupils.

Silent reading in year 1

SSR was practised by all classes in this school, although not at the same time. Initially the time devoted to it was no more than five minutes during daily sessions. This was gradually increased so that by the end of the autumn term it lasted for 10 minutes. By the end of the school year this had been extended to 15 minutes.

During SSR, pupils were required to read quietly and interruptions were discouraged. The reading materials consisted of books with a limited number of words and supplementary readers. Initially there had been chaos when the children were permitted to change their books as and when they wished. This ceased when they were allowed to have three different books to work with.

The teacher did not read but instead observed her pupils and anticipated difficulties. At the end of each session she discussed with the whole class what had taken place. In addition, she held regular small-group discussions and kept notes on pupils' individual choices. Enthusiasm for SSR was such that by the end of the autumn term most of the children were bringing in some of their own books to read. The teacher believed that her main function during SSR was to ensure that her young pupils developed the ability to make useful selections.

Silent reading in year 6

A small crowded classroom containing 30 pupils did not appear at first sight to be a propitious venue for SSR. There were, however, a number of old bookcases which contained a treasure trove of reading material, mainly fiction. It was particularly impressive that the books were a delightful mixture of old and new, freshly bought books alongside well-used ones. Such a range presented readers with an excellent variety of choice.

SSR was practised in every class on four occasions a week, years 3 and 4 reading for 20 minutes per session, and years 5 and 6 for 25 minutes. The pupils in this group read quietly and when questioned displayed an impressive knowledge of children's literature. Indeed the activity had been so successful that they were allowed to bring in comics for one session each week.

The records which they kept included information about the number of books which they failed to complete. Their teacher vigilantly checked this information, doing his best to break patterns of failure by helping pupils with their selections. Despite the initial impression of untidiness, it would be difficult to find many class-rooms where SSR was working better.

Recent problems

Yet something went wrong. In the late 1990s, SSR was once again regarded with suspicion. There were two main reasons for this. The first was the increased empha-sis on the technical aspects of the teaching of reading and on phonics in particular. SSR creates the impression that it is not an activity which directly teaches pupils effective skills. Thus, in their survey of the teaching of reading in the primary schools in three inner London boroughs, Ofsted (1996) was highly critical of the activity. It was not guided, it lacked purpose and even the well-tested ploy of the teacher acting as a role model was dismissed.

The second reason was the creation of the literacy hour which appeared, at first glance, to preclude SSR. How might SSR be defended? If this is not done effectively will 'the literate classroom' really be fully literate?

In general, teachers recognise the obvious. Sustained reading assists in learning how to read. This claim was backed up by Smith (1973) when he stated, admittedly rather controversially, that children learnt to read by reading. More recently Stainthorp (1997) has stated that the amount of reading which a child does has a direct influence on his/her progress.

Teachers need to marshal these arguments and show that they are aware of the procedures which are linked to SSR and how they can be adjusted to suit individual situations. They might also need to consider the following.

- SSR is not a separate reading programme; it is part of a whole school reading policy. Its links with the other parts needs to be shown.

- SSR is not an inflexible programme. To practise it week in, week out, might create the boredom which sometimes occurs when an activity becomes too routine.

- SSR might involve talking about books with fellow pupils and visitors to the school; by these means pupils can demonstrate their knowledge and enthusiasm.

- Most important of all, evaluative information needs to be compiled. This does not imply testing nor should it involve a laborious round of book reviews. It should involve records of which books pupils have completed, which they have left unfinished and how long it took to do both. With the exception of very young children, pupils can compile records such as this for themselves.

SSR revisited

The justification for SSR is still, I think, as valid as when I wrote my original chapter in 1998. However, much has happened since and, in terms of the activity's development, not all of it has been good. Let us revisit some of the evidence. In 1993, according to Wray and Lewis, most primary schools in this country appeared to be making use of SSR. It seems useful also at this point to elaborate on the survey conducted by Phil Reader and myself in 1997.

- Number of schools surveyed 50.
- Those who used SSR 95%.
- Of these,   42% practised it at KS2 only.
         40% practised it at both KS1 and KS2.
         18% practised it at KS1 only (all separate infant schools).
- In 68% of these schools it took place throughout the school simultaneously, in 32% it took place in individual classes at selected times.
- In 62% of the schools it was a compulsory activity.
- 92% of schools practised it throughout the school year.
- In 51% of the schools it was carried out daily, in 27% it was carried out at least three times a week.
- In 47% of the schools SSR lasted for 15 minutes, in 21% for longer and in 32% for less time.
- In 62% of the schools the teachers read during SSR sessions. In 35% this never occurred and in 3% it happened sometimes.

Towards the end of the 1990s, then, SSR seemed to be popular in primary schools and the arrangements for its use were, to some extent, varied. There was one further research result, albeit indirect, that was positive at that time. In their large-scale replication survey of children's reading choices, Hall and Coles (1999) discovered that there were small but statistically significant increases in the amount of reading done by both ten-year-old boys and girls when compared to the figures for the original research reported by Whitehead *et al.* in 1977. Of course, it is not possible to attribute this improvement directly to SSR but its increased use since 1977 suggests that the activity might well have been influential in this respect. Thereafter, the picture becomes gloomy. The criticism, already mentioned, of SSR by a small Ofsted survey in three London boroughs in 1996 had been unhelpful and gave the distinct impression that an agenda had already been set. For example, when an inspector asked a teacher why she read during SSR sessions, she replied that she was presenting herself as a role model for her pupils. Perhaps the children were not particularly responsive that day – we will never know – but as Wheldall and Entwistle demonstrated so conclusively in 1988, the teacher who models SSR usually makes a positive contribution to the activity's success. To dismiss it out of hand on the strength of one observation was, to say the least, cavalier. Nor did the establishment of the literacy hour prove to be helpful. When I expressed the view that it might be able to accommodate SSR I was wrong and those who disputed this were right. When I renewed contact with many of the schools that had contributed to our original survey it was obvious that SSR no longer played much part in the teaching of literacy in primary schools. The following quotes are typical.

- 'SSR? I'm not sure if we do it now. I'll ask my literacy adviser.'
- 'No, there are just too many other things to do now.'
- 'Yes, we are starting to sneak it in now, but it's entirely up to individual teachers.'

There were a number of statements like the last one – SSR by stealth – when it should be out in the open.

Two schools were exceptions. They stood out like great beacons of light. In one, the head of literacy, a distinguished writer himself, had encouraged an approach that concentrated on sustained reading and writing and, in particular, making both exciting. This dominated the literacy hour rather than vice versa. In the other, the large foyer was taken up by the school library. Children, singly and in groups, were evident there at all times of the school day. Although recognising that the hour had some virtues, teachers made use of it as and when they thought it was needed. The headteacher's policy might be termed Audenesque. He had stopped all the clocks as far as the hour was concerned and SSR continued to be practised every day in every classroom.

Both of these schools produced excellent results in many ways, not least in their SATs scores. This had given them the confidence to include SSR openly. It seems a pity that less successful schools are far less inclined to challenge the status quo, although it is understandable. It would, of course, be unfair to condemn the literacy hour out of hand. The latest results from PIRLS (2001) indicate that pupils from England are very high up on the international list when it comes to reading ability. We must give praise where it is due. Nevertheless, we are much further down the list in terms of reading for enjoyment. In this respect, have we turned full circle to a quarter of a century ago when Lunzer and Gardner (1979) found short-burst reading to be the norm and where Southgate *et al.* (1981) discovered that many young competent readers did not particularly enjoy the activity? The reply of one to the questions 'Why do you learn to read?' was 'So I can stop.'

I think, however, that there is the possibility that we took SSR too lightly. As the editor of this book has asked me, was it ever really understood? Is its decline due to complacency? Did it become so routine that we stopped thinking about it? In retrospect, the writing was on the wall well before the literacy hour. Robertson *et al.* (1996) in their small-scale study acknowledge that SSR was seen as an enjoyable activity in primary schools and that teachers regarded it, in general, as beneficial. But the underlying philosophy was rarely discussed and procedures were very much on a 'go as you please' basis and lacking in consistency. The authors concluded that what actually happened was by no means always in accordance with the guidelines described in the literature. It might well have been that in seeking to be flexible – and to be too prescriptive would, I think have been counter-productive – advocates of SSR allowed it to go too far the other way.

Today anyone who wanted advice on the subject would have to go a long way back in the literature. It has not been written about in this country for years. Yet there are still attempts to encourage children to read with enthusiasm. A recent one, *Reading Connects*, organised by the National Literacy Trust, encourages reading for pleasure. Its success was reported by Ward (2004) in the *Times Educational Supplement* recently. Another, *Read a Million Words* was reported on the same page. Clearly, there is still concern that children are not reading enough and these initiatives appear to be advocating sustained reading. It is unfortunate, however, that they have had to replace SSR when in fact they should have been supplementing it. Were we ever clear about what SSR could achieve? The many American accounts and the smaller number of British investigations tended to be subjective and full of enthusiasm. They seemed to take it for granted that the activity was a good thing. What might a more objective approach attempt? Well, it is well-nigh impossible to show that it might improve reading ability. There are far too many variables in that process to isolate one in a way that is ethical. But it is possible to encourage pupils to read more books and that can be easily measured. Let us remember here Stainthorp's (1997) finding that there is a link between children's reading ability and the amount of reading that they do. And there are a number of scales that can measure their attitudes and knowledge about books.

I am starting off a small-scale research in the course of the next school year that will involve encouraging SSR and measuring the consequences in the ways described above. I remain optimistic enough to think that it will help more children to see that they learn to read not so much to stop but to help them to move forward.

References

Belloc, H. (1930) *New Cautionary Tales*. London: Duckworth.

Brooks, G., Schagen, I. and Nastud, P. (1997) *Trends in Reading at 8*. London: NFER.

Campbell, R. (1988) 'Is it time for USSR, SSR, SQUIRT, DEAR or ERIC?', *Education 3–13*, June, 22–5.

Campbell, R. (1998) 'A literacy hour is only part of the story,' *Reading* 32, 2, 21–3.

Campbell, R. and Scrivens, J. (1995) 'The teacher's role during sustained, silent reading,' *Reading* 29, 2, 52–5.

Carsley, J. D. (1957) 'The interests of children, aged 10–11, in books', *British Journal of Educational Psychology* XXVII, 13–23.

Fenwick, G. (1988) *USSR in Theory and Practice*. Reading: Reading and Language Information Centre, The University of Reading, pp. 9–11.

Fenwick, G. and Burns, D. (1998) 'Sustained silent reading in the primary school', *Education Today*, 48, 2, 9–13.

Fenwick, G. and Reader, P. (1996) 'Sustained, silent reading', an unpublished paper from a primary school survey. Liverpool: John Moores University.

Freire, P. (1972) *Pedagogy of the Oppressed*. Harmondsworth: Penguin Books.

Hall, C. and Coles, M. (1999) *Children's Reading Choices*. London: Routledge.

Jenkinson, A. J. (1940) *What do Boys and Girls Read?* London: Methuen.

Lunzer, E. and Gardner, K. (1979) *The Effective Use of Reading*. London: Heinemann Educational Books.

Maybin, J. (1983) 'Whole school reading periods' in Hoffman, M., Jeffcoate, R., Maybin, J., and Mercer, N. (eds) (1993) *Children, Language and Literature*. Milton Keynes: Open University Press.

Moore, J. C., Jones, C. J. and Miller, D. (1980) 'What we know after a decade of sustained, silent reading,' *The Reading Teacher*, 33, 4, 445–50.

Ofsted (1996) *The Teaching of Reading in 45 Inner-London Schools*. London: Ofsted.

Perez, S. (1986) 'Children see, children do: teachers as reading models', *The Reading Teacher*, 40, May, 8–11.

Robertson, C., Keating, I., Shenton, L., and Roberts, I. (1996) 'Uninterrupted, Sustained, Silent Reading: the rhetoric and the practice', *Journal of Research in Reading*, 19, 1, pp. 25-35.

Sainsbury, M. (1998) *Literacy Hours – A Survey of the National Picture in the Spring Term of 1998*. Slough: NFER.

Smith, F. (1973) *Children's Reading*. London: Holt, Rhinehart and Winston.

Southgate, V., Arnold, H. and Johnson, S. (1981) *Extending Beginning Reading*. London: Heinemann Educational Books.

Stainthorp, R. (1997) 'Reading in the primary classroom' in *Effective Primary Teaching – Research Based Strategies* P. Croll, and W. Hastings, (eds). London: David Fulton Publishers.

Walker, P. (1980) 'Whole school reading', *The English Magazine* Summer, 28–31.

Ward, H. (2004) 'Fun makeover for reading', *Times Educational Supplement* 10 September, p. 6.

Wheldall, K. and Entwistle J. (1988) 'Back in the USSR', *Educational Psychology*, 8, 1–2, 51–6.

Whitehead, F. *et al.* (1977) *Children and their Books*. London: Macmillan.

Wray, D. and Lewis, M. (1993) 'The reading experiences and interests of junior school children,' *Children's Literature in Education*, 24, 4, 251–63.

Web links

Progress in International Reading Literacy Study PIRLS (2001).
http://www.standards.dfes.gov.uk/primary/publications/literacy/63521/ (accessed January 2005).

A sense of time and place: literature in the wider curriculum

Gillian Lathey

Introduction

A writer's sense of place is unique. Philippa Pearce's (1985) Cambridgeshire, scene of Tom and Hatty's magical race on ice skates across the frozen fens in *Tom's Midnight Garden*, is as different as can be from Jill Paton Walsh's (1987) lyrical and sometimes menacing evocation of the same watery landscape in *Gaffer Samson's Luck*. Do we, through reading these books, add to our knowledge of the geography of East Anglia? The answer is both yes and no; statistics and facts may remain as hazy as before, but we gain from each writer an unforgettable vision of the area coloured by the sensations, impressions and mood of her book. In the same way, a writer's sense of an historical period is an imaginative invention that may incidentally inspire and extend historical study. What literature offers us cannot, therefore, be directly harnessed to the service of subject or topic teaching without courting the danger of damaging the integrity of a writer's intention or a child's response. Stories, novels, plays and poetry must be read primarily for their qualities of language, imagination and thought so that pupils 'respond imaginatively to the plot, characters, ideas, vocabulary and organisation of language in literature' (programmes of study for reading key stage 2).

Given this starting point, however, there is no reason why a varied reading diet should not positively influence children's understanding of complex ideas across the curriculum. Alun Hicks and Dave Martin (1997) describe a successful cross-curricular project to teach both English and history through historical fiction in a secondary school: making significant links in this way while maintaining the essence of each discipline ought to be even more straightforward in the primary sector. By surveying the range of children's literature arising from one historical event – the Second World War – and offering examples of ways to work with specific texts in the upper primary (years 5 and 6) classroom, I hope to illustrate the kinds of connections between literature and history which can enhance both areas of learning without compromising either of them.

Within living memory

Because the Second World War is still – just – within living memory, there is a vast corpus of texts written for children set in the war years. Just as two views of Cambridgeshire may differ so markedly, these books cover a wide spectrum of responses and raise issues about human behaviour that span the whole curriculum. Fiction set in the Second World War may include reference to the war only as a backdrop and catalyst to a child's misunderstanding of the adult world (Bawden 1993), or dramatically portray a turning point in a child's understanding of adult behaviour: the realisation that war is no game but a matter of death and evil (Cooper 1974). Even novels featuring the most memorable effects of the war on British children, namely evacuation (Magorian 1981; Bawden 1993), or the fear and thrills of air raids (Westall 1995a, b; Rees 1978), differ in perspective and purpose. Children's encounters with stray German pilots (the numbers found in children's books bear no relation to reality!) provide an opportunity for an author to attempt a revision of attitudes to the German enemy in Westall's *The Machine-Gunners* (1977), Michael Morpurgo's *Friend or Foe* (1977) and James Riordan's *The Prisoner* (1999). Indeed, many British writers have looked beyond the British experience to place it in a European or world context: Ian Serraillier's (1960) *The Silver Sword*, first published in 1956, was groundbreaking in its treatment of the plight of child refugees in a devastated postwar Europe.

Translations take readers further into the world context, as well as fulfilling NLS requirements that children should read literature from other cultures. Hans Peter Richter's (1987a, b) autobiographical texts, for example, develop insights into the 'enemy's' point-of-view by offering an insider's view of a young German boy's growing personal involvement in the persecution of the Jews, while a child's response to the inhumanity of the concentration camps is the subject of the picture book *Rose Blanche* (Innocenti 1985). The allegorical novel *I am David* by the Danish author Anne Holm (1989) addresses the postwar fate of a concentration camp inmate, although the lack of historical context can be problematic. There are also compelling autobiographical accounts for the young by Jewish 'hidden children', namely *The Diary of a Young Girl* by Anne Frank (1997), *The Upstairs Room* by Johanna Reiss (1977), and *Tell No One Who You Are* by Walter Buchignani (1997), and by exiles, for example *When Hitler Stole Pink Rabbit* by Judith Kerr (1977). Finally, the war in the Far East is represented by Meindert de Jong's *The House of Sixty Fathers* (1966) and a distressingly direct picture book by Toshi Maruki, *The Hiroshima Story* (1983).

Teachers' choices from this varied set of texts will depend on the previous reading experience and current understanding of the children that they teach, as will the question as to when and how books might be linked to the wider curriculum. Selected books can be read alongside, before or even some time after the study of the history of the war during the final two years of primary school, since an opportunity to preview or revisit the theme of war in literary form may prove just as fruitful as an attempt to teach literature and history simultaneously. Whatever the timing, it is the matter of how the teacher engages children's interest in these texts that is, as always, of paramount importance. What I would like to suggest is a comparative approach that addresses the demands of the history National Curriculum in the course of an exploration of literary and aesthetic qualities. The comparison of selected texts and extracts encourages children to reflect on universal themes as well as differences in written style, narrative perspective and – in the case of picture books – the artist's choice of medium, colour, line and layout.

The books can be introduced to children in a number of ways: the teacher reading aloud affords access for all children to what are sometimes challenging texts, in addition to private reading both in school and at home. Two short stories can be read, discussed and compared within a week or two, whereas two novels would take a term or longer. Teachers of parallel classes could read aloud two contrasting novels inspired by the same experience, Nina Bawden's *Carrie's War* (1993) and Michelle Magorian's *Goodnight Mister Tom* (1981) for example, so that pairs or groups of children subsequently meet to summarise, reflect on and compare the reactions of the central characters Carrie and Willie to evacuation. Some of the strategies recommended for the literacy hour are also relevant. Group reading of short stories or novels can be guided towards the discussion of differences and similarities in texts set in the war years. Additionally, the close comparative analysis of carefully selected extracts from novels and stories, with an emphasis on figurative language and narrative point of view, fulfils the requirement for text level work. Comparison gives textual analysis a purpose, as indicated in the following examples that include whole texts, short stories and extracts.

War in the picture book: different views

In choosing texts suitable for comparison, I have in mind the expectation in the history National Curriculum that 'the history of Britain should be set in its European and world context' (programme of study, key stage 2). Reading literature across cultures enables British children to appreciate the repercussions of the war in the lives of children across the world. Although it is painful to take readers beyond stories of evacuation, air raids, stray pilots and spies to confront the inhumanity of the holocaust, I would argue that it is an essential element in any study of the

Second World War. A revealing introduction to this subject is to invite pupils to consider the fates of two children, one real and one imagined, in the pages of the prize-winning picture books *War Boy* by Michael Foreman (1989) and *Rose Blanche* by Roberto Innocenti (1985). *War Boy* is a delightful and delicately drawn account of Foreman's own early childhood spent in a village close to the 'front-line' town of Lowestoft. Although touched by sadness at the fate of the young men who went to war and never returned, a mood of innocent nostalgia predominates, expressed in humorous vignettes, luminous watercolour landscapes (yet another vision of East Anglia) and exact technical drawings copied from original sources. The enemy is clearly defined in the separation between the kindly brave British soldiers that the young Foreman meets in his mother's sweetshop, and the propaganda-induced image of the German soldier. The child at the centre of *War Boy* indulges in playful exploits such as 'bombing' school wastebaskets, imitating goose-stepping Nazis and enjoying the carnival-like atmosphere amongst cliff-top spectators as a 'doodlebug' explodes in spectacular fashion over the sea.

To read the whole or sections of *War Boy* to children and then, at a later date when the moment seems right, to read Roberto Innocenti's *Rose Blanche*, is to establish an immediate and evident contrast. Not for Rose Blanche the war-inspired games of an ingenuous child; she knows better and acts against the adult world of the Third Reich by smuggling food to children in a concentration camp. Rose's world is one of bleak contrasts, disturbing glimpses of cruelty and the necessity to act alone and in secrecy. To approach this subject at all requires a great deal of sensitive introduction on the teacher's part, plenty of time to revisit and talk about the text as a whole class, and subsequent opportunities for re-reading by individuals or groups. Catriona Nicholson, in Chapter 7, reveals in her account of work with year 6 pupils just how sophisticated and perceptive children's responses to *Rose Blanche* can be, given the right conditions. Text and images pose questions and tantalise the reader with what is left unsaid; this is a book which demands historical contextualisation as well as reflection on Rose's state of mind. After several readings of *Rose Blanche*, children can be guided to explore the difference between its profoundly troubling implications and the reassuring tone of *War Boy*; comparison highlights the enormity of the crimes and human suffering the book represents. Teachers can ask what each of the central figures witnesses and learns about war and human behaviour. The lightheartedness of Foreman's anecdotes emphasises the burden of responsibility that the young Rose Blanche carries and the terrible, unspecified fate of the camp inmates.

Children's responses to differing graphic and artistic styles can be linked to the stance of each book towards the war years, with a focus on particular illustrations. The glowing colours of Foreman's celebratory bonfire at the end of the war and the subdued tones of Innocenti's ruined town into which battle-weary troops are advancing, convey utterly different moods. The final pages of each book also give rise to a thought-provoking contrast. Both depict landscapes and appear at first glance to offer hope for the future. In *Rose Blanche*, flowers grow again over a devastated landscape, while Foreman's closing words, printed on the delicate wash of a Suffolk scene, set the world to rights with the comforting words of a popular song: 'So it was true, all the things the grown-ups had said during the dark days. Now the war was over everything would be all right, there'll be blue birds over the white cliffs.' However, the flowers in *Rose Blanche* only superficially mask the evidence of the camps, and the final image – of which Catriona Nicholson once again demonstrates children's appreciation – reminds the reader of Rose and her death. In commenting on these two closures, children can be guided to reflect on the contrasting resonances of each book, created in word and image.

Exploring the nature of persecution

If *Rose Blanche* gives children an insight into the fate of the Jews during the Third Reich, the cause of that fate – the pernicious progress of antisemitism in taking hold of hearts and minds – is central to any understanding of the causes of the holocaust. Children are constantly made aware of persecution in their own daily lives, for example in media coverage of the 'ethnic cleansing' during the conflict in the former Yugoslavia, or the treatment of asylum seekers in some parts of the UK. Racial persecution bridges the curriculum and is of immeasurable significance in human history. After learning that antisemitic persecution resulted in the concentration camps and genocide, children are certain to ask how such crimes could happen, and how individual Germans could develop such an irrational hatred of Jews. An ironic contrast that begins to answer these questions arises from the comparison of Hans Peter Richter's account of childhood in the Third Reich, and the subtle treatment of anti-German sentiment in Janni Howker's (1986) short story 'Reicker'.

Two extracts from Richter's (1987a) novel *Friedrich* illustrate the attraction for a young boy of the powerful corporate identity of the Hitler Youth, and the increasing social isolation of a Jewish child. Since the structure of the book is episodic, each section is self-contained and can be read in its own right after a short introduction. The scene 'In the swimming pool' points to the irrationality of a sudden change in behaviour by swimming pool attendants and other children when they discover that the narrator's friend Friedrich is Jewish. Questions can be posed about Richter's written style in relating this event. Sentences and paragraphs are brief; the episode is directly and simply related without comment. Readers are left to make up their own minds about events and to deduce Friedrich's feelings from one description of his behaviour: 'Friedrich blushed, lowered his eyes to the ground' (1987a: 78). With guidance, children can appreciate the purpose of this narrative strategy which compels the reader to draw moral conclusions, and which is at its most terse in accounts of the narrator's participation in attacks on Jewish property in the chapter entitled 'The pogrom'. The speed with which one statement follows the next as the action unfolds in this scene is punctuated by glimpses of the narrator's state of mind: 'All this was strangely exhilarating'; 'By now I was enjoying myself' (as he smashes a bookcase in a home for Jewish apprentices), until, finally, he is in tears at the end of the chapter as the flat of Friedrich's family is wrecked (pp. 91–2). Again, Richter allows the reader to draw conclusions from this emotional rollercoaster. The irony and guilt in the narrator's tears are contained, but not explained, in the last two lines of the chapter: 'Mother began to weep loudly. And I wept with her.'

By helping children to question this style and reflect on the reasons why Richter refrains from extensive comment on actions that were a part of his own childhood, teachers can initiate discussion on narrative style in autobiographical writing and the seductive dangers of prejudice.

Richter's novel and his subsequent eyewitness account (*I Was There*) are the work of a writer caught in a web of personal and national guilt. The reverberations of the past in the present are also the theme of Janni Howker's 'Reicker', a compelling story of murder and kidnapping which brings the Second World War into the 1980s, an era closer to children's own lives. The story opens with an unpleasant scene as two young boys shout 'Sieg Heil' and 'Nazi' at an elderly man as they imitate the goose-step and raise their arms in a Nazi salute. Reicker is a former German prisoner of war who worked on a local farm and stayed on after the war. In choosing her title, Janni Howker foregrounds a figure who is marginal to the story's plot but central to its meaning. A conversation about Reicker between one of the boys, Sean, and his father touches on the lingering pain of personal loss – Sean's uncle was killed during the war – and the lasting effects of wartime ideology. Sean's father speaks regretfully of his inability to see Reicker as a person: 'In wars most men fight for what they're told to believe in, I suppose. I don't blame Reicker. I just can't see *him*.' The boys do begin to regard Reicker as a person, however, when he finds a three-year-old girl who had been taken hostage in a local incident and gently sings her a German lullaby. Howker's artistry lies in the narrative structure of a story that has one final twist. The closing line is Reicker's response to Sean's stumbling apology for calling him a Nazi: 'When I was your age, I was'. No more is said, but the impact of that remark in linking the persecution that Reicker was involved in as a boy to the taunts he is subjected to in old age causes readers to interrogate their opinion of Reicker once again. A parallel reading of 'In the swimming pool' and 'The pogrom' from *Friedrich* will enhance children's appreciation of that last line. Guided group reading of 'Reicker', accompanied by discussion and a close focus on extracts such as the discussion between Sean and his father, can highlight both the deft touches of a skilled writer and the aftermath of historical events.

Family separation

My final example addresses a theme that speaks immediately to all children: the threat and actuality of family separation and the loss of a home. As domestic security is such a primary concern of the young, it is not surprising that so many British children's books address evacuation, or that the fates of hidden, refugee or exiled children should feature in books by British and continental European authors. *Carrie's War* (Bawden 1993) is one of the best known of all evacuation novels. Nina Bawden takes her own childhood wartime experience as the starting point for an exploration of the joys and misunderstandings of growing up; a departure from family roles and routines can lead to new opportunities. Nevertheless, it is the insecurity of wartime childhood that is caught in the scene where Carrie, her younger brother Nick and their friend Albert Sandwich await selection by a host family on their arrival in Wales. The reader is party to Carrie's fears throughout this passage: 'But she had already begun to feel ill with shame at the fear that no one would choose her, the way she always felt when they picked teams at school' (1993: 17). In discussing this passage and asking who is relating Carrie's thoughts, children's attention can be drawn to the way that a narrator takes us inside a character's mind, revealing as much about Carrie's general lack of self-confidence as about her current situation. This can be contrasted with similar scenes of arrival and family separation endured by Jewish children, where an examination of causes takes the reader into another dimension of history and human suffering.

In *The Upstairs Room* (1979) by Johanna Reiss, a book that also records personal experience, Annie and her sister Sini are Jewish girls hidden by a succession of Dutch families during the German occupation of the Netherlands. On arriving at the first of these hiding places, Annie's responses are recorded in a first-person narrative with the jerky immediacy of thought bites. When she and Sini are left alone: 'We looked at the bedspread. It was crocheted. We looked around some more. At the door – it was closed – and at each other' (1979: 44). Annie's anxiety is best conveyed by reading this section aloud, noting her fixation on insignificant details such as the crochet work on the bedspread. Reading passages from both *Carrie's War* and *The Upstairs Room* inspires empathy with both Carrie and Annie while emphasising the difference in their responses. Carrie is passively anxious as she waits to be chosen, but she does at least understand the reasons for her evacuation, whereas Annie, who is considerably younger, constantly and frantically questions the antisemitism that she has already experienced and the bewildering consequences of a world that appears to have gone mad.

A third and equally telling perspective on exile from home is that of Anne Frank, whose diary entries record history as it happens and place it in the context of a young girl's journey towards adulthood. The diary entry for the family's first complete day in the 'secret annexe' is remarkably upbeat in tone. While the rest of her family is irritated by the chiming of a clock, Anne comments: 'Not me, I liked it from the start; it sounds so reassuring, especially at night. You no doubt want to hear what I think of being in hiding. Well, all I can say is that I don't really know yet' (Saturday, 11 July 1942). Here there is no mediating narrator or act of memory involved; the reader has direct access to Anne's moods, hopes and fears as they change and develop. The early reactions of Anne, Annie and Carrie to the confrontation with a new life has a different historical background which requires explanation, just as each writer adopts different strategies in narrating lived history. Differences in the three extracts are sufficiently striking to lead to reflection on the personalities of the three girls portrayed, on the immediacy of Anne Frank's diary entries as opposed to the retrospective narratives of Nina Bawden and Johanna Reiss, and on narrative viewpoint in autobiographical writing.

There are many more potential starting points for comparison to be found in the literature introduced at the beginning of this chapter. Each author's sense of time *and* place – since the physical setting of many of these books plays a key role – animates an interest in individual histories and echoes of the past. At the same time as developing an appreciation of the art of the illustrator and the writer, reflection on human history as represented in children's literature both touches and goes beyond the whole curriculum. Indeed, narratives of the human experience of war deepen and extend children's understanding of what history actually *is*. As historical novelist Rosemary Sutcliff (1990) tells us: 'Sometimes there's a gap in known facts that can only be filled by the Truth of the Spirit.'

References

Bawden, N. (1993) *Carrie's War*. London: Puffin Modern Classics.

Buchignani, W. (1997) *Tell No One Who You Are*. London: Puffin Books.

Cooper, S. (1974) *Dawn of Fear*. London: Puffin Books.

De Jong, M. (1966) *The House of Sixty Fathers*. London: Puffin Books.

Foreman, M. (1989) *War Boy*. London: Pavilion Books.

Frank, A. (1997) *The Diary of a Young Girl*, transl. Susan Massotty. London: Penguin Books.

Hicks, A. and Martin, D. (1997) 'Teaching English and history through historical fiction', *Children's Literature in Education*, 28, 2, 49–58.

Holm, A. (1989) *I am David*, transl. L.W. Kingsland. London: Mammoth.

Howker, J. (1986) 'Reicker', in *Badger on the Barge*. London: Harper Collins.

Innocenti, R. (1985) *Rose Blanche*. London: Jonathan Cape.

Kerr, J. (1977) *When Hitler stole Pink Rabbit*. London: Harper Collins.

Magorian, M. (1981) *Goodnight Mister Tom*. London: Puffin Books.

Maruki, T. (1983) *The Hiroshima Story*, text by Elkin. London: A & C. Black.

Morpurgo, M. (1977) *Friend or Foe*. London: Mammoth.

Paton Walsh, J. (1987) *Gaffer Samson's Luck*. London: Puffin Books.

Pearce, P. (1958) *Tom's Midnight Garden*. Oxford: Oxford University Press.

Rees, D. (1978) *Exeter Blitz*. London: Hamish Hamilton.

Reiss, J. (1979) *The Upstairs Room*. London: Puffin Books.

Richter, H. P. (1987a) *Friedrich*, transl. Edite Kroll. London: Puffin Books.

Richter, H. P. (1987b) *I Was There*, transl. Edite Kroll. London: Puffin Books.

Riordan, James (1999) *The Prisoner*, Oxford: Oxford University Press.

Serraillier, I. (1960) *The Silver Sword*. London: Puffin Books.

Sutcliff, R. (1990) 'History and time', in *Travellers in Time*. Cambridge: CLNE.

Westall, R. (1977) *The Machine-Gunners*. London: Puffin Books.

Westall, R. (1995a) *Children of the Blitz*. London: Macmillan.

Westall, R. (1995b) *Blitz*. London: Harper Collins.

Reading the pictures: children's responses to *Rose Blanche*

Catriona Nicholson

Introduction

Underpinning the new Primary National Strategy (PNS) (DfES 2003a) initiative is an emphasis on the need to develop and promote creativity in all areas of the curriculum. Such 'official blessing' encourages us as teachers and educators to be creative in our interpretation of such documents as *The National Literacy Strategy (NLS) Framework for Teaching* (DfEE 1998). The speaking, listening, learning element of the PNS publication highlights the need for teachers to provide varied and imaginative classroom scenarios in which pupils can be 'taught' to become proficient and confident speakers and listeners. The poster pack advice buzzes with such words as 'active', 'responsive', 'encourage', 'extend', 'participate', 'reflect', 'evaluate', 'discuss', 'interact', 'converse'. Discussion is encouraged at all levels – partnered, paired, grouped, whole class, collective, child-led, teacher-led. This emphasis on oral activity links with what we have always known about teaching and learning – that we learn best by DOING: 'I do so I understand'. We learn to be readers by reading, to be writers by writing and to be speakers and listeners by being engaged in a purposeful way with those activities. Sharing responses to literature is one of the most meaningful ways in which good listening and good talking can be achieved.

Background

Central to any reading experience is the interaction between reader and text. Encouraging children to talk about their personal reading experiences with other readers has been acknowledged, through the inspiration and crusading zeal of educationalists such as Aidan Chambers (1993), as a prerequisite of good classroom practice. Teachers are now required, within *The National Literacy Strategy (NLS) Framework for Teaching* (DfEE 1998), to provide opportunities for pupils at key stage 2 to 'contribute constructively to shared discussion about literature, responding to and building on the views of others'. Wolfgang Iser (1974) asserts that the primary function of a fictional text is to tell a story in such a way and by such use of artistic devices or strategies as to stimulate a creative response in readers, namely to provoke readers to create for themselves the meaning and the 'reality' offered by the text. This dynamic concurrence between readers and texts characterises effective book share sessions within the primary school classroom, when individual reader responses contribute to communal understanding of a text. Having introduced book share sessions to groups of children over several years, I am aware of the challenges such a procedure presents in terms of classroom management. However, there is no doubt that the experience of sharing literary responses can promote linguistic development and heighten aesthetic and cultural awareness.

In Chapter 6, Gillian Lathey has identified the close relationship that exists between children's literature and history and she exemplifies ways in which these two components of the primary curriculum can be mutually supportive and illuminating. Jill Paton Walsh, to whom she refers, has identified the interface that exists between literature and history (Heins 1977). She suggests that a novel, being 'quintessentially a prose narrative' comments on history through story, character and event rather than through the temporal authenticity of its setting. Paton Walsh's aim as a writer of historical novels is 'to enshrine in the heart of the novel, in the very centre of its being, a truly historical insight'. Her conviction that 'you have to want to write what did happen and what it felt like' perfectly conveys the ideals expressed by Roberto Innocenti in the introduction to his picture book *Rose Blanche* (McEwan and Innocenti 1985) which became the focus for the series of year 5 and year 6 book share sessions to which I will be referring in this chapter. Not a novel, but undeniably a 'prose narrative', this starkly powerful text explores the nature of suffering, sacrifice and redemption in words by Ian McEwan[1] and pictures by Innocenti. The artist set himself the task of illustrating 'how a child experiences war without really understanding it'. Explaining his theme, he continues, 'I was a little child when the war passed in front of my door...my father did not want to answer my questions but I knew something terrible was happening'. One of my young readers confirmed that the book 'shows how war affects somebody ordinary...it could be you or me'.

The story[2], set in a drab, nameless village in the winter of 1944–5 near the end of the Second World War, is partly revealed through the eyes of a young German schoolgirl, Rose Blanche. Innocenti hoped the book would 'express a need for peace through images of war' and his title recalls the 'White Rose' movement, a small underground group of German students who were resistant to the war.

Children today are not made aware, unless exposed through book, film or photographic image, of the particular force for evil that generated the rise of Nazism and, by definition, 'sealed the fate of the Jews during the Third Reich' (see Chapter 6 by Gillian Lathey). In Innocenti's picture book, the inhumanity and sadism that prevailed during the Nazi occupation are seen from a child's perspective. The uncompromising poignancy of her vision is starkly relayed to the reader. The compelling full-plate illustrations show what cannot be conveyed in words. Throughout the book McEwan's restrained text locates a narrative for these telling and detailed images. I chose to make this text a focus for book shares because I believe that children at the right stage of development can, through engagement with stories which offer what Nina Bawden (1980: 17) refers to as 'emotional realism', receive a 'faithful account of the human condition' (Bawden 1980: 32) by glimpsing, from the safe distance of a book, a darker side of life. *Rose Blanche* is a text which compels a reader to respond. The shared experience of reading it enabled the children to explore ways of understanding aspects of human behaviour and to reflect upon the nature of good and evil.

From theory to practice

As with all good classroom practice, the concept of book sharing is underpinned by theoretical principles. Iser's (1974) study of the phenomenology of reading and the subsequent work of Aidan Chambers (1977) establish frameworks of reference for examining the responses of the children who shared *Rose Blanche*.

I have selected, from several hours of taped book share conversations, extracts from the opening and closing discussions for they exemplify Iser's assertion that the act of reading is 'a sense-making activity' (Iser 1978). The group of four year 5 children were unfamiliar with the book but the two year 6 boys had briefly examined it the previous year. The responses of the two boys support Iser's view that a second reading of a text elicits 'a kind of advance retrospection'. The responses of all six readers show how 'impressions that arise will vary from individual to individual' (Iser 1974). By way of introduction to the book, both groups concentrated on 'reading' the jacket illustration and, as they began to interpret the puzzle of its reflected war images, they began the process of 'establishing connections – filling in the gaps left by the text'. Rose Blanche stares from behind a curtained window on to an unseen outside. Behind her but apparently within her inside world are reflections of injured soldiers. There is compelling engagement between her disquieting gaze and the eye of the reader. Chambers (1977: 42) reminds us that 'In books where the implied reader is a child, authors...put at the centre of a story, a child through whose being everything is felt...the child...is thus wooed into the book...and led through whatever experience is offered'.

Articulating responses

Ian and David, encountering the book for the second time, having offered me remembrances of their initial reading, were clearly 'wooed' into the book:

David: She seems like she's an angel with the innocent blue eyes and yellow hair...she just needs curled hair and a fancy dress and she could live literally in a forest and be another Snow White.

CN: Can you describe her gaze?

David: Her eyes are just innocent.

Ian: She's somebody who doesn't seem to belong to any thing because of the war...her eyes have no depth...it's as if she's trying to get out the feeling of all the killing and hatred. The illustration doesn't give her eyes any depth...she's trying to repel something, she's just horrified. This reflection is the other side of war.

CN: Does what you see on this front cover encourage you to open the book?

Ian: It does me. If I was seeing it for the first time I'd think, 'well, what's inside?'

Discussing the impact of Rose Blanche's face on the front cover, both boys confirmed once again Chambers' proposal that the implied child reader is led through the book. Ian said:

> I can see the war through Rose Blanche's eyes because that's how the words have been written but with the pictures you kind of feel an onlooker at times because all through the book I remember you can see her and you can always see something in there which tells you that's where she was or that's where she is now.

David similarly demonstrates how 'advance retrospection' directs his thoughts as, with the benefit of a previous reading, he recalls the impact of the book:

> With the killing and the cruelty to come, if you try and shut it out you can't because of Rose Blanche. If she wasn't there you would shut it out.

The responses of the younger group bore out Iser's theory that a literary text (illustration) is 'something of an arena in which the reader and the author engage in a game of the imagination.' He refers to reading as a 'dynamic act of recreation' and proposes that the process is neither smooth nor continuous but one which:

> In its essence relies on interruptions of the flow...we look forward, we look back, we decide, we change our decisions, we form expectations, we are shocked by their non fulfilment, we question, we muse, and accept, we reject...we oscillate between the building and breaking of illusions.

> (Iser 1974: 288)

The unwritten narrative of the cover promoted animated discussion as the four readers made predictions, modified them and oscillated between the 'building and breaking of illusions'. They began to make sense of the cover illustration by constructing scenarios for the forthcoming narrative:

Sophie: Who is the girl?

James: She's looking out of a window but the men went off to the war but – um – didn't come back and she's seeing their ghosts...meeting their ghosts.

Rachel: 'Cos if you look at the window you sort of see cobwebby things hanging...Maybe it's after the war.

Anthony: I think it's the middle of the war.

Rachel: Maybe she's like a Florence Nightingale. She's been helping these people who are ill and um...um...she's been helping those people put bandages round their heads.

James: I think it's a reflection in a mirror...

Anthony: Maybe she's imagining it all. It's a reflection.

James: Yes, it's a reflection.

Rachel: Normally, if there's a reflection, it would be a different way round. I reckon she may be looking out of it.

Sophie: If you have a reflection, say, how can you reflect it? Unless there's a pond or something?

Anthony: She looks as if she's been evacuated.

Rachel: Maybe her father's been killed...or her mother.

Sophie: Is she the reflection?

As this group searched for narrative information, located pictorial clues, discarded ideas, hypothesised, hovered between sudden revelation and the conflict of uncertainties, they demonstrated how their expressive and varied conjectures verified Iser's (1974: 280) view that in reading 'the opportunity is given...to bring into play our own faculty for establishing connections – for filling in 'gaps' which are often so fragmentary that one's attention is...occupied with the search for connections between the fragments'.

Most of the discussion at this point centred around 'fragmentary' details and in particular the illusion created by the window reflection. The discussions reveal how, in group readings of a text, individual responses can be developed and modified by the contributions of others in a process of re-creation. As the younger group turned the pages, they took turns to read the written story and, in addition, modified their individual ideas, constantly sharing predictions of what the short- and long-term outcomes might be.

The illustrative inset of the title page established a reference for several recurring themes which were identified in the process of turning pages forward and then back: the red bow in Rose Blanche's hair, the tank tracks, the pools of still water which readers took to reflect 'gloom and winter' and 'sadness'. The distant running child was seen as 'running away', 'running to visit the soldiers' or 'running to say goodbye'. Each reader expected the story to be sombre and one reader proposed that the receding figure of the child was 'the only hopeful thing in the picture in her little red ribbon'.

Although the setting for the first full page illustration was unfamiliar to them, the younger readers began to identify and connect familiar pictorial clues: the German helmet and the 'Nazi cross', the foreign signs and architecture. They turned back to the introductory inset illustration and observed that the mud tracks matched the tyres on the lorry or car shown in the left foreground of this full plate. Summing up after heated discussion they referred again to the jacket illustration and, using knowledge of social and historical concepts, tried to make sense of the images:

James: It's the German soldiers going off, waving goodbye. We know it's defi-nitely Germans because there's the German cross.
Rachel: I think her father dies because she's wearing different clothes than on the cover because on the cover she's wearing black clothes, like Queen Victoria. And that's the sort of thing that's going to happen in the story... that person dressed in black on this page is getting us ready for it.

The older readers in their discussion of the title page illustration spoke with second reading assurance, informed by what Iser calls 'a repertoire of familiar literary patterns':

Ian: The first small picture is of Rose Blanche running across a muddy track and I think that's pretty symbolic because she's there and she's got the bright red hairband. Everything else just blends around her. What do you think, David?
David: You can obviously see it's well used by tanks and trucks because of the tracks. Rose Blanche... she's the only mark of colour... It's all dismal; grey, dark, dark greens mixed with browns. You see her as a glimmer of hope.
Ian: The track looks everlasting, doesn't it?
David: Yes, and she's heading into the mist and that's telling us something.

Both groups deliberated over details which might connect their earlier expectations with forthcoming narrative events or experiences. Initially they freely exchanged ideas about how they, as individuals, would feel about being involved in a war but, as the readings proceeded, the discussions began to focus on symbolic images which appeared to convey Rose Blanche's plight; recurring images of barbed wire, fences, barriers and the enclosure were commented upon. At one point David expressed his own concerned involvement as a reader:

You're an onlooker onto Rose Blanche...You see it all through her eyes. The SS officer looks as though out of the side of his eye he's looking at you...He's trying to see what you're doing. I just hate it...it's awful.

As the regular pattern of the child's visits to the camp become established, the tenor of response within both groups became less animated and the children spoke with feeling and marked compassion:

Rachel: She looks so pale.
Anthony: I feel so sorry for her.
James: We feel like we're Rose Blanche.
Sophie: Because you can't see her (in the double-spread concentration camp depiction) it feels like you're Rose Blanche.
James: I know they are Jewish and they are children like us.
Sophie: Just imagine having to walk away from them.
Rachel: It's the way you're looking at them and the way they're looking at you...

Through sombre ever-darkening shades of colour, Innnocenti uses effective means to convey the sadness and desolation of war and to confront the terrible realms of man's inhumanity. As the ironic tragedy of Rose Blanche's final visit to the site of the concentration camp is revealed, these young readers reached for and found, in the simple eloquence of their words, a language which matched the poignancy of their reading experience. Their response to the mystery and metaphor of the final double page spread is evidence enough that the sharing and interrogating of texts is essentially a creative process that enables readers to 'talk well' about books and thereby to gain insight into the nature of human suffering. Here is an extract from the younger readers' interpretations of that significant page:

James: Those flowers represent the children of the camps and that single flower represents Rose Blanche.
Rachel: Gentleness over the barbed wire, gentleness over cruelty.
Anthony: If the artist hadn't shown that flower bent over the barbed wire, I wouldn't have known Rose Blanche was dead. You've got to read the pictures for a long time to realise the meaning of things like that flower...If you just turned over you wouldn't understand anything because you wouldn't be looking at it properly. You really got to look into the picture to find out the meaning. The pictures are the description.
Sophie: It's like hope is expressed in light and colour...
James: And all these flowers they represent the good of the bad...
Anthony: It's like an invasion of all the Spring and the explosions of colour defeat all the bad things.

Talking well

The case for promoting reader response activities through group reading rests on the quality and depth of talk that such discussions generate. The year 6 readers, Ian and David, discussing the final double spread in detail, revealed extraordinary insight. In responding to this text each drew on a language of tenderness, revealing astute powers of discrimination. I offer the transcript of their final discussion as evidence of how their creative sharing of the text has enabled them to glimpse coherence behind the chaos of war, to make sense of the past and to confirm their faith in the endurance of the human spirit:

David: This [illustration] with the piece that Ian read, the explosions, the uniforms, the parades, the positions of the birds, and the triumph, it's just like the war and now... it looks exactly the same scene as when Rose Blanche was shot, and on the barbed wire you can see the very flower that she was holding. And under it there are flowers of the same variety. The tank tracks are now covered in grass the... um... barbed wire fence looks as if it was being attacked by creepers. The trees are crowding in and you can hardly see the broken branches – they're all sprouting new. But then when you think how many people have suffered here the beauty is taken away.

Ian: This is where the prison camp used to be.

David: Yeah, and the steel girders have also been attacked by creepers.

Ian: It's really as though it's a war of good against a war of evil and that's what the author Roberto Innocenti is trying to get over to you.

David: (to himself) This picture is just brilliant.

Ian: Yeah... and the flower that Rose Blanche had put there had really, by the looks of things, given up hope and then that seed has spread... it's like Adam and Eve populating the world.

David: Really, if you took away the steel girders and the fence, you'd see a perfect piece of the countryside, you wouldn't really notice it had been the war at one stage... the only signs are the fence, the girders and a small section of tank track.

Ian: Yeah... even that pan which was in... (turns back two pages)... which was in that picture where it was all muddy, is still there in the same position. The way that the author has changed scenes from the beginning where everything was desolate, everything was dead, like people's morale, everything was dead, and then suddenly spring comes and morale is lifted but it's the morale of the countryside really. It is just excellent this book. I can see why it's been controversial and I recognise that... this tells how horrible war really is. You can get war books and I'm not saying you shouldn't read them but they just don't tell you what war is really, really like…so many…*Island on Bird Street* does…uh…*Echoes of War* does but this is better than either of them in some ways because (speaks emphatically) the pictures tell the story (in measured tones). This…is…the advance…of…peace.

David: In the last motif (before the endpaper) there's the flower which Rose Blanche was holding…on the barbed wire and it's covered in rain…

Ian: And it's bedraggled…when you see that, its almost as if there's another war on because there's that dark background and you can see sheet-like rain if you look closely, and the barbed wire. But there's that flower…even though it's dead it's…it's…between two spikes of the wire and it's as though it's separating the two sides in the war – the one on the left is the German spike and the one on the right represents the Allies. It's as if the flower is stopping the war from happening any more…with a book like this though you have to let everyone interpret the meaning of the story in their own way.

Roberto Innocenti established the focus for his own partially understood childhood experience in the fictional experiences of the child Rose Blanche. Readers respond to the impact of a relentlessly harrowing narrative which we receive through the filter of her vision. The responses of these six present-day readers became my experience of their experience of Rose Blanche's experience; what was seen but not understood by the young Innocenti has, through a perfect blend of words and pictures, been made visible to the next generation.

Notes

1   There are two versions of the picture book *Rose Blanche*. The illustrations, by Roberto Innocenti, remain the same but the texts differ markedly. One, published by Creative Education (1985) in the USA, has an original text by Christophe Gollaz and Roberto Innocenti. The version discussed in this chapter, with text by Ian McEwan, is 'based on a story by Christophe Gollaz'. McEwan, at the request of Jonathan Cape, translated the Gollaz story and wrote a new text for Innocenti's illustrations. Several interesting and intriguing questions arise from a study of both narratives.

2   The story opens in late autumn with Rose Blanche and her mother waving goodbye to men from the town who are leaving to fight in the war. Apart from queues at food shops, daily life and the routines of home and school remain the same. One day Rose witnesses the violent arrest of a small boy and, furious at the kidnapping, she follows the lorry into which he was bundled, through the streets of the town and out into the countryside. Her trek brings her to the outskirts of a concentration camp where in a clearing 'dozens of silent, motionless children stared at her from behind a barbed wire fence'. This awesome experience marks the turning point in Rose's life. Her humanity and the pity that she feels for the starving prisoners lead her to make daily and nightly visits to the camp where she passes her hoarded offerings of food through the wire fence. Eventually, threatened by invasion, the townsfolk leave but Rose Blanche returns to the forest where, in a moment of confusion, the 'sharp and terrible sound of a shot' is heard as a retreating soldier fires instinctively at any movement in the misty gloom of the forest. A desolate wintry landscape, ravaged by the destructive savagery and the ugly barricades of war, frames our last view of Rose, whose tired face, now a death mask, communicates unutterable sadness. A blue flower that she holds rests lightly against broken wire. Poignantly recalling this scene two pages later, Innocenti uses a luminous diffusion of colour and light to convey the symbolic representation of the child and of hope within the 'invasion' of a burgeoning spring. Blue flowers bloom below the strands of barbed wire.

References

Bawden, N. (1980) 'Emotional realism in books for young people', *The Horn Book Magazine*, LVI, 1, 17–33.

Chambers, A. (1977) *Booktalk*. London: The Bodley Head.

Chambers, A. (1993) *Tell Me: Children, Reading and Talk*. Stroud, Gloucestershire: The Thimble Press.

DfEE (1998) *The National Literacy Strategy: Framework for Teaching*. London: DfEE.

DfES (2003a) *Excellence and Enjoyment: A strategy for primary schools*. London: DfES.

DfES (2003b) *Speaking, Listening, Learning: Working with Children in Key Stages 1 and 2*. London: DfES.

Heins, P. (1977) 'Crosscurrents of criticism', *Horn Book Essays 1968–1977*. Boston, MA: The Horn Book Inc., pp.219–25.

Iser, W. (1974) *The Implied Reader*. Boston, MA: Johns Hopkins University Press.

Iser, W. (1978) *The Act of Reading: A Theory of Aesthetic Response*. Baltimore and London: Johns Hopkins University Press.

McEwan, I. and Innocenti, R. (1985) *Rose Blanche*. London: Jonathan Cape.

Becoming writers

Motivating children to write with purpose and passion

Teresa Grainger

Introduction

Teaching writing is a balancing act; real time and space need to be created for developing children's knowledge about language as well as their ability to use and apply this knowledge creatively and effectively. The balance between process and product also needs to be considered and the relevance and purpose of writing constantly highlighted, so that young learners experience the meaning potential of writing and perceive themselves as writers. Six-year-old Shona, in observing her teacher's somewhat glum demeanour one afternoon, wrote the following post-it note and stuck it on the register.

FIGURE 8.1 Shona's post-it note

Shona knew, albeit implicitly, that writer's write because they have something to say to someone, a story to tell, a view to express or information to remember. Yet too often in school, children 'learn to write for the circular purpose of learning to write' (Frater 2004) and find little personal purpose or value in it. If writing is reduced to a series of formulae which must be followed and a toolkit approach to the knowledge and skills required is adopted, then the act of writing is divorced from the writer and disinterest and disaffection may well develop (Packwood and Messenheimer 2003). As two nine-year-olds commented recently, 'I hate being told what to do and how to do it' and 'I don't like writing, it's nothing to do with me' (Grainger *et al.* 2003). This chapter focuses on motivating young writers to write with passion, and helping them find pleasure in writing as they use it for their own purposes. Several key issues are examined, including the need for an extended model of composition, the power of texts and creative contexts to tempt young writers to engage and the importance of teaching skills in context. The significance of talking about writing and of choice, voice and space are also explored.

The extended process of composition

Writing involves time and experience, reflection and evaluation, so the process of composition needs to be an extended one (Bearne 2003) encompassing considerable talk and drama, discussion and exploration as young writers play their way thoughtfully forwards. Creative opportunities enable children to try out possibilities and reflect upon what it is that they are trying to say, although their ideas will be further developed and shaped when they actually write them down. In a three week unit of work on traditional tales for example, we may plan for periods of storytelling, dramatic investigations and considerable focused reading, writing, sharing and discussing. Our explicit teaching of textual features will also be woven into this time, although some learning about folk and fairy tales will develop through immersion in the genre in shared, guided and independent reading, reading aloud and through storytelling. As the National Literacy Strategy acknowledges, 'Much of what children need to learn about writing, from story structure to written language features and punctuation, can be gained from storytelling, shared reading and the oral interaction stimulated by them' (DfES 2001).

The long-term aim in this unit might be to produce a class anthology of folktales, which will be known from the outset and consciously travelled towards, but the route actually taken will depend on the children's interests, responses, questions and needs. The planned writing opportunities will be imaginatively framed in support of the long-term goal, but others will be seized as they surface and related objectives will be explored in context. To support their storytelling, children may, for example, represent narrative structure in the form of story maps, mountains, seeds or hands (Grainger *et al.* 2004) and move through imitation towards innovation and re-creation. Delighting in the oral opportunity to entertain and engage others as the tellers of tales, they will lean on the structure, characters and language of stories they have heard and told, as six-year-old Gary's taped tale indicates...

> Once upon a time there lived a king, a queen and a prince. The king and queen had something to tell the prince and so that night he went looking for something and he'd forgotten what he went looking for but then he finally remembered. So he went looking for a girl and there was this lovely pretty house covered in pink paint and blue little bits of blue and then he knocked on the door and he said would you like to come for dinner and the girl said yes but she was expecting somebody else and this was their first date when she thought it was him so they went round to the house and they had chips, sausages and beans and the princess says I will come round on Monday, Wednesday, Friday and Sunday so this day was Saturday and the prince went round to the ring shop and he spended and he got his money out and he said he had ten pounds and there was only a ring for nine pounds so he bought the ring and that night he said he had a surprise for the girl in the living room when she came round and he went down on both knees and said will you marry me and the girl had half an hour of thinking about it and then she came into the living room and said yes and the king and queen organised a great wedding and they both lived happily ever after but there was one row in the end and then they lived happily ever after until they died.

The extended process of composition allows time for children such as Gary to engage fully with a range of motivating activities which lead towards purposeful writing, and enables us as their teachers to lead by framing and inspiring, but also by following their interests and sensitively shaping the unfolding exploration with them.

Potent texts to lean on and learn from

As reading and writing are closely related, it is essential that we help children lean on literature, both oral and written, to enrich their storehouse of possibilities (Fox 1993). The kinds of literary texts that are most supportive to children as writers at KS2 are, according to Barrs and Cork (2001) traditional tales, stories containing 'poeticised speech' and emotionally powerful texts. Younger writers are also drawn in through affective engagement with powerful literature, with film, television and the lyrics of popular music and these are potent tools for prompting writing. When children's personal responses are honoured and connections are made with the texts of popular culture and their interests, their involvement and pleasure in learning and writing increases. Investigating the texts we read is an integral part of the extended process of composition and can occur in a multitude of ways, alongside teaching about language forms and features. However, such focused teaching of reading/writing, despite its emphasis on literary devices, should not be at the expense of the meaning or purpose of the text, but should enable children to apply any new knowledge and skills to their own writing, as the Teaching Reading and Writing Links Project showed (Corden 2003). The breadth and variety of textual forms that exist represent a rich resource that children can lean on and learn from, so as teachers we need to steep them in exciting texts and develop creative contexts in which their thoughts and responses can be represented in a variety of ways.

Creative contexts to generate ideas

To motivate young writers we need to invite children to take part in creative contexts to generate ideas, manipulate objects, talk and draw and create meaning together: this will shape both their ongoing and their later writing. As children play with the possibilities of texts they know through the extended process of composition, they may create and craft visually, orally, physically and/or in written form. Their multimodal explorations may, for example, involve them in discussing issues, hotseating characters, playing with puppets or story boxes, interviewing people, dancing, drawing, making music and much more besides. In such contexts, the desire to mean, to make, to understand and to write is fostered and the learners are actively involved in shaping their understanding. The play scripts, PowerPoint presentations or persuasive arguments eventually produced will have emerged through this active process of reading, exploring, creating, generating and representing texts in such engaging creative contexts.

Stepping inside texts imaginatively fosters children's creative capacity as writers since writing in role in imagined contexts has increased authenticity and often a real sense of audience (Barrs and Cork 2001; Grainger 2004). For example, during a drama based around *Little Wolf's Book of Badness* by Ian Whybrow, Nathan wrote in role as Little Wolf to his parents back home (see Figure 8.2). In his letter he reflects upon the narrative that he and his friends had improvised, refers to the missing whisky bottle and builds upon the interior monologue that he had voiced within the drama. In this piece of writing, Nathan evokes a real sense of Little Wolf's playful demeanour and humorous tone of voice in both words and visual presentation. The drama had been a kind of oral rehearsal for writing that helped shape the letter and prompted Nathan's involvement and interest. He read it aloud with pride and passion, taking up Little Wolf's role again as he did so. Recent Primary National Strategy research clearly indicates that both drama and film can make a marked difference to attitude and attainment in writing (Bearne and Grainger 2004) contributing to excellence and enjoyment in education (DfES 2003).

Through imaginatively using talk during the extended process of composition, children are able to voice their views and express their feelings, trying out, absorbing and transforming others' voices, as they begin to trust and stretch their own.

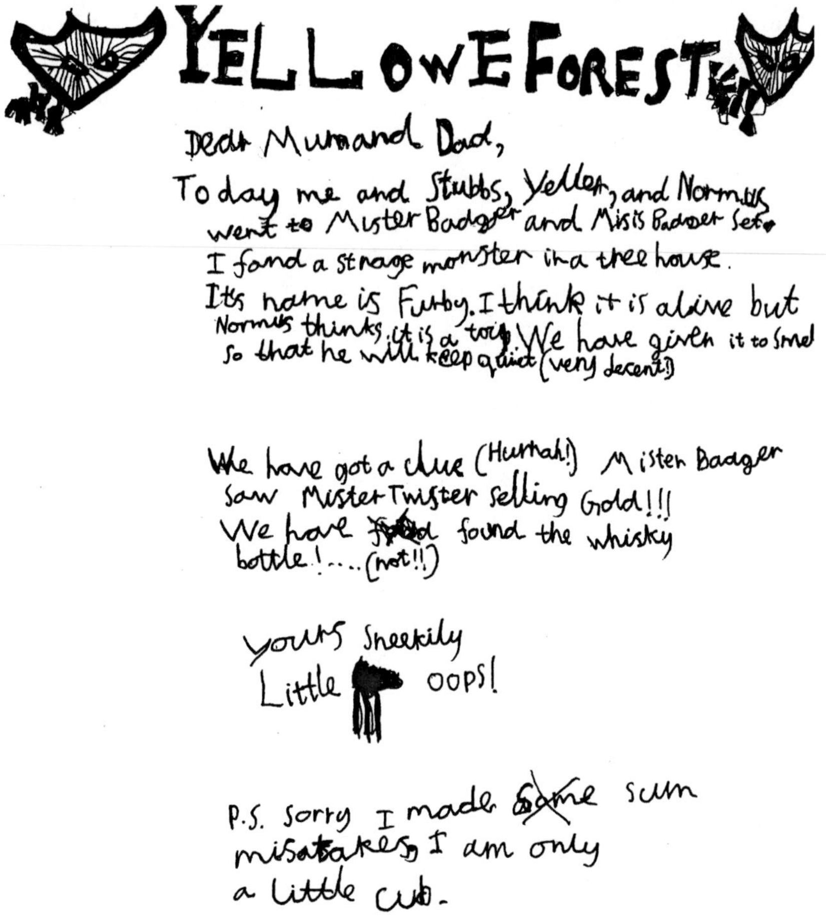

YELLOWE FOREST

Dear Mum and Dad,

Today me and Stubbs, Yeller, and Normus went to Mister Badger and Misis Badger Set.
I fond a stnage monster in a tree house.
Its name is Furby. I think it is alive but Normus thinks it is a toy. We have given it to Smol so that he will keep qaiet (very decent!)

We have got a clue (Hurrah!) Mister Badger saw Mister Twister selling Gold!!!
We have found the whisky bottle!....(not!!)

yours sneekily
Little 🐾 oops!

P.S. Sorry I made some sum misatakes I am only a little cub.

FIGURE 8.2 Nathan's letter to his parents

The use of drama, storytelling and other interactive activities helps them take risks with ideas, words and images. In such contexts they are affectively and intellectually involved which encourages openness to learning, so that the move into writing is more meaningful and is experienced as a somewhat seamless shift. Writing in such contexts is not perceived as a separate tiresome task to be undertaken, but as an extension of the engaging enterprise in which they are involved. Children deserve support in developing their ideas and this requires considerably more than a brief conversation with their partner prior to writing. Through inhabiting creative contexts in the extended compositional process they can take the time to explore and reflect upon themes, issues and characters, generating ideas as well as following through their trains of thought, pursuing and extending their ideas in action as well as through reflection and critique.

Explicit teaching in engaging contexts

During a unit of work which involves talk focused and often playful and imaginative contexts, children may use writing to make notes, label diagrams, tell tales, write reports, and reflect upon both lived and imagined experience. Their writing, based on potent texts and developed through inspiring contexts, also needs to pay attention to technical skills and employ their knowledge about language. Such knowledge must be taught for 'creativity and knowledge are two sides of the same psychological coin, not opposing forces' (Boden 2001: 102). However, skills transfer more easily if they are embedded in a meaningful framework and are employed for real outcomes and purposes. For example, in role playing the heated discussion between Tim and his dad in Jaqueline Wilson's *Cliffhanger*, ideas about how dad might persuade his timid son to go on an adventure holiday will be improvised in action. Tim's own defensive position will also be created. After some generative drama time, the substantive content of the persuasive argument could be recorded in shared writing, so the teacher could then choose to examine the use and placement of speech verbs, speech marks, adverbs to describe intonation and manner, speech presentation, and so on. Such teaching is contextualised and can be applied to the children's own writing as they work in pairs to resolve the argument on paper. Research into effective teachers of literacy (Wray *et al.* 2002) shows that the explicit teaching of word, sentence and text level features was a regular part of the practice of these professionals, who set such instruction in contexts which were meaningful to the children. They also carefully explained the purpose of these features. Whole texts, not extracts, must be employed for teaching and modelling should be used extensively as an integral and integrated part of instruction in the extended process of comprehension and composition. As teachers we need to develop children's knowledge about genres of writing and we may well set targets which relate to punctuation and spelling, for example, but these need to be in the context of treating children first and foremost as authors, communicators and meaning makers.

Talking about writing

Close collaboration over writing and frequent conversations about writing can help involve and motivate children, enabling them to focus on their content, audience and purpose. Through talking about their own and others' texts they can widen their understanding about writing, as thought is not simply expressed in words but comes into existence through them (Vygotsky 1978). The Essex Writing Project found that talking about writing, before, during and after writing raises standards (Essex County Council 2003). It can also be motivating and empowering if strong relationships of trust and respect are created in school. Young writers may, however, need help to respond to one another's work with interest and insight, but with careful modelling and sensitive teaching, children can become effective response partners, who respond to both the writer and the writing. In discussing their writing, children need the chance to talk about what they were trying to achieve and the strategies they employed to keep the reader interested. Such conversations can help them develop a metalanguage to describe language and become more conscious of the choices they are making as authors who appreciate that writing involves both creating and crafting. As teachers we must try to make time to discuss children's writing with them at the draft stage and focus on their meanings as well as read their work back to them, giving it life and breath and helping them hear the tunes and patterns they have created (Barrs and Cork 2001). Teacher intervention and peer discussions during drafting can undoubtedly facilitate reflective activity and enrich the quality of the writing (for example, Wells *et al.* 1990; Corden 2002).

As teachers we must model the reflective process of writing, writing publicly and authentically in front of the children and verbalising our thoughts about our intentions for this writing as we reflect on its emerging message or meaning. We may also focus on the text's construction and the language itself or we may choose to highlight the processes of planning, drafting, editing and proofreading our work. As writers in the classroom, we need to show children the importance of re-reading our writing as we compose and asking questions of ourselves, for example: 'What am I trying to achieve? How else could I phrase it? What does it sound like?' and so forth. If we invite the children to help us shape our writing and comment on its strengths as well as suggest possible ways forward, then gradually they will learn to see us as writers too and begin to evaluate their own writing also. Teachers who write alongside their pupils, both in demonstration writing and in independent writing, find that they gain considerable insight into the writing process and understand more fully the demands of writing in school; this often challenges such teachers to construct more creatively engaging contexts and to offer more choice (Grainger 2005).

Choice and voice

To develop children's independence as writers we must build choice into activities, encouraging them to make decisions for themselves. The NC (DfEE 1999) states that at key stage 2 children should be taught to choose the form and content of their writing to suit their purpose, but choice is important at all ages. In a large survey of young writers, both the KS1 and KS2 children involved, expressed a strong desire for more autonomy in writing. They did not like having the content, form and shape of their written work too tightly prescribed and valued all opportunities when they themselves had some agency in the process (Grainger *et al.* 2003). If, given the choice, young writers often use writing to reflect upon subjects that have relevance and interest to them, they may make more use of texts from popular culture and make connections to their inner affective existence. Through writing regularly about what matters to them, children experience the potential of writing more fully and invest more of themselves in the process. For example, in one school a group of ten- and eleven-year-old boys found both pleasure and purpose in writing through collaboratively publishing their own magazine entitled *Bonkerz*. The ten issues contained jokes and comic strips, historical information and recipes, a pets' corner, quizzes about *The Simpsons*, diary entries, word searches, and so on, all created by the *Bonkerz* crew in their own free time at home and at school. Their commitment to this publication, which they sold in aid of charity, was remarkable and highlights their growing independence as writers and their pleasure in writing. These youngsters had found a way to explore their different strengths and identities through writing and wrote for a receptive KS2 audience. Figure 8.3 shows three extracts from an issue of this magazine.

Another vehicle for offering choice which has grown in popularity in recent years is writing journals. In these journals, which are covered and decorated individually, children often choose to write about their lives, their concerns and interests, fads and fashions, experience and expertise, and many appear to return to earlier entries to redraft some of this work which they share with enthusiasm (Graham and Johnson 2003). In the process they reveal something of themselves as young people, with a growing sense of self and identity and particular passions and desires. In order to help children take increased ownership of their writing in their journals and elsewhere, we need to provide support for the selection of ideas and time to share their work with one another in the classroom community of writers. In such contexts as they write for and of themselves on subjects about which they are knowledgeable, children find their voices, that sense of their uniqueness as a writer (Grainger *et al.* 2005). Choice can be built into work in the literacy hour too, when, for example, a film such as *Finding Nemo* or *Toy Story* is being watched and the use of the music to evoke mood and character is being examined. In such contexts, the teacher can offer choice knowing that the children can draw upon their experience, knowledge and interest in the movie and may, for example, like to write a letter from Marlin, a poem about Nemo or create another undersea adventure for these characters.

Physical and conceptual space

To motivate and involve young writers we need to ensure there is sufficient physical space for children to converse, improvise, explore and negotiate meanings and possibilities together. Resources of various kinds will be needed, including, for example: props, puppets, gel pens, percussion instruments and drawing materials. Role play areas, message boards, home writing displays, a writing table, audio cassette recorders and computers can also be invaluable, enabling children to make use of what they need when they are working independently. In addition to physi-

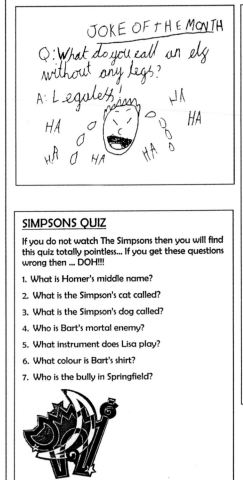

JOKE OF THE MONTH

Q: What do you call an elg without any legs?

A: Legaless!

HA HA HA HA HA HA

SIMPSONS QUIZ

If you do not watch The Simpsons then you will find this quiz totally pointless... If you get these questions wrong then ... DOH!!!

1. What is Homer's middle name?
2. What is the Simpson's cat called?
3. What is the Simpson's dog called?
4. Who is Bart's mortal enemy?
5. What instrument does Lisa play?
6. What colour is Bart's shirt?
7. Who is the bully in Springfield?

HILARIOUS HISTORY

Maths lessons are full of problems but English lessons are quite another story. Music lessons break all records but history is full of hoaxes like: some say he died somewhere else, this is a memorial, others say this is his grave. No one knows, but would you like to prove the teacher wrong?

Egyptians pyramids. They were built by aliens from outer space who landed on Mount Etna, that's why it's erupting.

Tutankhamen's tomb:
He was actually buried in a bus that fell through a time warp from 2002 AD.

The Nile delta:
It was actually dug by Rameses II because he thought it would make a nice view from the pyramids.

NB This is a load of rubbish, poppycock and anything else you can possibly think of except the truth.

History quiz

Q1 Who built the pyramids? a: Aliens b: The Egyptians c: Bob the Builder
Q2 Where was Tutankhamen buried in? a: A bus b: A tomb c: A time warp
Q3 Who dug the Nile delta? a: Rameses II b: Mother Nature c: Peter Pan

TRUE ANSWERS
IF A, YOU BELIEVE ANY THING YOU READ. IF B, YOU'RE SMART. IF C, YOU'RE MAD!!!!!!!!!!

FIGURE 8.3 Extracts from *Bonkerz*

cal space, creative contexts provide conceptual space for young writers to generate ideas, to imagine and to play their way forwards (Craft 2002). In such open environments of possibility, there is space to make choices, to take the initiative, to make suggestions and try out alternative ideas and oppositional stances. This is not, however, a shapeless environment. The teacher will give form and shape to many of the activities, and may model, for example, a musical interpretation of a poem with accompanying body percussion and an ostinato to highlight the poem's meaning. On the journey towards writing children will engage, respond, imagine and investigate texts through a process of deep immersion, playful investigation and considered reflection. So the social and intellectual environment of the classroom becomes a kind of 'third teacher' (Edwards *et al.* 1998) that motivates and supports young writers.

Creative teachers of writing

As teachers, if we adopt a flexible yet informed frameset, we can offer engaging invitations to learn about writing through engaging in writing and we can motivate young writers to actively use, notice and study language attentively, creatively and effectively. If we take a full part alongside them in the extended process of composition, and develop our own creative potential as we too tell tales and take up roles in drama, for example, we can show them that we also use writing for our own purposes and find pleasure in it. Together, we can find inspirational and involving ways forward that build on the children's interests, capture their imaginations, and energise their emotions so that a desire to write is developed and their voices are activated through deep creative engagement and considered reflection.

Acknowledgements

Thanks to Emma Goff from St James Infants for sharing Graham's work with me and to Kathy Goouch and Andrew Lambirth for their collaboration in the *We're writers* research which enriched my thinking and thus this chapter.

References

Barrs, M. and Cork, V. (2001) *The Reader in the Writer*. London: Centre for Literacy in Primary Education.

Bearne, E. (2003) *Making Progress in Writing*. London: Routledge.

Bearne, E. and Grainger, T. (2004) 'Raising boys' achievement in writing: joint PNS/UKLA pilot research project', *Literacy*, 38, 3.

Boden, M. (2001) 'Creativity and knowledge', in A. Craft, B. Jeffrey, and M. Liebling, (eds) *Creativity in Education*. London: Continuum.

Corden, R. (2001) 'Teaching reading-writing links (TRAWL) project', *Reading, Literacy and Language*, 35, 1, 37–40.

Corden, R. (2002) *Literacy and Learning through Talk: Strategies for the Classroom*. Buckingham: Open University Press.

Corden, R. (2003) 'Writing is more than "exciting": equipping primary children to become reflective writers', *Reading, Literacy and Language*, 37, 1, pp. 18–26.

Craft, A. (2002) *Creativity and Early Years Education*. London: Continuum.

DfEE (1999) *National Curriculum for English Programme of Study*. London: DfEE/QCA.

DfES (2001) *The National Literacy Strategy, Teaching Writing: Support Material for Text Level Objectives*, DfES 0531/2001. London: DfES.

DfES (2003) *Excellence and Enjoyment: A Strategy for Primary Schools*. Nottingham: DfES.

Edwards, C., Gandini, L. and Forman, G. (eds) (1998) *The Hundred Languages of Children* (2nd edition). Greenwich, CT: Ablex.

Essex County Council (2003) *Visually Speaking using Multimedia Texts to Improve Boys' Writing*, The English team, Essex Advisory and Inspection Service.

Fox, C. (1993) *At the very Edge of the Forest: The Influence of Literature on Storytelling by Children*. London: Cassell.

Frater, G. (2004) 'Improving Dean's writing: what shall we tell the children', *Literacy*, 38, 2.

Graham, L. and Johnson, A. (2003) *Writing Journals.* Cambridge: UKLA.

Grainger, T., Goouch, K. and Lambirth, A. (2003) 'Playing the game called writing: children's views and voices', *English in Education*, 37, 2, 4–15.

Grainger, T., Lambrith, A., Goouch, K. Oliver, M. (2004) *Creative Activities for Plot, Character and Setting, Ages 5–7.* Leamington Spa: Scholastic.

Grainger, T. (2004) 'Drama and writing: enlivening their prose' in P. Goodwin, (ed.) *Literacy through Creativity.* London: David Fulton.

Grainger, T. Goouch, K. and Lambirth, A. (2005) *Creativity and Writing: Developing Voice and Verve in the Classroom.* London: RoutledgeFalmer.

Grainger, T. (2005) 'Teachers as writers: travelling forwards together', *English in Education*, 38, 1.

Myhill, D. (2001) 'Crafting and creating', *English in Education*, 35, 3, pp. 13–20.

Packwood, A. and Messenheimer, T. (2003) 'Back to the future: developing children as writers', in E. Bearne, H. Dombey, and T. Grainger. *Classroom Interactions in Literacy.* Buckinghamshire: Open University Press.

Wells, G., Chang, G. and Maher, A. (1990) *Creating Classroom Communities of Literature Thinkers, Cooperative Learning.* New York: Praeger.

Whybrow, I. (2001) *Little Wolf's Book of Badness.* London: Collins.

Wilson, J. (1995) *Cliffhanger.* London: Corgi Childrens.

Winnicott, D. (1974) *Playing and Reality.* Harmondsworth, Middlesex: Penguin.

Wray, D., Medwell, J., Poulson, L. and Fox, R. (2002) *Teaching Literacy Effectively in the Primary School.* London: RoutledgeFalmer.

Vygotsky, L. (1978) *Mind in Society.* Cambridge, MA: Harvard University Press.

Developing children's narrative writing using story structures

Maureen Lewis

Introduction

Following her work through the EXEL Project (see Chapter 10), Maureen Lewis addressed the concerns expressed by primary practitioners over children's ability to write stories. In this chapter, Lewis describes some of the ways in which she worked with colleagues in supporting young writers of fiction.

The problem

'They're all right on beginnings. It's the middle where it all gets lost. How can I help them with middles and ends?' This remark, made by a key stage 2 teacher attending an in-service course on writing, was greeted with nods and murmurs of agreement from the rest of the key stage 1 and key stage 2 teachers present. There was general agreement that, although children might write a developed opening with some skill, for example, writing a detailed and imaginative description of the characters or the setting, the overall shape of the story could still be weak and unclear. Many pupils, these teachers felt, could write a simple sequence of events (an 'and then' story as one teacher described it) but attempts to write more complex stories had often become confused and incoherent.

The problem identified by this group of teachers echoes comments from the reports by the SCAA (1997a, b) evaluating the 1996 SATs. In the writing task, SCAA (1997a) found that a key difference in children's writing (and the levels that they scored) was 'the way the writing was structured' and that some children spent 'all their time and energy in explaining the opening'. They noted that some of the texts 'were based on *well-defined structures* with which children were evidently *familiar*' and that, 'where children did not have this kind of support, they had more difficulty in producing an *appropriately organised* piece of writing. This was particularly the case with stories where unshaped rambling pieces contained undeveloped events following one another in rapid succession and lacking a conclusion' (my italics throughout).

The problem for teaching and learning appears to be twofold:

■ How to help children to recognise that stories have structures beyond a simplistic beginning, middle and end

■ How to help them to use this understanding to support their own story planning and writing

SCAA (1997a) recommend that teachers should 'provide children with opportunities to work on structuring and concluding their stories'. One effective strategy for this, they suggest, is 'the use of literary models, the organisational features of which can be explicitly discussed with the children.

The strategy of using a book as a literary model is well established. Many teachers, for example, might use a book such as *Rosie's Walk* (Hutchins 1970) as a model for writing a story of a walk around the playground, or *Funnybones* (Ahlberg and Ahlberg 1990) as a model for a story of the skeleton living in a school and exploring the school at night. However, such work can be taken further and in this chapter I shall discuss how using groups of books which share a common story structure can be used to enhance children's story writing. Working with a class of year 4 children and their teacher, using picture books as models, we were interested to discover whether the following were true:

■ We could identify a range of common story structures.

■ Children could identify these structures for themselves.

■ The use of graphic story structure frames helped children to record the story structures that they had identified and to plan their own stories.

■ The occasional, focused use of writing frames scaffolded some children in writing.

■ The children's ability to write stories improved.

The theoretical background

One starting point for the work was based on insights from story grammar. Much of our knowledge about story structure comes from literary critics such as Vladimir Propp (1968) who searched for a universal story structure to be found in popular Russian folk tales, and also from the work on story grammar developed throughout the 1970s and early 1980s. At that time, cognitive psychologists became interested in individuals' mental representations (schema) of story components and how such components fitted together (Mandler and Johnson 1977). Story grammar is characterised as 'a set of rules that will define both a text's structure and an individual's mental representation of story structure' (Whaley 1981). Several researchers developed story grammars (Mandler and Johnson 1977; Rumelhart 1978; Stein and Glenn 1979). Mandler and Johnson, for example, argued that there are six major story elements: setting, beginning, reaction, attempt, outcome and ending. It is argued that, as our experience of stories grows, so does our knowledge about stories and we can draw on this knowledge to help us to predict and understand what is happening when we meet new stories. Others have proposed alternative structures but, whatever the particular structures used, researchers have generally agreed that readers and listeners use story schema in three ways:

- As a set of expectations for the structure of a story
- To facilitate comprehension of a story
- To improve memory and recall of a story

Strategies such as prediction tasks, scrambled stories, cloze tasks and retelling tasks were recommended (Whaley 1981) to help children to draw on and develop their story schema. From this early work on story structures, other classroom practices have been developed to help children explicitly to recognise the story structures that they encountered. Story mapping (Benton and Fox 1985), story shapes (Bentley and Rowe 1990), story comparison charts (Worthy and Bloodgood 1993) and story structure charts (Newman 1989) are now sometimes used to enhance children's understanding of the books and stories that they encounter. Such practices help pupils to recognise key events in a story, can help them to develop insights into characters' motives and can help them to develop character sketches and to appreciate the importance of setting. It is clear from the many accounts of such strategies and their popularity in classrooms that all these activities are viewed as useful in developing children's story schema.

However, many of these activities are based upon helping children to make explicit what they have learnt from reading or listening to a text. More recently, work on textual genres has encouraged teachers to deconstruct written texts with children as a precursor to then constructing further texts using the same structural features (Derewianka 1990; Wing Jan 1991; Lewis and Wray 1995). One strategy which has been developed to help children to make the link between non-fiction textual structures and their own writing is the use of writing frames (Lewis and Wray 1996). The success of this strategy in scaffolding children's writing suggested that frames might also prove useful in narrative writing.

The work in school

Although the account and work samples that follow are all from year 4 children, the ideas can easily be adapted for older or younger pupils. Each week a selection of picture books was assembled, all of which shared a similar story structure. The story structures identified were as follows:

- Cumulative stories (add-on stories)
- Reverse cumulative stories (take-away stories)
- Journey stories: linear journeys (from A to B), return journeys (from A to B to A) and circular journeys (from A to A)
- Turning point stories: character, circumstances or physical characteristics
- Wasted-wishes stories
- Simple problem and resolution stories
- Days-of-the-week stories

Further details of these, together with examples, are given in an appendix at the end of this chapter.

Picture books were ideal for our purpose for, not only are they appealing texts in their own right, they also offer a complete text in brief and so allow children to sample several examples in a relatively short space of time (Lewis 1997). They also allow the teacher to differentiate the text for varied reading abilities, for example, *Rosie's Walk* (Hutchins 1968) and *Hail to the Mail* (Marshak 1992) both provide models of a circular journey text but make very different reading demands during their use in independent activities. Once a selection of books was assembled, a five-step sequence was followed as each set of books were used.

The five-step approach

Immersion in the text type

At the start of the session the children were told that that they were going to hear some stories and that, although all these books and stories were different, there was something the same about them. They were asked to pay particular attention to the 'pattern' of the story. Later this terminology was changed to 'structure' of the story. The children coped well with this metalanguage, having experienced what it meant in context. Two or three of the selected books were read to the whole class (or sometimes this activity was undertaken as oral storytelling) and the children encouraged to enjoy and respond to the stories.

Explicit discussion of structure and concrete recording of the structure

The children were then asked about the structure of the story and how it was the same in all the examples that they had enjoyed. The structure was explicitly discussed and this was followed by some kind of whole-class mapping and graphic representation of one of the shared books. This visual representation of the story structure was drawn or scribed by the teacher and the links between the graphic representation and the story were also re-articulated as teacher 'think alouds' as the drawing progressed This move, from recognition into a visual representation of the structure, was important for many of the children and seemed to help them to fix the structure in their minds by moving from an internal abstract concept to an external explicit object.

Independent recording of the structure

The children then worked in pairs to read and map a further example of a story which had a similar structure to that shared in the whole-class activity. Here books could be differentiated according to reading ability. Figure 9.1 shows an example of a mapping of an A-to-B journey story structure. This structure is as follows: start of journey, events en route (either people or physical landmarks met), reaching destination and concluding act. The events en route usually represent problems encountered and overcome.

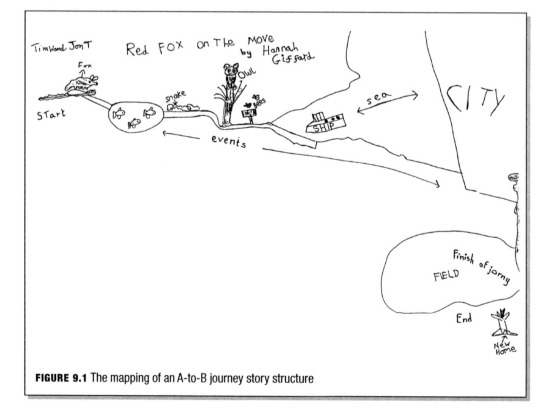

FIGURE 9.1 The mapping of an A-to-B journey story structure

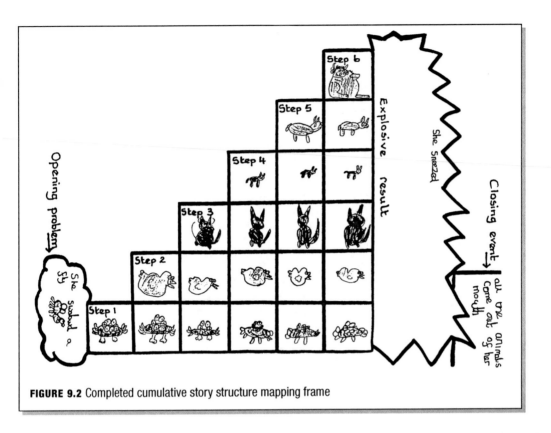

FIGURE 9.2 Completed cumulative story structure mapping frame

On some occasions the children were given a mapping frame on which to record the structure of the story that they had read. These mapping frames provided a visual prompt to the story structure. Figure 9.2 shows a completed cumulative story structure mapping frame. The design of this frame helps the child to recognise the elements of the structure: opening event or problem, the addition of one new element each time, the explosive climax when overload is reached, and the concluding event to close the story – or to start the sequence again. We also used further graphic mapping frames designed to reflect the story structure for turning point stories, circular stories and 'take-away' stories.

Using the structure to plan their own story

From independent recording of the story structure, the children then moved into planning their own story using the same structure. For some children this involved moving straight into a written story plan but for many children it involved some kind of planning frame to help them. This planning frame was often a further blank version of the mapping frame that they had just used, enabling them to see the links clearly. Figures 9.3 and 9.4 show a child's mapping of *Mrs Armitage on Wheels* (Blake 1987) using a text deconstruction frame, followed by his planning frame for his own story based on the structure.

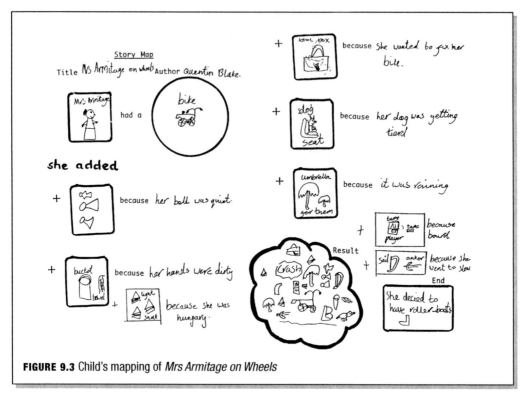

FIGURE 9.3 Child's mapping of *Mrs Armitage on Wheels*

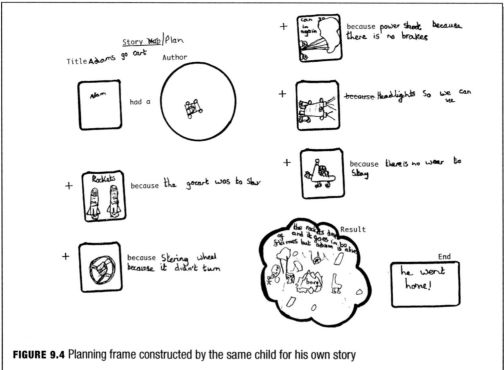

FIGURE 9.4 Planning frame constructed by the same child for his own story

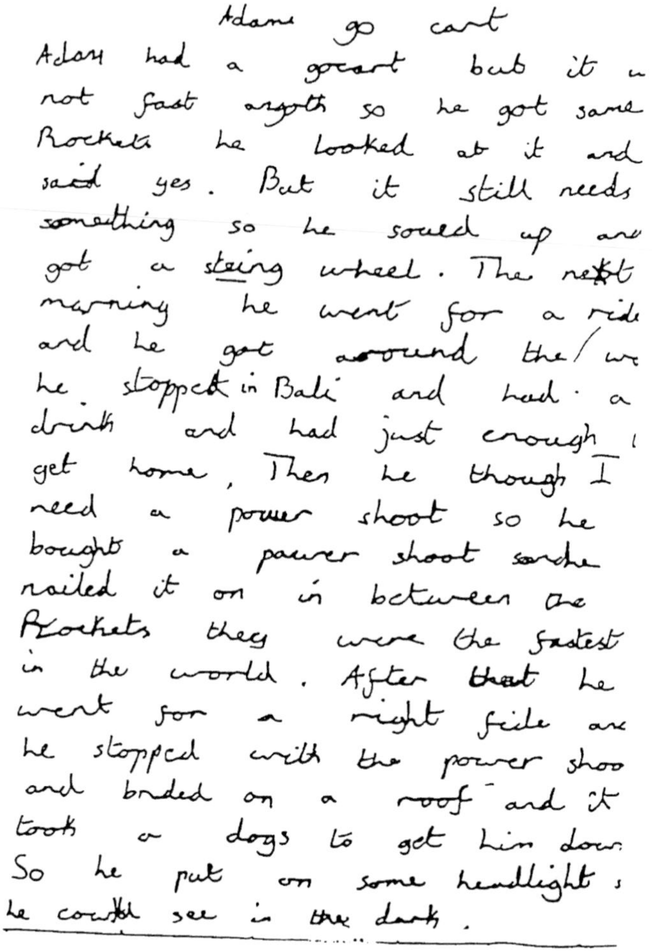

Adams go cart
Adam had a gocart but it w
not fast anogth so he got some
Rockets he Looked at it and
said yes. But it still needs
something so he soued up and
got a steing wheel. The next
morning he went for a ride
and he got around the/wo
he stopped in Bali and had a
drink and had just enough t
get home, Then he though I
need a power shoot so he
bought a power shoot so he
nailed it on in between the
Rockets they were the fastest
in the world. After that he
went for a night fide and
he stopped with the power shoo
and landed on a roof and it
took a dogs to get him down
So he put on some headlights
he could see in the dark.

FIGURE 9.5 First draft of the story based on the mapping in Figure 9.3 and the planning frame in Figure 9.4

Drafting the story and sharing the drafts in a plenary

The plans were then used to write a first draft of a story and these drafts were shared in a plenary session, when the rest of the class listened and commented on whether the structure was clear and the story coherent. We never had time within one session to complete the writing process but often the children redrafted and finished their stories during the rest of the week. Figure 9.5 shows the first draft of the cumulative story based on the mapping and planning structures shown in Figures 9.3 and 9.4.

At the first draft stage some children had simple writing frames with sentence starters to help them. Often these were placed on the computer. Figure 9.6 shows the first draft of a cumulative story written by two less able writers using a frame to help them. The given frame is underlined.

Did it make a difference?

In judging whether the work had any impact, we can look at evidence from the children's behaviour during the sessions, the children's work, child interview data, incidents that occurred outside the writing sessions and the class teacher's views.

The class contained the usual mix of children with a variety of attitudes and skills but throughout the term the children appeared fascinated by what they did. Brian Cambourne (1997) argues that two of the criteria for judging successful literacy teaching strategies are 'active engagement' and 'spill-over' (i.e. evidence that the children spontaneously apply what they have learnt on other occasions and make links within other areas of the curriculum). Both of these features appeared to be evident:

Interviewer: What about 'active engagement'?

Class teacher: I thought that they were superb because they had all morning and there was very little sign of anybody starting to mess around or whatever. There were large numbers who were always keen to carry on and finish – even after two and a half hours. And it wasn't novelty value ... it would have easily worn off before the end. They were very well engaged.

Similarly, many of the children interviewed talked about their interest in what they had done and how they wanted to continue. Ellie's comments are typical: 'Those story patterns. They were really interesting. It made me want to write a story. I thought my "take-away" story was really good. It was funny.'

'Spill-over' occurred on many occasions with children finding books in their reading sessions which demonstrated structures that they recognised, or elements of a story where they spotted a link. It might have been useful to start a class list or database to which they could have added their discoveries.

John: I was hearing my little brother read the end bit of *The Gingerbread Man*. That's kind of a 'take-away' story, isn't it? Not all of it. The bit where the fox eats him bit by bit. And it's 'add on' too – all those people who chase him.

Class teacher: Kylie said that she went home and read after we'd done our session together. She then went home and looked for the same kind of patterns. So she was clearly up and away.

The class teacher felt that the work had had an effect on the quality of work of many of the children and was particularly pleased with its effect on the quality of the writing of the less able children.

One suny morning miss mcintosh was in the stockroom getting books Suddenly the door slammed . "Help! Help! Get me out," shouted miss mcintosh. So mr statton pulled but the door did not open.Then miss lewis came to help. and they both pulled, but the door did not open. Then Jason came to help.Mr statton and miss lewis and Jason pulled,but the door did not open.Then Tracey came to help.Mr statton and miss lewis and Jason and Tracey pulled and pulled.

THE DOOR OPENED and everyone all fell down . miss mcintosh was saved so everyone shouted hurrah. and had a cup of tea.

FIGURE 9.6 First draft of a cumulative story written by two less able children using a writing frame

Class teacher: To start with they did find it a bit difficult – when they were doing that first one some of them found it difficult but last weekend I took all their books home and went through the last story and most had got a structure – some sort of pattern – and the less able children too.

Many children claimed in their interviews that using a structure frame to help them to plan had been helpful and they were all able to talk, with varying degrees of fluency, about story structures that they now knew. The class teacher felt that the children had moved on in their use of story plans because of the explicit teaching.

Class teacher: When we did stories, the plans for stories were character and setting. But I could never get my head around finding some sort of structure to base the story on because I always believed it was up to them actually to think of the structure themselves, whereas now I can see far better how to guide them, and the results are definitely better just reading what they've come up with.

One of the criticisms that can be levelled against such a structured approach to supporting children's writing and the use of frames is that it can stifle individuality and creativity. There was little evidence of this with the work produced. The wide variety of individual stories that the class wrote each week showed that children still used very different characters, settings and ideas within the structures that they were using.

Interviewer: Can it stifle children's creative initiative?

Class teacher: I don't think you do stifle that. Because I remember way back to when I qualified, we weren't allowed to teach them how to paint were we? They had to express themselves. I rarely got anything good in art, whereas now art is quite structured. You do drawings from life or whatever. You do looking at other artist's work – all those sort of things and the quality of art is much better. You see those three-dimensional things, in the class (indicates). I long since realised that you've got to teach them something, because people can only actually be expressive when they can build on some inner knowledge. I think with structures for stories in English we're doing the same thing. They can be as imaginative as they like because they have the tools with which to build. We owe it to them to give them the groundwork. That's what primary education is about. We give them the groundwork and then, when they are able, they can take off. They can fly. There are children now who I am sure can write without the mapping or writing frames any more but can use the knowledge that is now their own.

Conclusion

This chapter has described one term's work with one class of children and so any claims that can be drawn from it must be limited. However, these children's increasingly confident use of story structures and the improvements in their ability to produce a coherent story suggest that explicit teaching about story structure and making links between structure mapping and planning is a useful strategy, worthy of further exploration.

Appendix

Cumulative stories

In these step-by-step stories, events or objects or characters are continuously added to preceding events, objects or characters until a climax (often explosive) is reached.

- The *Enormous Turnip* – traditional.
- *Hairy McClarey from Donaldson's Dairy* by Lynley Dodd (1985). London: Penguin Children's Books.
- *Mr Gumpy's Outing* by John Burningham (1978). London: Penguin Children's Books.

Reverse cumulative stories

In these stories, something is progressively diminished until it disappears altogether or something returns to the status quo.

- 'The story of Horace', in *The Faber Story Book* edited by Kathleen Lines (1961). London: Faber and Faber.
- *Five Little Ducks* by Ian Beck (1993). London: Orchard.

Journey stories

In journey stories the participant usually meets people, animals or physical landmarks along the route. These meetings provide a moment where something happens – often a problem and resolution.

- Linear journeys (from A to B)
- *Red Fox on the Move* by Hannah Gifford (1995). London: Francis Lincoln.
- *On the Way Home* by Jill Murphy (1984). London: Macmillan.
- Return journeys (from A to B to A)
- *The Shopping Basket* by John Burningham (1980). London: Jonathan Cape.
- *We're Going on a Bear Hunt* by Michael Rosen (1993). London: Walker Books.
- Circular journeys (from A to A)
- *Rosie's Walk* by Pat Hutchins (1970). London: Penguin Children's Books.
- *The Bad-tempered Ladybird* by Eric Carle (1982). London: Penguin Children's Books.

Circular stories (not journeys)

A series of acts at the end of which the character is back at the beginning. A variant of this is the wasted-wishes circular tale. In these stories, wishes are granted in return for some good deed but these are wasted owing to some flaw (for example, greed or stupidity) in the character and they end up back where they started.

- *There's a Hole in My Bucket* – traditional song.
- *The Old Woman Who Lived in a Vinegar Bottle* – traditional.

Turning-point stories: character, circumstances or physical characteristics

In these stories some distinctive aspect of a character's personality, circumstances or physical appearance is foregrounded. An event takes place because of this characteristic, as a result of which the character is changed by the end of the story. Often a 'bad' characteristic is changed or punished, and a good character is recognised and rewarded.

- *King Midas and the Golden Touch* – traditional.
- *The Frog Prince* – traditional.

The problem and resolution structure

This is a very common structure. It is best first introduced in a simple form of one problem, solved quickly. More complex versions can then be introduced.

- *Alfie Gets in First* by Shirley Hughes (1991). London: Red Fox.
- *Are You There Bear?* by Ron Marris (1986). London: Penguin Children's Books.

The days-of-the-week structure

The days of the weeks are gone through sequentially and on each day a same but different event occurs (for example, the caterpillar eats each day but different food); on the final day a climax is reached and something new happens.

- *The Very Hungry Caterpillar* by Eric Carle (1974). London: Penguin Children's Books.

References

Ahlberg, A. and Ahlberg, J. (1990) *Funnybones*. London: Mammoth.

Beck, I. (1993) *Five Little Ducks*. London: Orchard.

Bentley. D. and Rowe, A. (1990) *Group Reading in the Primary Classroom*. Reading: Reading and Language Information Centre, The University of Reading.

Benton, M. and Fox, G. (1985) *Teaching Literature 9–14*. Oxford: Oxford University Press.

Blake, Q. (1987) *Mrs Armitage on Wheels*. London: Jonathan Cape.

Burningham, J. (1978) *Mr Grumpy's Outing*. London: Penguin Children's Books.

Burningham, J. (1980) *The Shopping Basket*. London: Jonathan Cape.

Cambourne, B. (1997) 'Key principles of good literacy teaching', Talk and unpublished conference paper. Manchester, United Kingdom Reading Association.

Carle, E. (1974) *The Very Hungry Caterpillar*. London: Penguin Children's Books.

Carle, E. (1982) *The Bad-tempered Ladybird*. London: Penguin Children's Books.

Derewianka, B. (1990) *Exploring How Texts Work*. Newtown, New South Wales: PETA.

DfEE (1988) *The National Literacy Strategy Framework for Teaching*. London: DfEE.

Dodd, L. (1985) *Hairy McClarey from Donaldson's Dairy*. London: Penguin Children's Books.

Gifford, H. (1988) *Red Fox on the Move*. London: Frances Lincoln.

Hughes, S. (1991) *Alfie Gets in First*. London: Red Fox.

Hutchins, P. (1968) *Rosie's Walk*. London: Bodley Head Children's Books.

Lewis D. H. (1997) 'Working with picture books in the primary classroom.' Talk and unpublished conference paper. Manchester, United Kingdom Reading Association.

Lewis, M. and Wray, D. (1995) *Developing Children's Non-fiction Writing: Working with Writing Frames*. Leamington Spa: Scholastic.

Lewis, M. and Wray, D. (1996) *Writing Frames: Scaffolding Children's Non-fiction Writing*. Reading: Reading and Language Information Centre, The University of Reading.

Lines, K. (ed.) (1961) *The Faber Story Book*. London: Faber and Faber.

Mandler, J. M. and Johnson, N. S. (1977) 'Remembrance of things parsed: story structure and recall,' *Cognitive Psychology*, 9, 111–51.

Marshak, S. (1992) *Hail to the Mail*. London: Bodley Head Children's Books.

Maris, R. (1986) *Are You There Bear?* London: Penguin Children's Books.

Murphy, J. (1984) *On the Way Home*. London: Macmillan.

Newman, J. M. (1989) 'Online: the flexible page', *Language Arts*, 66, 4, 457–64.

Propp, V. (1968) *The Morphology of the Folktale*, 2nd edn, transl. L. Law Scott, Baltimore: Port City Press.

Rosen, M. (1993) *We're Going on a Bear Hunt*. London: Walker Books.

Rumelhart, D. E. (1978) 'Understanding and summarising brief stories,' in *Basic Processes in Reading: Perception and Comprehension*, D. LaBerge, and S. J. Samuels, (eds) Hillsdale, New Jersey: Lawrence Erlbaum Associates.

SCAA (1997a) *Standards at Key Stage 1. English and Mathematics. Report on the 1996 National Curriculum Assessments for 7-year-olds*. London: HMSO.

SCAA (1997b) *Standards at Key Stage 2. English, Mathematics and Science. Report on the 1996 National Curriculum Assessments for 11-year-olds*. London: HMSO.

Stein N. L. and Glenn C. (1979) 'An analysis of story comprehension in elementary school children', in *New Directions in Discourse Proceeding*, R. O. Freedie (ed.). Norwood, New Jersey: Ablex.

Whaley, J. F. (1981) 'Story grammars and reading instruction,' *The Reading Teacher*, 34, 8, 762–71.

Wing Jan, L. (1991) *Write Ways. Modelling Writing Forms*. Oxford: Oxford University Press.

Worthy, M. J. and Bloodgood, J. W. (1993) 'Enhancing reading instruction through Cinderella tales,' *The Reading Teacher*, 6, 4, 290–301.

10

The problems and possibilities of non-fiction writing

David Wray and Maureen Lewis

Looking at non-fiction writing

We shall begin by looking at three pieces of non-fiction writing.

Danny is a year 7 pupil who has been asked to write in a science lesson on how the solar system was made. Here is his explanation:

> How was our solar system made. One day a man called god woke up and fancied a change. He said I will have a red planet a green and blue planet and one with rings round it. And a few glowing spots to make it look pretty and I will play basketball spin shots so some spin. Two hours later a massive energy bang it blew god house down. When he opened his eyes he saw his creation and then he lived for 2 whole years after that he died. Before he died he created two humans called Adam and Eve and if it wasn't for him we would not be here today. Nobody knows if there was life on these planets all we know is people live on earth exsept for god he died. We don't know what it looks like here is a picture of what I think it looks like.

Adam (year 6) has been asked to write an account of the Spanish Armada. Here is the first half page (of three pages altogether) of what he wrote:

> 'Spainish Armada'
> A long time ago in 1588 King Philip II wanted to invade England. Suddenly a letter came from the Netherlands and it said 'I'm sorry but I'm not going to fight with you because I feel sick.' So the genral said none of them are coming to fight us and so it looks like just us and England this time. But in Spain they were building a very big ship called the armada. When they had builte it they had 130 ship in side the armada had 8,000 sailors and 20,000 soldirs and 180 priests to make people Cathlic again.

Finally Edward (year 5) has written a discussion paper about life in Tudor times. Here are some extracts from his piece:

'Tudor Times'

The issue we are discussing is whether women and children were treated harshly in Tudor times.

Most people living in Tudor times did not think so. They might have argued that children were untamed beasts and when they beat them they would become more tame.

Men might also have argued that women should know their place so that beating them was not wrong .

Nowadays, however, most people think that women and children in Tudor times were treated harshly. They claim that men chose their wives and the parents chose a husband for their daughter which is not fair because they might not love them.

Furthermore they argue that poor people in Tudor times had to work hard at a young age.

My own opinion is that women and children were treated harshly in Tudor times. I believe this because women and children were not treated as individuals.

Most teachers would agree that, while each of these three pieces of writing may be interesting and 'creative', the first two are inadequate responses to the task the children were set. They are both written in ways which owe more to imaginative stories than to the structures expected of writing in science and history respectively. A large number of children appear to have similar problems in writing and their difficulty is one of matching the way that you write, the style that you choose and the structure that you use to the particular purposes for writing that you encounter in various curriculum subjects.

Yet, in the third piece of writing, the child has apparently solved this problem. His writing is structured to fit the demands of a discussion paper; it shows evidence of appropriate choice of vocabulary and sentence structure. Because of these features it gives the appearance of a much more mature piece of writing. Yet the author, while clearly a reasonably bright child, was younger than the authors of the first two pieces and, in fact, not noticeably a higher achiever in other aspects of school work. How then has he been enabled to produce such writing? It is central to the argument of this chapter that the answer to this question lies in the nature of the teaching that Edward has received, teaching which has ensured that he is aware of the structural and language demands of particular writing tasks and does not approach them with misguided assumptions about how writing works in this context.

What are the essential characteristics of this teaching? These are twofold. First, it rests upon an analysis of the problems that children face in producing effective non-fiction writing and attempts to help them to overcome these problems. Second, it is guided by a model of effective teaching. We shall explore both these aspects.

The problems of non-fiction writing

Writing causes several problems for those not skilled at it (and even for those who are!). From talking to teachers and observing children during the Exeter Extending

Literacy (EXEL) Project,[1] funded by the Nuffield Foundation, we have identified four major problem areas:

- The problem of the blank page
- The difference between writing and talking
- The 'and then' syndrome
- The structure of texts

We shall now discuss these in more detail.

The problem of the blank page

Most writers will agree that the most difficult part of writing anything is the first line or two. Getting started can be so difficult, even for experienced writers, that they invent a number of 'delaying tactics' (sharpening pencils, making coffee and walking around the room) to put off the awful moment. A blank page can be very daunting and for many less experienced writers it can result in abandonment of the writing task. 'Please Miss, I can't think what to write' will be recognisable to many teachers as a familiar response of some children to writing tasks. The blank page has overwhelmed them.

The difference between writing and talking

When talking to another person, the language user receives constant support for his or her language. Talking usually takes the form of a dialogue, namely one person says something and this prompts the other person to say something, which in turn prompts the first person to reply, and so on. Talkers thus receive continual prompts for their language production. These prompts also help to model the register in which the language user can join in the ongoing dialogue. We naturally adapt the way that we speak depending upon our relationship with the person that we are speaking with, and clues as to an appropriate way to join in a conversation come from the way that the other person speaks.

Writers, on the other hand, do not receive such prompts. They are by themselves, forced to produce language without support from another and to work out for themselves an appropriate register for that language.

Of course, in a classroom, there is potentially support available, from a teacher who may be at a child's shoulder prompting with such suggestions as: 'That's an interesting idea. Tell us more about that.' 'You've described that well. Can you give some more information about why it was there?' 'How exciting! And what will happen next?'

It is difficult, however, in a classroom which may contain up to 35 child writers, for a teacher to be able to provide sufficient of this support to meet the needs of the whole class.

The 'and then' syndrome

Inexperienced writers tend to have a limited range of ways of joining together ideas in writing. Most primary teachers will recognise this by the prevalence of 'and then' in their pupils' writing, as if this were the only way of linking ideas in writing. Mature writing, of course, is characterised by more elaborate ways of joining together ideas, using such connectives as 'furthermore', 'moreover', 'nevertheless', 'on the other hand' and so on. Teachers need to find ways of deliberately introducing these alternative connectives to children and helping them to use them effectively in their writing.

The structure of texts

It does seem to be the case that children often lack experience of different types of text, especially non-fiction texts, and their organisational structures. They need some support in distinguishing between these types in terms of linguistic features such as vocabulary, connectives and structure. A concept which can help to explain and categorise these linguistic differences is that of text genre.

According to genre theory, pieces of writing which share a common purpose will tend to share a common structure. One language purpose might be to provide instructions for someone else to carry out a task, for instance in a recipe. Such instructions, be they spoken or written, will tend to follow the following pattern:

- A statement of the goal (for example, this is how to make a chocolate cake)
- A list of materials necessary to achieve this (for example, you will need ...)
- A series of steps to carry out (for example, first you ... , then ...)

Language patterns such as this tend to become so routine that we are barely aware of them; yet clearly they have to be learnt. Many children will find such structures difficult because they do not have the right expectations about texts. It is quite common, for example, for children to write instructions in the form of a narrative: 'I got some sugar and put it in a mixing bowl. Then I ...'. This suggests that teachers need to teach children to use a range of appropriate language structures for appropriate purposes.

In order to do this, teachers need themselves to be aware of various text structures. As we have outlined elsewhere (Lewis and Wray 1995) there appear to be six basic factual genres: recount, report, discussion, persuasion, explanation and instructions. Research suggests that primary children obtain a great deal of experience of writing recounts but rarely experience the other genres. This imbalance is important because in later school life and in adulthood these other genres are very heavily used and are crucial to success. Secondary school examinations, for example, demand the ability to write cogent arguments and discussions and if children have not been taught how to structure these forms of writing they will be disadvantaged.

Non-fiction writing – some possibilities

A model for teaching

The model of teaching upon which we have based the work of the EXEL Project is summarised as follows (the thinking underpinning this model has been fully outlined by Wray and Lewis (1997)):

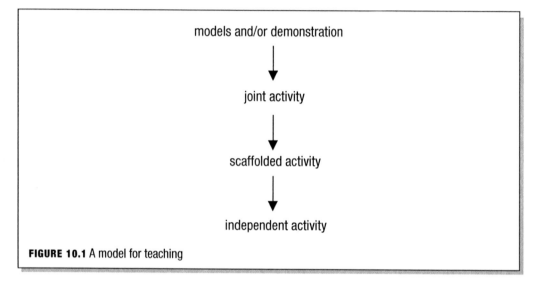

FIGURE 10.1 A model for teaching

The model stems from the ideas of Vygotsky (1978), who put forward the notion that children first experience a particular cognitive activity in collaboration with expert practitioners. The child is first a spectator as the majority of the cognitive work is done by the expert (parent or teacher), and then a novice as he or she starts to take over some of the work under the close supervision of the expert. As the child grows in experience and capability of performing the task, the expert passes over greater and greater responsibility but still acts as a guide, assisting the child at problematic points. Eventually, the child assumes full responsibility for the task with the expert still present in the role of a supportive audience. The model seems to make good theoretical sense; yet it can be a little difficult to apply it fully to teaching in a busy over-populated classroom. In particular, it seems that children are too often expected to move into the independent writing phase before they are really ready and often the pressure to do so is based on the practical problem that teachers are unable to find the time to spend with them in individual support. What is needed is something to span the joint activity and independent activity phases.

We have called this the scaffolded phase, a phase where we offer our pupils strategies to aid writing but strategies that they can use without an adult necessarily being alongside them. One such strategy that we have developed which has become popular is the use of writing frames. These can act both as a way of increasing a child's experience of a particular type of non-fiction writing and as a substitute for the teacher's direct interventions which encourage children to extend their writing.

Some example writing frames

We have space here for only a few examples of the writing frames that we have developed. Further, photocopiable examples can be found in the books by Lewis and Wray (1997, 1998) and a more extensive account of the thinking behind writing frames in the book by Lewis and Wray (1995).

Recount genre

Before I read about this topic I thought that...
But when I read about it I learnt that...
I also learnt that...
Furthermore I learnt that...
The final thing I learnt was that...

Explanation genre

I want to explain why...
The are many reasons for this. The chief reason is...
Another reason is...
A further reason is...
So now you can see why...

Persuasion genre

Some people argue that...
But I want to argue that...
I have several reasons for arguing for this point of view. My first reason is...
Another reason is...
Furthermore...
Therefore, although some people argue that...
I think that I have shown that...

Note how writing with the frame overcomes the four writing problems highlighted earlier.

- It no longer presents writers with a blank page. There is comfort in the fact that there is already some writing on this page. We have found that this alone can be enough to encourage weaker writers to write at greater length.
- The frame provides a series of prompts to pupils' writing. Using the frame is rather like having a dialogue with the page and the prompts serve to model the register of that particular piece of writing.

- The frame deliberately includes connectives beyond the simple 'and then'. We have found that extended use of frames such as this can result in pupils spontaneously using these more elaborate connectives in other writing.
- The frame is designed around the typical structure of a particular genre. It thus gives pupils access to this structure and implicitly teaches them a way of writing non-fiction.

How to use writing frames

Use of a frame should always begin with discussion and teacher modelling before moving on to joint construction (teacher and child or children together) and then to the child undertaking writing supported by the frame. This oral 'teacher-modelling' joint construction pattern of teaching is vital, for it not only models the generic form and teaches the words that signal connections and transitions but also provides opportunities for developing children's oral language and their thinking. Some children, especially children with learning difficulties, may need many oral sessions and sessions in which their teacher acts as a scribe before they are ready to attempt their own writing.

It would be useful for teachers to make 'big' versions of the frames for use in the teacher-modelling and joint construction phases. These large frames can be used for shared writing. It is important that the child and the teacher understand that the frame is a supportive draft and words may be crossed out or substituted. Extra sentences may be added or surplus starters crossed out. The frame should be treated as a flexible aid and not a rigid form.

We are convinced that writing in a range of genres is most effective if it is located in meaningful experiences. The concept of 'situated learning' (Lave and Wenger 1991) suggests that learning is always context dependent. For this reason, we have tended to use the frames within class topic work rather than in isolated study skills lessons. When the children have a purpose for writing, you may decide to offer them a frame as follows:

- When they first attempt independent writing in an unfamiliar genre and a scaffold might be helpful to them.
- When a child or group of children appear stuck in a particular mode of writing, for example, constantly using 'and then' . . . 'and then' when writing an account.
- When they 'wander' between genres in a way that demonstrates a lack of understanding of a particular genre usage, for example, while writing an instructional text such as a recipe, they start in the second person (first you beat the egg) but then shift into a recount (next I stirred in the flour). Mixing genres can of course be a deliberate and creative decision. We must take care to differentiate between those occasions when a child purposely moves between genres and those where different genres are confused.

- When they have written something in one genre (often a personal recount) which would be more appropriate in a different genre, for example, writing up a science experiment as a personal recount. Although writing accounts from personal experience is a vital part of the process of becoming a writer, we must judge when a child needs help to adopt other genres.

In all these situations we would stress that writing frames are just one of a range of strategies and writing experiences that a teacher would offer to assist the children.

Using frames with a range of writers

We have found writing frames helpful to children of all ages and all abilities (indeed their wide applicability is one of their features). However, teachers have found the frames particularly useful with children of average writing ability and with those who find writing difficult. Teachers have commented on the improved quality (and quantity) of writing that has resulted from using the frames with these children.

It would of course be unnecessary to use the frame with writers already confident and fluent in a particular genre but they can be used to introduce such writers to new genres. Teachers have noted an initial dip in the quality of the writing when comparing the framed 'new genre' writing with the fluent recount writing of an able child. What they have later discovered, however, is that, after only one or two uses of a frame, fluent language users add the genre and its language features to their repertoires and, without using a frame, produce fluent writing of high quality in the genre. The aim with all children is for them to reach this stage of assimilating the generic structures and language features into their writing repertoires.

Children need to use the frames less and less as their knowledge of a particular form increases. At this later stage, when children begin to show evidence of independent usage, the teacher may need only to have a master copy of the frames available as help cards for those occasions when children need a prompt. A box of such help cards could be a part of the writing area in which children are encouraged to refer to many different aids to their writing. Such a support fits with the general 'procedural facilitation' strategy for children's writing suggested by Bereiter and Scardamalia (1987). It also seems to be a way into encouraging children to begin to make independent decisions about their own learning.

Also, as pupils become familiar with the frame structures, there is a number of alternative support structures which can be used, such as prompt sheets containing lists of possible ways of connecting ideas together. A number of these may be found in the book by Lewis and Wray (1998).

Pupils' responses to the frames

Using a discussion frame, Mark (year 6) wrote about the arguments for and against a new building project. The frame helped to structure the writing and allowed the pupil access to a difficult form:

'Environmental change'

In our group we had a discussion about whether it was a good idea to build a new super-market in the field beside our school.

Some people thought it was a good idea because it you needed some think after school. If you needed some milk you only a couple of yards away.

Other thought it was a really bad idea because the fumes will drift into the playground.

However, I think the main point is the road will be busy and children will be in danger. After considering all the evidence and points of view I think it is a bad idea.

Marissa (year 4) used a persuasion writing frame to help her to put forward an argument concerning the number of computers in the class:

'Computers'

Althuogh not evrybody would agree, I want to argue that we need to have more comput-ers in our classrooms. I have several reasons for this point of view. My first reason is that everyone can have their own computer, and they don't have to wait to take turns.

Furthermore so that the teacher can keep an eye on everyone. Some people might argue they don't want more computers becasue they might fill up the classroom. I think I have shown that comnputers are very intelligent things. If we had own computers we might get intelligent too and we won't have to argue over them.

These two pieces of writing represent only a very small selection of those we have collected so far from children across the country. They suggest that the use of writ-ing frames as a teaching strategy for non-fiction writing can significantly enhance children's writing achievements. Writing frames offer one exciting possibility for developing writing.

Note

1   The EXEL Project, co-directed by David Wray and Maureen Lewis, has, since 1992, been working with teachers at key stages 1, 2 and 3 across the country to develop teaching strategies to improve children's reading and writing for information.

References

Bereiter, C. and Scardamalia, M. (1987) *The Psychology of Written Composition*. Hillsdale, NJ: Lawrence Erlbaum Associates.

Lave, J. and Wenger, E. (1991) *Situated Learning*. Cambridge: Cambridge University Press.

Lewis, M. and Wray, D. (1995) *Developing Children's Non-fiction Writing*. Leamington Spa: Scholastic.

Lewis, M. and Wray, D. (1997) *Writing Frames*. Reading: Reading and Language Information Centre, The University of Reading.

Lewis, M. and Wray, D. (1998) *Writing Across the Curriculum*. Reading: Reading and Language Information Centre, The University of Reading.

Vygotsky, L. (1978) *Mind in Society: The Development of Higher Psychological Processes*. Cambridge, MA: Harvard University Press.

Wray, D. and Lewis, M. (1997) *Extending Literacy*. London: Routledge.

Teaching and learning spelling

Olivia O'Sullivan

Introduction

There have been many different views of how children learn to spell. Spelling has been seen as a process of memorisation, a perceptual or visual process, a skill 'picked up' from reading, a kinaesthetic process linked to handwriting, a developmental process, a linguistic process and as a process linked to developing phonological or phonemic awareness.

Many teachers therefore find teaching spelling to be a complex and sometimes confusing process. While the National Literacy Strategy (DfEE 1998), used widely in England as the basis for spelling teaching, offers many detailed teaching objectives for word level work, it does not provide a set of key principles or an underlying pedagogy which primary teachers can confidently adapt to meet the wide variety of spelling needs within their classrooms.

This chapter sets out some principles about children's spelling development and practical guidelines for teaching spelling based on the findings of a three-year study in three London primary schools (O'Sullivan and Thomas 2000). The project looked at teachers teaching spelling and children learning to spell. Thirty-one children were tracked over the three years, ranging from reception to year 6. They were a mixture of boys and girls, language backgrounds and spelling abilities.

Learning to spell in English: stages of development or different sources of knowledge?

There is a widely held view that children's spelling development falls into identifiable stages (Gentry 1991; Read 1986; Temple *et al.* 1988; Redfern 1993).

It is argued, that as children make progress in spelling, the word 'monster' might be spelt in the following ways.

TABLE 11.1 Spellings of 'monster'

Child's spelling	Description	'Stage'
(scribble)	Scribble/play writing	Pre-literate
TxMLI	Strings of letters	Pre-literate
msr	Main sounds heard phonetically	Semi-phonetic
mnstr	Sounds heard phonetically fully represented	Phonetic
monstir	Visual aspects represented, though not necessarily in standard form	Visual or transitional
monster	Correct spelling	Standard spelling

Most experienced teachers working with young children know that children use all of these strategies as they progress towards standard spellings. Through our case studies, however, we found out that children often used *many different strategies* at the same time within a single piece of writing. The above 'stages', therefore, are far from being invariable or discrete.

Samantha (reception, term 2) wrote:

To Mr Gumpy (words provided by teacher on flip chart)
Sorry for hoppg anbt
Thak you for litg me come
on your doat
Love from (words provided by teacher on flip chart)
the ribbt

(Dear Mr Gumpy, Sorry for hopping about, thank you for letting me come on your boat. Love from the rabbit.)

In this short piece of writing Samantha used the following strategies:

- She copied some words for example, 'Mr Gumpy'.
- She had a repertoire of known words for example, 'for', 'you', 'me', 'come'.
- She used phonetic strategies – for example, 'thak' (thank).
- She used visual strategies – the 'oa' in 'doat' (boat), the 'pp' in 'hoppg'.
- She may have been beginning to make analogies – 'hoppg' ('hopping') and 'litg' ('letting').

She had begun the year by writing strings of letters.

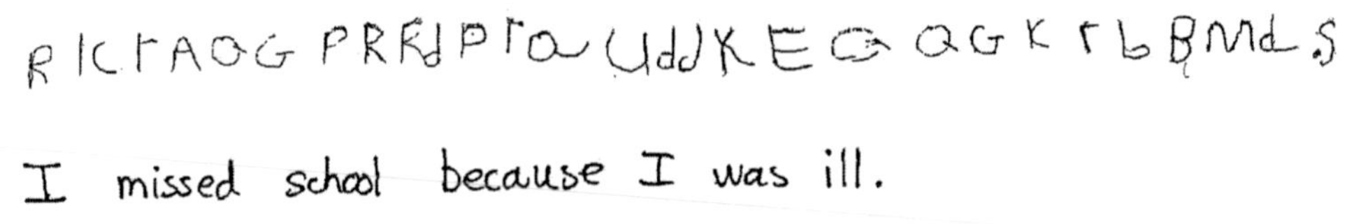

RICTAOG PRRJPTaUJJKEG aGKTLBMLS

I missed school because I was ill.

FIGURE 11.1 Samantha's progress in writing

By the end of her second term she was drawing on many different sources of knowledge and spelling strategies.

Learning styles

Young children approach the spelling system in different ways. Some children, like Samantha in the example above, tend to represent what they can remember visually of a word rather than what they can hear – for example, she uses the 'oa' in 'doat' (boat) or the 'pp' in 'hoppg'. These letters cannot be heard, only remembered visually.

Other children prefer a phonetic route into spelling. The following piece from Robert, a year 1 child observed recently, shows the use of high frequency words spelt in standard form together with plausible phonetic spellings.

I went to Eejipt.

It was very hot and sandy.

Then I met a fero. He was rich and he had a goldin crawn it was no ordery crawn it went dowen intil it reechd on to the top ov his bac.

Just then, a shado cam oet ov the distnts. Fero sed to me that shado is the blac primid. Then fero said theat eevl fero the eevl fero. I hid in the sand and lisind. Then I herd fero say. Cum cum cum drc fero cum drc fero. Then my hiding plas clapst. I had to dig a hol fast. Then the hed on tbe primid wen up. Then the feros strtid to fit. Robert, year 1, term 1

I went to Egypt. It was very hot and sandy.

Then I met a pharaoh. He was rich and he had a golden crown. it was no ordinary crown it went down until it reached on to the top of his back.

Just then, a shadow came out of the distance. Pharaoh said to me that shadow is the black pyramid. Then pharaoh said that evil pharoah the evil pharaoh. I hid in the sand and listened.

Then I heard pharaoh say. Come come come dark pharaoh come dark pharaoh. Then my hiding place collapsed. I had to dig a hole fast. Then the head on the pyramid went up. Then the pharaohs started to fight.

FIGURE 11.2 Robert's holiday in Egypt

The two children have distinct preferences about the way they tackle spelling. What is important though in terms of future progress is that Robert, who spells words in terms of what he can hear, gradually needs to focus more consciously on the visual aspects of the spelling system, namely that all is not as it sounds. Samantha, who writes what she remembers visually, needs to do so in the context of developing a better understanding of sound/symbol relationships in English spelling. For children who do not make these connections, problems may occur, to a greater or lesser degree.

Children as writers and readers

It is also important to recognise the broader factors which underpin the achievements of competently developing spellers such as Samantha and Robert:

- They are encouraged by their teachers to write interesting texts – their engagement in writing is apparent.
- They feel confident to write, to tackle new texts and new words – this also has its roots in the classroom environment.
- They are all rapidly developing competence as readers.

Our research found that the teacher's role in establishing this kind of classroom ethos could not be underestimated.

All the very competent spellers in our study were fluent readers. For many children, learning to read marked a real leap forward in their spelling competence. The following two extracts from narratives written by Alfie in year 2, observed recently, are separated by only six months. The first piece contains many phonetic attempts at words; the second, an extract from a five chapter story, is spelt almost entirely in standard form. What happened in between the two pieces is that his reading really took off.

the submarine dove depar wene they sore a opaninG that began to lite up. turn the lits on professor said Biff. I wich this submarine was thiner said wilf. You sore a witch said profesor tanGol. then the profesor point a buton and a smal box choc up then the profeser opend the Box puld uote a tyoos pluGd it in and the lits turnd on LukoLee thay just mist the rocks. (Alfie, year 2, October, term 1)

The submarine dove deeper when they saw a opening that began to light up. Turn the lights on professor said Biff. I wish this submarine was thinner said wilf. You saw a witch said Professor Tangol, then the professor point a button and a small box shook up then the professor opened the box pulled out a tyoos? plugged it in and the lights turned on Luckily they just missed the rocks.

Chapter one

In a land far far away a dragon lived. in the middle of a forst (forest) lay a small cottage. In the court yard was tons and tones (tons) of gold. On the gold were two dragons. a red welsh dragon and a green saxon dragon.

All the other thousand dragons had gone to the evil spirit nogard except the red welsh dragon and the green saxon dragon.

The master nogard was a bionicle and hard to defeat. (Alfie, year 2, March, term 2)

On the other hand, some children who became fairly fluent readers did not 'pick up' spelling from their reading and did not develop a similar competence as spellers. These children did not attend to the patterning of the spelling system, and did not make links between words.

Jonathan was a competent reader who had some difficulties with spelling:

Henry VIII had blue eyes. He was fat because he ate to (too) mutc (much). He wears a cloack (cloak), tunic, tite (tights), a hat, rope belt and Julry (jewellery). He was boold (bald) so his hat could fit him. He had these weard (weird) shoes like duck bekes (beaks). He had lots and lots of patons (patterns) on his cloth's (clothes) as he got older he got very ugly. He was very rich and his faverout (favourite) ship was the marry rose. He had six wives. Henry VIII was a stubben (stubborn) man he liked plays and pageants. He was a nasty man and he killed two of his wives. He broke his religen (religion) by getting divorced. (Jonathan, year 4)

Although he writes with confidence, Jonathan has difficulties in choosing the 'right' pattern for words – in fact he usually tends to choose the phonetic option, as in 'tites' for 'tights'. He also has difficulties with words like 'julry' (jewellery). He does not make the connection with the root word, 'jewel'. Word endings such as 'ite' as in 'favourite', and 'ion' as in 'religion' also prove troublesome. All of these aspects can form the focus for teaching.

Key areas of spelling knowledge

Phonological awareness and analogy-making

Our research demonstrated that the main aspects of phonological awareness which have been identified in studies of children reading – syllabification, onset and rime and phonemic awareness – were relevant to children's development as spellers.

Many very young children initially adopt a phonemic approach to their early spelling. Shakira, in reception, wrote:

I pd w mi s sk (*I played with my street shark*)

Shakira is at the beginning of learning how to encode spellings. Her developing phonemic awareness in spelling will help her to formulate her understanding not only of how the spelling system works but also help her to begin to analyse words in reading.

Research into phonological awareness shows that children use onsets (or word beginnings, for example, 'b' in 'bat' or 'str' in 'string') and rimes (or word endings, for example, 'at' in 'bat' and 'ing' in 'string') to make analogies in order help them read unfamiliar words. For example – if a child can read 'c-at' he or she can, by making analogies, read 's-at', 'b-at', 'r-at', and so on (Goswami and Bryant 1990; Goswami 1995; Goswami 1999).

Analogy-making strategies were used spontaneously by children who were successful spellers in our project, in that they used their knowledge of one word to attempt the spelling of unfamiliar words. While the most competent spellers made links between words, children who were less successful as spellers tended to see each word as a separate, unrelated challenge.

Vowels in English are particularly tricky because vowels on their own do not consistently represent the same sounds. For example, the letter 'a' makes a different sound in 'cat', 'call', 'car', 'cake'. However, when the vowel is attached to a group of consonants (as in 'c-all', 'b-all', 'f-all', and so on, vowel consistency increases considerably (Treiman 1994). Children who are encouraged to hear and see the similarities between words with similar rimes are therefore learning an important strategy for spelling as well as for reading.

Onset and rime activities are important for older children who are experiencing severe spelling problems, who are usually experiencing difficulties in reading as well. Dean in year 5, despite support, experienced severe problems.

On the way to kfc I cun nley tat the
cein as it malt in my mafa I wooc
troow the door I shie swcolnon matin
in the batar I get my food and I get
a set and I get a pees of
cicin out of the bacit and
I am leecin my leepss

On the way to KFC I can nearly taste the
Chicken as it melts in my mouth I walk
Through the door I see sweetcorn melting
In the butter I get my food and I get
A seat and I get a piece of
Chicken out of the bucket and
I am licking my lips.

An initial strategy used to support Daniel in year 5 was the collection of words with similar patterns based on words arising from his writing, such as 'can', 'lips', 'get', 'my', At this point in his development, he had no clear sense of straightforward spelling patterns. He improved considerably as a speller as his reading developed in fluency, by the beginning of year 6, and was beginning to make analogies spontaneously.

Word structures and meanings

Many aspects of the spelling system are concerned with within-word units, or morphemes, which denote particular functions or meanings. For example, 'ed' at the end of the 'walked', 'wanted' and 'rained' is pronounced differently each time although it attaches the same meaning to the word. Children interpret this in many ways through their independent spelling: Robert writes 'lisind' (listened), 'clpst' (collapsed) and 'strtid' (started). Children may use all of these forms, and others, before settling on the final form of 'ed'. Such developments in their spelling represent experience of written language, teaching, and a movement away from what they can hear towards what they are beginning to know about the visual patterning of words and their structural aspects.

To summarise, children learning to spell draw on a wide range of influences and sources of knowledge:

- Extensive experience of written language as readers and writers
- Phonological awareness
- Knowledge of letter names
- Known words
- Visual awareness
- Awareness of common letter strings and word patterns
- Knowledge of word structures and meanings
- Growing independence – knowing how and where to get help, how to proofread and check their writing
- Making analogies and deducing rules

Teaching spelling

The broad range of competences that children need to acquire as spellers means that teaching spelling involves much more than handing out word lists and intervening in children's writing.

Teachers who teach spelling effectively pay attention to:

- The classroom climate or ethos with regard to spelling. Children are encouraged to try out spellings and are actively involved in their own learning.
- Classroom resources, provision and the literacy environment – and how children are encouraged to use these.
- The inclusion of spelling in the broad routines of literacy teaching – in shared reading and writing, in writing workshops, in geography or history lessons.
- Promoting involvement and interest in words through *active, oral* and *investigative* approaches to spelling and word study – routines and activities which support particular areas of spelling knowledge.
- The provision of regular opportunities to discuss spelling.
- Setting up spelling and writing partnerships in the classroom.
- How intervention can positively support individual children's spelling progress.
- Ways children can be involved in monitoring their own progress.

These points should form the basis of a whole class, and preferably a whole school, approach, which is also shared with families.

It is beyond the scope of this chapter to discuss all the successful teaching approaches identified in our research, but the principal areas will be highlighted.

Classroom resources and environment

A wide range of resources for spelling is a basic means of promoting spelling development. These resources should be situated in the context of a classroom which promotes reading, writing and talk in a range of formal and informal contexts: provision of a range of books, book and writing areas, displays of children's writing, labelling in English and community languages.

TABLE 11.2 Spelling resources

Spelling resources for reception and key stage 1	Spelling resources for key stage 2
Resources to support early spelling Alphabet cards and strips to support writing Range of alphabet books and early dictionaries Name cards showing names in upper and lower case Days of the week/month charts Word banks Small desktop word banks of other common words Word banks from core books and class topics on display Collections of words with common initial letters, rhymes, letter patterns Computer software which promotes attention to letters and words	*Word banks created as a result classroom investigations* Common words, topic words Words using the same letter string, eg words using 'ough' Words with common prefixes and suffixes (and their meanings) A range of dictionaries and thesauruses *A range of handwriting resources including:* Examples of handwriting style, showing letter joins Guide rules Handwriting and calligraphy pens
Handwriting resources Charts with examples of handwriting style showing letter formation with 'exit' stroke guide rules *Computer and spelling software, online access*	*Computer and spelling software, online access*

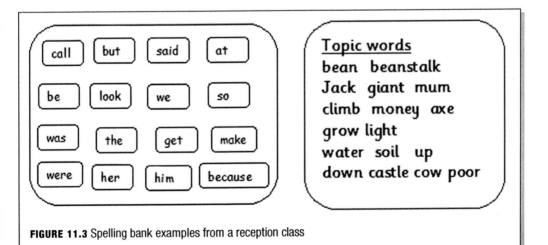

Topic words
bean beanstalk
Jack giant mum
climb money axe
grow light
water soil up
down castle cow poor

call but said at
be look we so
was the get make
were her him because

FIGURE 11.3 Spelling bank examples from a reception class

Including spelling in literacy routines

The major classroom literacy teaching routines – shared writing, reading, group reading and collaborative writing contexts – provide key opportunities for promoting an interest in words, their uses, meanings, spellings and structures from reception to key stage 2.

Regular word study sessions in whole class or group contexts become more central to the teaching of spelling at key stage 2.

Spelling journals and logs

Increasingly (certainly from year 3 onwards) spelling journals can be used for word and language study – to work on words with similar spelling patterns, to work out rules and generalisations, to define word meanings or record word webs. Journals can play an important role in promoting interest in spelling.

As children get older, they can be encouraged to use their spelling journals or logs to practise particular words using Look-Say-Cover-Write-Check. Spelling journal sessions can form a regular part of literacy hour routines and help to:

- Make links between issues arising in individual children's writing and whole class focuses

- Reduce the use of work sheets

- Provide an effective record for teacher and child of spelling development

FIGURE 11.4 A spelling journal

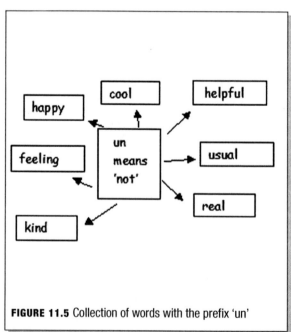

FIGURE 11.5 Collection of words with the prefix 'un'

Handwriting teaching

Handwriting teaching in the early stages, particularly working in groups, helps children to establish the correct shape and formation of letters and to meet common letter patterns. Spelling is helped by seeing the connections between groups of letters (Cripps 1990).

- Short frequent teaching and practice sessions are most effective.
- Each letter should be carefully introduced, with demonstrations of how it is formed (the teacher needs to demonstrate with her back to the children). Children can trace the letter in the air before practising it on paper.
- Letters can be taught in groups according to their formation, for example, i l t u y/r n m h b p k/c a d g q o e/s f/v w x z j, or according to frequency of use, for example, by teaching common letters, such as i, t, p, n, s, first.
- Always teach letters using the exit stroke – to allow for ease of joining (Sassoon 1990; Jarman 1990).
- Later on use letter strings and patterns which link to a weekly focus in handwriting practice sessions.
- alphabet strips (lower and upper case) using correct letter formation should be on children's tables during writing.
- later, well known songs, rhymes, poems and proverbs can be used for practice.

By the beginning of key stage 2 cursive handwriting should be introduced if it has not happened earlier. This will necessitate regular handwriting practice sessions and practice can be linked to particular spelling patterns and word structures (Cripps 1990). Handwriting should also be linked to issues of presentation: final drafts of some pieces of work can be used for handwriting practice, as can the copying out of favourite poems, songs or proverbs for class anthologies.

Computers

Computers can be used in a variety of ways to support the teaching of spelling. All aspects of writing, spelling and editing can be demonstrated by the teacher on a large screen or whiteboard. However, children should also have the opportunity to work in pairs or individually. Children can also use computers to create word banks, posters and lists of words with similar patterns, meanings and structures. The use of computers encourages reluctant writers through increasing the amount of writing they do (Safford, O'Sullivan, Barrs 2004). Children who are less successful spellers also find it easier to detect misspellings on screen than in their handwritten texts, and find use of the keyboard easier than handwriting. With older children, the use of the spellchecker can be introduced.

Computer programs directed to teaching the alphabet or a range of spelling competences can be helpful for a wide range of children, particularly if supported by a teaching assistant. Practice of this kind is often more helpful when carried out in a pair or small group, where discussion of word features can take place. *ABC Talking Animated Alphabet*, *Starspell* and *Word Shark* (for older children) are commonly used programs.

An increasing number of websites provide resources and activities online:

- A range of downloadable games to print off, such as 'double letter bingo', mainly suitable for upper key stage 2 can be found at
  http://www.collaborativelearning.org/literacyonline.html

- The Ambleside school website has an astounding array of literacy activities including an online 'Look Cover Write Check' game
  http://www.amblesideprimary.com/ambleweb/literacy.htm

- Two BBC websites could be used as group and whole class activities – if your classroom is online

  - The Spellits
    http://www.bbc.co.uk/schools/spellits/

  - *Revisewise* has both spelling and grammar activities (key stage 2)
    http://www.bbc.co.uk/schools/revisewise/english/spelling/

Routines to establish independence in spelling

A range of spelling strategies

Encourage children to develop a wide range of spelling strategies:

- To write down what they can of unknown words using a mixture of what they can hear, their knowledge of probable letter patterns, and word meanings

- To list the ways in which a word might be spelt, using what they know, and then to make decisions about which version is correct, using the look of the word

- To syllabify longer words

- To make analogies with known words

- To draw on rules or generalisations where they are helpful, for example, consonant doubling

- To focus on word roots, families or meanings, for example, 'medic-ine' and 'medic-al'

Proofreading routines

Teachers can establish regular routines for proofreading in the classroom by encouraging self-checking for meaning, accuracy of spelling and punctuation, involving regular spelling partners and setting up an editing table in the classroom

TABLE 11.3 Activities to develop spelling knowledge

Class and group activities which develop spelling knowledge in reception and key stage 1	Class and group activities which develop spelling knowledge in key stage 2
The following skills are important for both spelling and reading. Activities can be planned for the whole class or groups *Syllabification*, eg clap out names, favourite foods *Awareness of rhyme* Sing songs and rhymes, use wordplay, rhyming texts, talk about rhymes, make collections of rhyming words, shared writing. *Onsets and rimes* Make collections of words with the same onsets or rimes. Use magnetic letters to build words Create 'snap' and 'pairs' card games from words with the same onsets and rimes. *Alphabets* Make a classroom alphabet book or frieze based on children's own names or a theme. Make cards with class names for games and activities. Sing alphabet songs and rhymes. Play alphabet games, eg I went shopping and I bought an apple, a ball, etc. *Whole words* Read and re-read a core of familiar books – make collections of words from these texts. Book-based games, made from a familiar book, provide opportunities for children to meet and observe familiar words in context (Bromley 2000). Create a big class dictionary/word bank of known words which can be added to week by week and be used as a class resource. *Visual patterns and word structures* Make collections of spellings that do not follow 'straightforward' phonic patterns, eg 'ight' Make 'snap' and 'pairs' games with words using visual patterns, eg 'ight' and 'ite' words, 'eet' and 'eat' words. Note that some groups of bilingual children whose first languages are written in phonically regular ways may need help with the visual nature of the English spelling system. Make collections and games based on compound words – words made up of words, eg *break-fast*.	*Letter strings and patterns* Involve children in making word collections, and in highlighting words with similar patterns and letter strings in text extracts, poems, newspaper articles. Bilingual children will benefit from working collaboratively with monolingual English speakers on these issues so that meanings and derivations can be discussed. It is important to include letter strings and patterns in words which look and sound alike, eg: *-ack* as in *sack, black, attack* *-igh* as *sigh, might, frighten, delightful* and in words which look alike and may sound different, eg: *-ood* as in *good, food, wood* *-ear* as in *tear, near, bear, clear, learn* *Word structures and meanings* Analysing a word like *un/help/ful/ness* draws attention to the role of prefixes and suffixes. Encourage children to make collections of words beginning with similar prefixes or ending with the same suffix. *Word and spelling study* At key stage 2 a collection of dictionaries, including etymological dictionaries (giving word origins), rhyming dictionaries, name and placename dictionaries, thesauruses, and dictionaries of phrases, proverbs and sayings, provides an invaluable resource for word and spelling study. These investigations can be carried out individually, in pairs and small groups and can be recorded in spelling logs or journals.

where resources for checking spelling are kept, and where children can check their spellings alone and with others.

Establish a look-say-cover-write-check system

Teachers can develop a whole class approach to the use of look-say-cover-write-check system:

Look	at the word carefully and mark any parts which are causing problems.
Say	the word to yourself.
Cover	the word and close your eyes. Remember the word by trying to see it in your head. Say it slowly in a way that helps you remember it.
Write	the word down.
Check	the spelling to see if you have got it right.

Children and teachers can identify together words to be worked on, such as topic words, frequently misspelt words or words with a particular pattern. Children should then practise the words during the week in their spelling log using look-say-cover-write-check, and check their spellings regularly with a spelling partner. The teacher monitors progress regularly.

Conclusion

In summary, our research pointed to a number of significant factors in children's spelling development. Children did not necessarily follow a linear model of development, and took different routes into spelling. Learning to spell is not just a rote learning exercise: children need to take risks and make errors as they progress towards standard spelling. They also need to broaden their range of strategies, and to make analogies in spelling unfamiliar words – not only sound–letter relationships, but in relation to grammatical and linguistic features. Some children who were fluent readers did not develop effective spelling strategies; children who were at the early stages of reading found it difficult to make progress as spellers. Both of these groups of children need particular support and teaching.

Our research found that the role of the teacher is critical in promoting children's progress as spellers. The teacher determines the range and variety of writing and reading that children do, and can promote an interest and involvement in words and their spellings. Teacher demonstrations in shared writing provide a key context for discussing all aspects of spelling. Teachers help children by encouraging them to take an active role in their own development through discussion, editing, self-correction, and working with a partner.

Acknowledgements

I would like to express my complete indebtedness to my co-researcher in the project and co-author of *Understanding Spelling*, Anne Thomas, formerly of the Centre for

Literacy in Primary Education, and to the staff of CLPE who are my learning community.

My continuing gratitude goes to the children and staff of the three project schools, Berger Primary School (Hackney), Gallions Mount Primary School (Greenwich), St Luke's CE Primary School (Lambeth).

I would like to thank Alfie Manser (Edmund Waller School, London) and Robert Adamczyk-Hedley (Cragside Primary School, Newcastle) for permission to use extracts from their writing.

References

Bromley, H. (2000) *Book-based Reading Games*. London: CLPE

Cripps, C. (1990) *Joining the ABC: How and Why Handwriting and Spelling Should be Taught Together*. Wisbech: LDA.

Peters, M. (1985) *Spelling Caught or Taught?* London: Routledge.

Gentry, J. R. (1991) *SPEL... is a Four Letter Word*. Leamington Spa: Scholastic.

Goswami, U. (1995) 'Phonological development and reading by analogy: what is analogy and what is not?' *Journal of Research in Reading*, 18, 2.

Goswami, U. (1999) 'Causal connections in beginning reading: the importance of rhyme,' *Journal of Research in Reading*, 22, 3.

Goswami, U. and Bryant, P. (1990) *Phonological Skills and Learning to Read*. New Jersey, USA: Lawrence and Erlbaum.

Jarman, C. (1990) *The Development of Handwriting Skills*. London: Simon and Schuster.

O'Sullivan, O. and Thomas, A. (2000) *Understanding Spelling*, London: CLPE.

Read, C. (1986) *Children's Creative Spelling*. London: Routledge and Kegan Paul.

Redfern, A. (1993) *Practical Ways to Teach Spelling*. Reading: Reading and Language Information Centre.

Safford, K., O'Sullivan. O. and Barrs, M. (2004) *Boys on the Margin*, London: CLPE.

Sassoon, R (1990) *Handwriting: The Way to Teach It*. Cheltenham: Stanley Thornes Ltd.

Temple, C.A., Nathan R.G. and Burris, N.A. (1988) *The Beginnings of Writing*, 2nd edn. Boston, MA: Allyn and Bacon.

Treiman, R. (1994) 'Sources of information used by beginning spellers' in *Handbook of Spelling Theory: Process and Intervention*, D. Gordon, A. Brown, and N. C. Ellis, (eds), Chichester: John Wiley and Sons.

Computer software

ABC Talking Animated Alphabet, available from www.rm.com/Primary/Products/ (accessed January 2005).

Starspell, available from www.fishermarriott.com/starspel.htm (accessed January 2005).

WordShark, available from www.wordshark.co.uk/ (accessed January 2005).

The struggle to punctuate: a brief case study of two children learning

Nigel Hall

Introduction

In this chapter, I want to explore the experience of two children as they learnt to punctuate during year 1 and year 2. The children responded in very different ways to the challenge and reached quite different points in their development. Part of the function of this chapter is to describe their pathways and to explore the factors that might account for the differences. The study from which the material is drawn was completed before the inception of the National Literacy Strategy and, at the end of this chapter, I will be considering the extent to which the methodology and content of the *National Literacy Strategy's Framework for Teaching* might or might not make a difference to the progress of such children in the future.

In key stage 1 punctuation is, on the whole, a late arrival in literacy education. For most of this century, and particularly in the second half, teachers of the youngest children concentrated on encouraging children to write meaningfully rather than to worry too much about punctuation. It was usually junior school teachers who were faced with introducing children to the nature and function of punctuation. The catalyst for change was a series of reports from various government agencies, starting with *Language Matters* (Department of Education and Science 1984). For the first time in almost a hundred years a proposal was made about expectations for achievement of all children in English. History does not yet record how these decisions were made, but amongst them was the claim that by the age of seven years children should be able to 'use full stops and capital letters appropriately' (Department of Education and Science 1984: 6).

What is certain is that there did not exist any research evidence for the appropriateness of this claim. Indeed, retrospectively, one of the most remarkable things about learning to punctuate was its invisibility in the research literature. So where did these expectations come from? It is my guess that it happened by default. The conventional age at which children moved from infant to junior education was seven; full stops are pretty basic and probably seemed to be the first things that should be learnt about punctuation. Whatever the reason, the decision, once made, stuck.

The Kingman Report (Department of Education and Science 1988) appeared to mellow in its requirements. On page 34 of that report, alongside an example of writing from a seven-year-old, is the comment: 'Her spelling errors show that she has begun to comprehend the patterns of English spelling. But this is the work of a seven-year old. As Anne progresses she will learn about the placing of full stops.' Nevertheless, comes on page 55, the demand that, by the age of seven, children should be able to achieve the following: 'Use simple sentences, using full stops, capital letters and commas, word spacing and appropriate word forms. Understand sentence boundaries, namely what a full stop and a capital letter are for.' A year later, the Cox committee suggested (Department of Education and Science 1989) that, by the age of seven, children should be able to 'produce, independently, pieces of writing using complete sentences, some of them demarcated with capital letters and full stops or question marks' – a prescription which became a quasilegal requirement when it was enshrined in the first version of the National Curriculum English document (Department of Education and Science 1989).

This stipulation was uncomfortable for many teachers of young children. When Robinson (1996) interviewed a range of teachers, she found some common concerns:

- 'I don't think that they actually have a lot of experience of reading and writing actually to see the point to punctuation.'
- 'They are just on the edge of development in their writing and to teach them punctuation would stop that for some children . . . put them off, you know. I think they expect too much.'
- 'I think that they are having to learn it before they are ready to understand it.'

While criticising the national curriculum expectations, the teachers were not dismissing punctuation as unimportant, in either the long term or the short term, but their concern was for a possible contradiction between encouraging children to write with fluency and comfort, and the demand for accurate punctuation. Allied to this was the problem experienced by all the teachers that at no time in their pre-service or in-service education had they ever been shown how to teach punctuation. To make matters even worse, as has already been stated, there was nowhere for them to turn for guidance. The evidence which would even begin to answer their questions did not exist (Hall 1996).

The study to be partly described below predated the National Literacy Strategy, so for the moment this will be ignored. However, in the final section of this chapter it will be considered in relation to the possible later development of the children's understanding of punctuation.

The study

It was in relation to the uncertainties outlined above that a research project was set up to examine how children came to make sense of punctuation. The study was designed to take a very intensive look at how children learnt within the classroom setting. As a consequence it focused upon a relatively small number of children, but followed their experiences in great detail. The aim was not to reach firm conclusions about how to teach punctuation but to identify a range of issues that might help set future research agendas. In other words, the study was designed to provoke thinking and to open up an area for discussion, and not to provide quick and easy answers.

The school in which the study took place was situated in an urban area of northwest England and had achieved national recognition for its work on parental and community relationships. It served a multicultural and socially diverse population and was staffed mostly by young but experienced teachers. There was a large range of social problems experienced by the children and every year, as a result of government housing regulations, a large number of children moved into or on from the school. Thus a major concern was with providing a stable and warm environment in which children worked at an appropriate pace.

At the time that the study was carried out the national curriculum was in progress, but at that time government ministers had repeatedly claimed that they were setting targets and not making stipulations about the methodologies to be used by teachers. Thus schools still made their own choices about how to develop literacy knowledge and skills. The dominant choice in this school was common at the time and was essentially child centred. The teacher operated the classroom in a way which Bernstein (1997) termed a 'competence model'. In this model there are relatively few defined pedagogic spaces; the emphasis is on the learner's product and their intellectual construction of it. Criteria are more implicit and diffuse. Learners have a relatively high degree of autonomy, and explicit formal instruction is less common. This did not mean that things to be learnt were not featured significantly in the classroom. For instance, during the first term in year 1 the children were introduced to punctuation in many different ways. It was talked about. It featured on the concept keyboard and in *Breakthrough to Literacy* folders. It was displayed in many kinds of ways and the children were encouraged to look for it in the world of print around them in the classroom.

Punctuation was a presence in this room. The children saw it as something curious, interesting and an object to be explored. The approach of both the year 1 and the year 2 teachers was to provide opportunities, experience, evidence and feedback rather than formal direct instruction. The consequence was that, although children's interest in and exploration of punctuation was actively encouraged, the teaching and learning of punctuation were not formally defined pedagogic activities as they are now in the *Framework for Teaching* structure.

The two children

The two girls examined in this case study had both been in the school since the beginning of reception class. Both were quiet children and enjoyed writing. Fhamida was aged 5.1 years at the start of the study. She was from a Bangladeshi background and had a number of elder brothers and sisters; although her parents spoke only limited English, her father insisted that at home the children spoke as much English as possible. She was effectively bilingual and even at the age of six, had sometimes been used as a translator by her parents. Lian was 5.7 years at the start of the study, was the eldest child in the family and had two younger sisters, one of whom was a new baby.

In this relatively short chapter it is possible to illustrate only a few aspects of the development of the children. However, these are drawn from a continuously gathered collection of written work, observations and discussions. The first piece of independent writing that we have for either child was a short piece written on 7 October 1994. Figure 12.1 shows what Lian wrote. She reported that it said, 'I was a potato in our harvest' (festival). The word 'harvest' was copied. Lian was extremely anxious about writing independently, and hence the reversion to copying for the final word. Figure 12.2 shows what Fhamida wrote. At first she read this as 'I O T L O T...l' using the letter names, and it was only after hearing other children read their pieces as meaningful texts that she claimed it said, 'I was an old lady in our harvest.'

FIGURE 12.1 Lian's first piece of independent writing

FIGURE 12.2 Fhamida's first piece of independent writing

At this point both children seem confused and uncertain about the act of writing. It did not seem to make much sense to either of them and was seen as an activity that involved putting letters down in any order, and then making a claim that they said something. To all intents and purposes the children appeared to be level at this point. However, this similarity did not last very long.

Fhamida

While the general classroom experiences of the children were very similar, Fhamida soon began to reveal a much greater awareness of punctuation. In January of year 1, in the guise of a handwriting task, all the children in the class were asked to copy a piece of text. "Hello!" said the old man. "Where are you going?" The boy just looked at him. "I don't know." The boy was lost. He didn't know where to go.' If capital letters are included, then there are 21 independent punctuation marks. In her copy, Lian included nine, six of which were capital letters, two were exclamation marks and one was the terminal full stop. Fhamida successfully copied all 21 and was able to discuss what they were. She was, however, unclear about their functions.

Teacher: What are full stops for?
Fhamida: To make a space.
Teacher: When do you use them?
Fhamida: At the end of words.

This copying exercise proved to be quite a subtle way of revealing differences in awareness of punctuation (and in an earlier version Fhamida had managed to omit all the full stops). That the influence of attention to punctuation was having an effect in this classroom is revealed by a comparison with a class, a year older, who took the test at the same time. The younger class significantly outscored the older class.

A few days later Fhamida was independently writing a letter to the character 'Martin' in the book *Dear Martin*. Figure 12.3 shows what she wrote. A 'translation' of this follows.

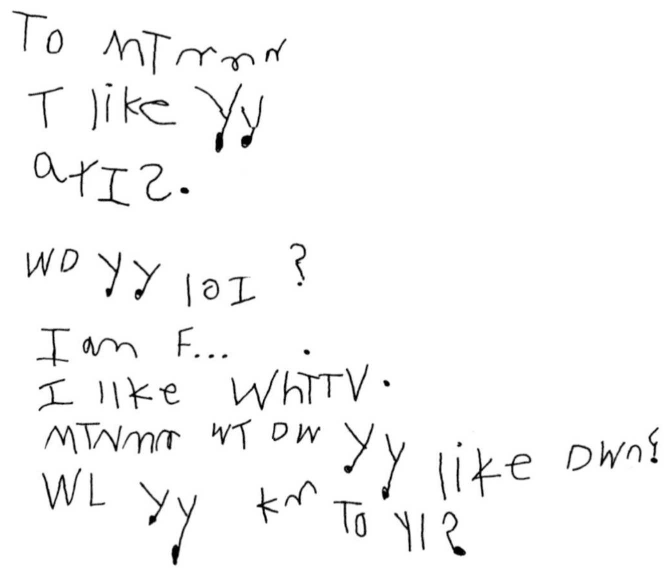

FIGURE 12.3 Fhamida's letter to Martin

To Martin

I like you
(indecipherable).
Would you (??)?
I am Fhamida.
I like watching TV.
Martin what do you like doing?
Will you come to Year 1?

Fhamida had become curious about punctuation, was noticing it in her reading, contributing to class discussions about it and talking about it to other children. Her movement towards conventional spelling was enabling her to write more frequently, for a wider range of purposes, and at greater length. An example of this enthusiasm for punctuation occurred when the class had been reading a poem laid out graphically without commas:

Miss Mary Mack
        Mack
        Mack
Dressed in black
     black
     black

Another teacher bought in a copy laid out using commas:

Miss Mary Mack, Mack, Mack,
Dressed in black, black, black.

The whole class became fascinated by these differences. Within a few days Fhamida had produced a six-page poem based upon *Red Riding Hood* but using the structure of 'Miss Mary Mack' (Figure 12.4). The 'translation' is *Red Riding Hood, Hood, Hood,*

FIGURE 12.4 Fhamida's poem based upon *Red Riding Hood*

Perhaps the most significant evidence of a conceptual move forward came in April that year. She was with two other children who dictated a description to a researcher who scribed it on a large sheet of paper. During a discussion afterwards there was a heated debate about the position of a full stop (for a full discussion of this see Hall and Holden-Sim (1996)). Part of the text was as follows:

and she shouts a lot and
she tells us to do our work

One child wanted to put a full stop after 'lot' because full stops 'could go in the middle', while another instantly said that they had to go at the end of lines. Neither child was using a linguistic principle for their choice; middle and end of line are graphic principles. It was Fhamida who said the full stop could go after 'lot' as the 'and' belonged to 'she tells us'. The significance of this is that, for the first time in the classroom, a child was explaining the use of a full stop using a linguistic principle.

One month later Fhamida used mid-line full stops in her independent writing as shown in Figure 12.5, the 'translation' of which follows.

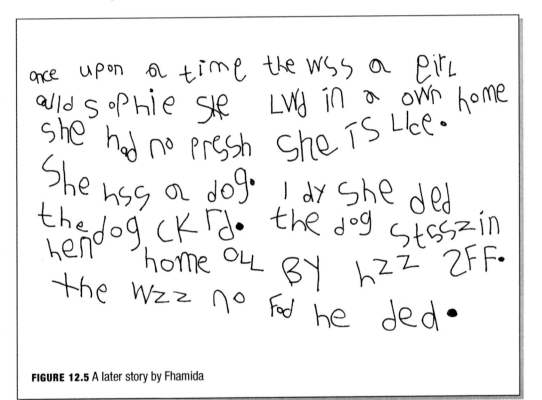

FIGURE 12.5 A later story by Fhamida

Once upon a time there was a girl
called Sophie she lived in her own home
She had no friends she is lonely.
She has a dog. One day she died
the dog cried. The dog stayed in
the hen's house all by itself.
There was no food and he died.

Thus, towards the end of year 1, Fhamida was satisfying the general criteria of the English national curriculum document and demarcating some of her sentences using full stops, although frequently without using capital letters. In year 2 this move towards linguistic punctuation continued. In a very long story written in February 1996 she at first put in only two full stops. When asked if there was anything she wanted to add, she put in several more full stops. While each one correctly marked the end of a linguistic unit (always the end of a sentence), some of these units included more than one conventional sentence. According to Kress (1982), this was a typical move towards conventional linguistic punctuation. She was grouping by topic (rather than by sentence), although in many cases these units were conventional sentences (for an illustration of this see Hall (1998a)). On 9 July of year 2 she was writing

> I like you very very very much! You
> are very kind. You hardly shout.
> Do you remember the eid party
> and we played and ate lots of
> food and remember the Christmas party
> and I got a pencil case.
> Remember when we first came
> in Year 2 i was so scared and
> when you read a story i
> wasn't scared then. You
> shouted because some of us didnt
> colour neatly. You shouted at
> some of us because we did'nt
> write neatly.

It is clear that Fhamida had succeeded in meeting the criteria without losing interest in writing. She would be able to move on to key stage 2 with a fairly good notion of how to punctuate a text simply but conventionally.

Lian

Lian, while appearing to start at the same point as Fhamida, never did solve the problem of punctuation. She remained dominated, even at the end of year 2, by non-linguistic beliefs about punctuation.

On the same day that Fhamida was writing to Martin (Figure 12.3) Lian was writing the words shown in Figure 12.6, the 'translation' of which follows.

FIGURE 12.6 Lian's early attempt at writing

To Mrs S
Can we have a fair.

In the three intervening months, Lian, despite following an additional special programme which provided specialist teaching with phonics and reading, was able to convey meaning in writing only through the initial letter sounds of words. Despite what seemed a difficulty, Lian enjoyed writing and was proud of what she achieved. Four months later she was writing at greater length but almost always failing to put in any punctuation. Occasionally, after a reminder from the teacher, a full stop might be added right at the end. The failure to use punctuation was not because Lian was unaware of it. If asked, she could name several marks and draw them and even repeat formulae about 'rests'.

In June of year 1 Lian wrote an extended piece which appeared to use punctuation in an interesting way (Figure 12.7). Its 'corrected translation' is as follows:

Mum was making cooking. Dad said, 'Is it ready?' and Mum said, 'No, it is not.' So (he) went out in the garden.

However, it is likely that, if it had not been for an accident, the punctuation would have been missing. As she was sitting down to write, another child sat down, picked up his pencil and said, 'I'm going to do a full stop.' He then simply put a full stop on his blank piece of paper. Lian, having written 'Mum', watched him do this and promptly put a full stop after 'Mum'. As she wrote her piece, she then added more full stops. At the end, thinking that she had finished, the researcher looked away. As he did so, Lian got her pencils and sprinkled some more full stops through the piece. Lian was unable to offer any explanation for her use of full stops; they appeared randomly distributed.

Lian continued into year 2, becoming more confident in her ability to write meaningfully, to spell conventionally and to write at greater length. However,

FIGURE 12.7 Another piece by Lian

punctuation was largely ignored except when working with the teacher and receiving constant reminders. On 9 July (the same date as Fhamida's last piece) Lian wrote an interesting text with only one full stop. She was asked if there was anything she wanted to add; she thought and said, 'Those rest things'. She then added some full stops to the piece (Figure 12.8), the 'corrected translation' of which is as follows:

> I like you. You have nice shoes. I really like Ginn maths. I wish I could do some every day because it is good. It is my favourite. I like playing. I (??) think I am good at them. Do you like the trip the best? It was the best. I kept on going on the slide and I never got off it because it's good. I call it a twirly whirly because it looks like a twirly. Does it to you? It does to me. you have nice clothes. I like the trips what you take us on. I like the name what you have got.

This time, perhaps more confident, Lian was able to offer explanations for the placement of the full stops as follows:

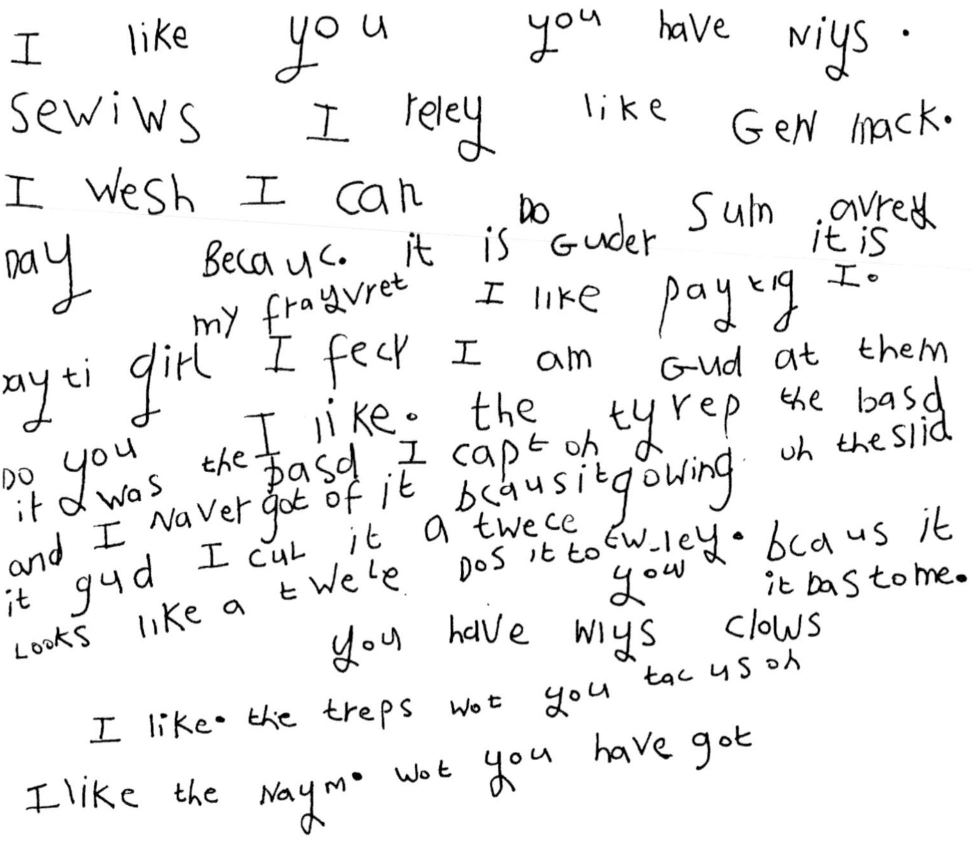

I like you you have niys .

Sewiws I reley like Gen mack.

I wesh I can do Suln avreu
day Becauc. it is Guder it is
my fraqvret I like payorig I.
ayti qirl I fecl I am Gud at them
Do you I like. the tyrep the basd
it was the basd I capt oh uh theslid
and I Naver got of it bcausitgowing
it gud I cul it a twece Dos it to Ew-ley. bcaus it
Looks like a twele you it bas tome.
you have wiys clows
I like. the treps wot you tac us oh
I like the Naym wot you have got

FIGURE 12.8 A later piece by Lian

- because it's a bit long;
- 'cos I didn't put one in that line, so I did it there;
- 'cos it's a bit long, from there, there's a lot of words to there;
- 'cos it's long as well.

The explanations have nothing to do with linguistic principles but invoke 'long', 'from there to there' and 'not putting one in the line above'. This is placement and explanation based upon graphic principles. The distribution is according to graphic balance; there needs to be so many; they must not be too close together nor must they be too far apart. Thus, at the end of key stage 1, Lian is using underlying principles to punctuate that have nothing to do with the linguistic structure of the texts but have everything to do with what a text looks like as a graphic object. Although this particular example is uncommon, this reasoning is shared by all those children (and for a while in their development this means almost everyone) who put full stops at the ends of lines, at ends of stories and at the end of pages regardless of whether they are sentences (Hall 1998a, 2001).

Comparisons

The first point that must be made is that while Lian and Fhamida appeared to start at the same point, it is probably an illusion generated by their previous school experience. If the children were not able, or had not been given the opportunity, to develop independent writing skills, then differences are likely to be obscured. Second, while it was not the function of this project to test the children psychologically, it was quickly clear that in general Fhamida was much more able than Lian. She progressed more quickly in all subjects, was always curious about the world and was a reflective child. There may also have been some less obvious advantages. Fhamida was clearly influenced by her elder brothers and sisters, and the appearance of ditto marks and apostrophes in her texts she explained in terms of having seen them in her sister's writing. Fhamida had asked her sister about them. It is also possible that her bilingualism made her more aware of the linguistic properties of text. A child who can switch between languages may well be more metalinguistically aware than one who cannot (Mohanty and Perregaux 1997).

To say that children have different abilities and therefore progress at different rates may seem to be obvious, and the different achievements of these two children may not be difficult to explain. However, the point of this small case study is to illustrate the qualitatively different ways in which these children understand the object of punctuation. For Fhamida it is becoming an intrinsic part of the meaning-making process. For Lian it is an object that is linked to writing solely by the teacher's demand for it to be included. It serves no function in her writing and shares no relationship with meaning making; it is an object which has separate roots from those of written language. Alongside the effort of getting readable words onto the page, the tiny marks of punctuation seem insignificant and irrelevant to the task of authorship.

The children's futures as users of punctuation

The most powerful stage in the government's control of the literacy curriculum came after this case study had been carried out, with the development of a National Literacy Strategy and the production of the document, *Framework for Teaching* (DfEE 1998). This highly prescriptive curriculum set out a relatively detailed set of expectations for children for each year of primary schooling. Punctuation (with the exception of the omissive apostrophe) was contained within the sentence level work (subtitled, 'Grammar and Punctuation'). By the end of year 2 children should be able to 'use commas in lists', 'write in clear sentences using capital letters and full stops accurately,' 'add question marks', 'read aloud with intonation and expression appropriate to grammar and punctuation', 'identify speech marks in reading, understand their purpose, use the terms correctly,' 'to recognise and take account of commas and exclamation marks in reading aloud,' and 'revise knowledge about other uses of capitalisation, for example, for names, headings, titles, emphasis, and begin to use in own writing.' In year 3, the new focus is primarily on the punctuation of speech, additional uses for capitalisation (although they seem pretty much the same as the year 2 expectations), and more understanding of comma usage. In year 4 children are expected to conquer the possessive apostrophe, understand the relationship between commas and clauses and identify semi-colons, colons, dashes and hyphens. Year 5 seems to be mostly consolidation, but includes understanding the use of commas to punctuate embedded clauses. The stipulations for year 6 are so slight that it seems children should know pretty much all there is to know about punctuation by the end of year 5 and mostly revise or consolidate this knowledge in year 6.

Alongside the shift in expectations about literacy knowledge came a move towards more explicit teaching. Would having been exposed to the teaching structures of the *Framework for Teaching* have made any difference to their level of knowledge at age seven? And, would following the *Framework for Teaching* during years 3–6 have taken both children to a confident knowledge of punctuation in its entirety? This can only be explored hypothetically as these children were not part of a later, larger research project that collected data from over 400 children and followed in detail 96 children, 24 for each of the years 3–6 (Hall, Sing and Wassouf 2001). It was clear that there were at the start of the project still many children like Lian who, on moving into year 3, had no grasp of what punctuation was for and had no understanding of its relationship to written language. It was also clear that there were many children in the year 6 classrooms whose knowledge of punctuation was very shaky, and who exhibited major confusions about it. At the same time there were many children like Fhamida who had worked out the basic relationship and who by the age of ten were punctuating relatively intrinsically, that is automatically punctuating their work as they write. For them punctuation was an integral part of the composing process. While they would check work and change or add punctuation, it was largely included as they put pen to paper, or put fingers to keyboard.

However, it would be untrue to see their progression as seamless, and in most cases the older children's punctuation was still relatively intuitive. To explain their choices they tended to draw on technically incorrect language; still most children in year 6 called speech marks 'sixty-sixes' and 'ninety-nines' – despite the *Framework for Teaching's* expectations that this would have been learnt in year 2. In year 6 many children still relied excessively on listening for pauses when deciding about the use of a comma or full stop. The stupidity of this was beautifully revealed when, faced with such a problem, one child read aloud a short text extract with a pause and claimed it needed a comma, while another child read it aloud without a pause and claimed it didn't. It is clearly not a helpful basis on which to make decisions. In many detailed and complex discussions with these children there was only one occasion in which a year-6 child produced a grammatical explanation for the use of a full stop or comma.

The difficulty for young children is that new learning does not necessarily make understanding the world easier. When learning to spell, the first major conceptual move is recognising that there is a fundamental relationship between letters and the sounds that we make when speaking. However, this huge leap in understanding is soon made more problematic as children meet the mass of inconsistencies in the English spelling system. As they learn strategies for these, so the spelling knowledge resources on which they can draw increase, but so do the possible alternative strategies for spelling. Thus the children are left with more decisions to make and more confusions to experience. A similar pattern occurs in learning to punctuate. The first major conceptual leap is to appreciate that there is a basic relationship between punctuation and the structure of written language, an understanding attained by Fhamida. However, making this break-through is followed by having to sort out a mass of inconsistencies that abound both within punctuation itself and in the ways in which punctuation is taught. Fhamida's success is likely to be followed by considerable confusion, some of it inherent in the nature of punctuation, but a lot of it caused by the difficulties of teaching some abstract concepts. Thus children are still largely left with sorting punctuation out for themselves, and they use the language that seems to them to make sense. Sometimes this works, but sometimes it does not, hence the year 6 children who still relied on weak or contradictory explanations. This research project did reveal significant development in children's ability to use punctuation during the primary years, but even in year 6 for many children it was still a very confusing area of written language.

Acknowledgements

The material in this chapter derives from research funded by the Economic and Social Research Council.

References

Arthur, C. (1996) 'Learning about punctuation: a look at one lesson', in *Learning about Punctuation*. N. Hall, and A. Robinson, (eds), pp. 92–108. Clevedon: Multilingual Matters.

Bernstein, B. (1997) *Pedagogy, Symbolic Control and Identity: Theory, Research, Critique*. London: Taylor and Francis.

Department of Education and Science (1984) *English from 5 to 16: Curriculum Matters 1*. London: HMSO.

Department of Education and Science (1988) *Report of the Committee of Enquiry into the Teaching of the English Language (The Kingman Report)*. London: HMSO.

Department of Education and Science (1989) *National Curriculum English for Ages 5–16 (The Cox Report)*. London: HMSO.

DfEE (1998) *National Literacy Strategy: Framework for Teaching*. London. DfEE.

Hall, N. (1996) 'Learning about punctuation', in *Learning about Punctuation*. N. Hall, and A. Robinson, (eds) pp. 5–36. Clevedon: Multilingual Matters.

Hall, N. (1998a) *Punctuation in the Primary School*. Reading: Reading and Language Information Centre, The University of Reading.

Hall, N. (1998b) 'Young children and resistance to punctuation', in *Research in Education*, 60, 29–40.

Hall, N. (1999) 'Young children's use of graphic punctuation.' *Language and Education: An International Journal*, 13, 3, 178-93.

Hall, N. (2001) 'Developing understanding of punctuation with young writers and readers', in *The Writing Classroom: Aspects of Writing and the Primary Child*. J. Evans, (ed.) Portsmouth, NH: Heinemann Books and London: David Fulton Publishers, pp. 143–53.

Hall, N. and Holden-Sim, K. (1996) 'Debating punctuation: six-year-olds figure it out', in *Listening to Children Think: Exploring Talk in the Early Years*. Hall, N. and Martello, J. (eds) London: Hodder and Stoughton, pp. 86–99.

Hall, N. and Robinson, A. (eds) (1996) *Learning about Punctuation*. Clevedon: Multilingual Matters.

Hall, N., Sing. S. and Wassouf, C. (2001) *The Development of Punctuation Knowledge in Children Aged Seven to Eleven: Final Report*. ERSRC Project, R000238348.

Kress, G. (1982) *Learning to Write*. London: Routledge and Kegan Paul.

Mohanty, A. and Perregaux, C. (1997) 'Language acquisition and bilingualism', in *Handbook of Cross-cultural Psychology: Basic Processes and Human Development*, Vol 2. J. W. Berry, P. R. Dasen, and T. S. Saraswathi (eds), Boston: Allyn and Bacon.

Robinson, A. (1996) 'Conversations with teachers about punctuation', in *Learning about Punctuation*, N. Hall, and A. Robinson, (eds) Clevedon: Multilingual Matters, pp. 92–108.

The world of literacy

Working with words: vocabulary development in the primary school

George Hunt

Introduction

From very early in their lives, children acquire vocabularies that enable them to make sense of the world around them and to process new ideas and meanings. In this chapter, George Hunt considers the development of vocabulary in children and its importance to successful learning – especially literacy learning. He provides an outline of word acquisition, a description of the research which underpins explicit support to children as they develop their vocabularies and some practical suggestions about ways that teachers can incorporate working with words into everyday learning activities.

Some issues in vocabulary development

The scale and rapidity of children's acquisition of vocabulary are probably the most impressive aspects of language development. Most children produce their first recognisable word somewhere between their tenth and fourteenth months. Other words follow very rapidly, so that by the age of 18 months the 'average' child can produce about 50 words, and understand five times as many (Crystal 1986). Although estimates of vocabulary size after the child passes the 200-word mark (typically at around two years old) are bewilderingly variable, some studies have put the recognition vocabulary of children starting school at roughly 10,000 words (Anglin 1993). Unlike grammatical and phonological development, where the most dramatic achievements occur in early childhood, vocabulary development is a life-long process. Although the rate of vocabulary acquisition is certainly impressive in the pre-school years, there is ample evidence that in some respects it is even more dramatic in the early and middle school years (Anglin 1993).

There are problems when estimating vocabulary size, however, as there are problems in defining both what we mean by a *word*, and what is meant by saying that somebody *knows* a word. Should *schoolchildren*, for example, count as one word or two? Are *swim, swimming, swimmer, swam* and *swum* separate words, or variants of the first term? What about phrases such as *lamb to the slaughter* and *gets on with*, where the seemingly distinct words represent a single concept? The issues surrounding word knowledge are even pricklier as the ability to understand a word does not imply the ability to use it. Consider the word right:

My right shoe leaks.
He's my right-hand man.
Drive on the right.
Turn right at the lights.
Turn through a right angle.
Keep on the right path.
Keep right on to the end of the road.
It's right here.
It's miles away; right over there.
Right, let's get going.
Right, I understand you now.
You are in the right.
You have no right.
That's the right answer.
That's the right stuff!
He's right in his belief.
He's very far right in his beliefs.

A complex network of connotations binds these different usages, involving affect, metaphor and shades of meaning. It is the learner's comprehension of this network that would have to be assessed if we were to try to determine whether or not a child knew this word. That is to say, vocabulary size is intimately related to vocabulary depth.

There are important educational implications here. Research is unanimous in identifying close links between the vocabulary size and measures of educational success, including reading and writing ability (McKeown and Curtis 1987). The more words that children have in their vocabularies, the more likely it is that they will be able to process printed words. A large vocabulary also helps a writer to express more precise meanings (Shaughnessy 1978). Conversely, deficits in learners' vocabularies are related to educational failure. At the most obvious level, a shortage of words will result in difficulties in speaking and listening, although the number of children who suffer from this degree of deficit is fewer than is popularly believed (Hughes 1994). At a more subtle level, deficits in particular types of word can have serious effects on learning. Perera (1979) has pointed out how ignorance of sentence adverbs such as *however, hence, therefore*, and so on, can make an otherwise 'readable' text incomprehensible; she also pointed out problems arising from readers' failure to appreciate unfamiliar meanings for familiar words such as *vacuum* and *liquid*. We cannot, however, deduce from this that efforts to increase vocabulary by rote learning of sets of words will bring about educational improvement. There is no implication that vocabulary size *produces* academic achievement. Both common sense and research suggest that the relationship between vocabulary size and proficient reading, for example, is reciprocal (Adams 1990). Furthermore, there is no reliable evidence that the memorisation of word lists is an effective strategy for expanding a learner's vocabulary. What *would* be effective is an important concern for any teacher attempting to create a literate classroom. Although we cannot prove that knowing words causes academic achievement, there is evidence that not knowing them contributes to 'Matthew effects' (from the Gospel of Matthew 25: 29), whereby the rich get richer and the poor get poorer (Stanovich 1986: 381).

> The very children who are reading well and who have good vocabularies will read more, learn more word meanings and hence read even better. Children with inadequate vocabularies – who read slowly and without enjoyment – read less, and as a result have slower development of vocabulary knowledge, which inhibits further growth in reading ability.

In order to address the question of what teachers can do to help to develop children's vocabulary, it would be useful to look at four procedures which have been held to be effective in this respect: direct instruction of vocabulary, learning words from context, learning words from dictionaries, and morphological problem solving.

Direct instruction of vocabulary

Given the rapid growth in children's vocabulary, it seems likely that only a fraction of the words that children learn in the primary years are acquired through direct instruction or word lists. Most children learn more words than anyone has time to teach them (Miller and Gildea 1987). This is not to say that there is no role for direct instruction; it is often necessary to teach specialist vocabulary for specific purposes. In one of the most thorough attempts to teach vocabulary through direct instruction, Beck *et al.* (1987) taught the meanings of 104 words to grade 4 children over a five-month period and achieved an 80 per cent success rate (namely an average of 80 per cent of the words were retained three weeks later). Although this does not sound impressive compared with the 20 words a day of largely uninstructed learning discovered by Anglin, the following aspects of this programme are worth considering.

- Words were grouped according to meaning.
- Children received multiple exposures to words in a variety of illustrative contexts.

- They received rich and varied information about each word, including how it related to words already known, and to other aspects of current knowledge and experience.
- A strong word play element was included.

Beck *et al.* (1987: 157) concluded that the active learning approach and the appeal of playful exploration stimulated word awareness and enabled them to seek out words independently: 'We reasoned that because children were being inundated with words and having enjoyable, successful experiences with them, they might become more aware of new words in their environment and more likely to expend effort understanding them.'

Learning words from context

A factor that seems to be more feasible than direct instruction in accounting for the rapid vocabulary growth in children is the capacity to learn words incidentally from context, particularly when reading. Much research has indicated that this is an effective source of vocabulary learning for children (Nagy and Andersen 1984; Shu *et al.* 1995), but *only* when they have become reasonably fluent readers. Unskilled readers cannot learn new words purely from the printed context because until decoding becomes automatic, there is not enough capacity available to make the inferences necessary for the acquisition of new words (Adams 1990). There is also the problem that many of the contexts in which unfamiliar words occur do not provide the novice reader with unambiguous clues about the meanings of such words.

Helping children to learn from context through adult–child discussion of word meanings in texts is a fruitful source of vocabulary acquisition. Collaborative discussion of texts in the classroom is likely to help children to learn specific words from a text and useful strategies of inference which will increase independence with reading.

Learning words from dictionaries

One of the most common vocabulary exercises given to children is to look up words in a dictionary and then to write sentences based on the definitions that they find. One problem with this approach is its dullness and lack of purpose. Another is the quality of some dictionaries. Research by Miller and Gildea (1987) showed that inadequacies in the language of definition caused children to make 'fragment selection errors'. For example, a child looking up the word *erode* wrote the sentence, 'My family erodes a lot' after misinterpreting the familiar phrase *eats out* in the definition. Most teachers will be familiar with gaffes of this nature, and they may well be tempted to despair of using dictionaries as anything other than old-fashioned versions of spellcheckers. However, there have been many interesting developments in lexicography in the years since Miller and Gildea wrote their paper. Most recent dictionaries for children use 'transparent' definitions rather than the traditional phrases. For example, the definition of *right* in the adult Oxford paperback dictionary begins: '1 (of conduct or actions, etc.) morally good, in accordance with justice'. In the Collins Pocket Primary the definition reads; 'Your right hand is the hand that most people write with'. While this definition reduces one of the most complex and contentious words in the language to its most simple use, its form is more accessible to a youngster than traditional 'definese' (McKeown 1993). As well as the greater clarity of definese (the style of writing in which definitions are expressed), recent children's dictionaries include example sentences which give further clues to the meanings and grammatical forms of words. Dictionaries are also better illustrated, and their typography is clearer. All these factors should establish the modern dictionary in vocabulary development, but only if children are encouraged to explore them as sources of enjoyment.

Morphological problem solving

Morphemes are units of meaning. Anglin (1993) coined the phrase 'morphological problem solving' to describe how children figure out words which are 'potentially knowable' by relating them to words that they already know. He found that much of the vocabulary growth that occurs in the school years can be explained by children's growing awareness of the structure of words. He also found that children construct meanings by identifying and blending morphemes in unfamiliar words. This study also emphasised that the learners' personal vocabulary is highly structured (Miller 1993):

> The mental dictionary is not a homogenous list of concept utterance pairs that have been memorised by rote. Words are related to one another in many ways and it is by taking advantage of those relations that children are able to develop their vocabularies so rapidly.

An emphasis on the learner actively discovering and creatively developing relationships between words and meanings underlies the classroom activities outlined in the rest of this chapter.

Some suggestions for vocabulary investigations in the classroom

The following activities are meant to do three things: to teach children about words, namely their origins, anatomy and usages; to teach children specific sets of words and meanings; to teach children a sensitivity towards words in general. They are compatible with the vocabulary extension objectives laid out in the word level work in the National Literacy Strategy. Many also can be used to support spelling, phonics, sentence and text level.

Stimulating curiosity about words

Word of the day; word family of the week

Select a word which is relevant to a topical theme and display it in the classroom. Discuss its meaning, spelling and, if appropriate, morphological structure (there is no need to use technical vocabulary when doing this). Ask the children for any words that they know related to the word of the day.

Register games

Ask the children to answer the register by giving a word related to a particular theme. Keep this quick and playful; if a child cannot give a word, supply one yourself and pass on. Themes could include colours, towns, animals, size words, words with specific spelling patterns, and words from other languages.

Words from other languages

Children who speak languages other than English can be asked to contribute mother tongue equivalents for words which the class are currently investigating. For example, children could compare weather terminology in different languages to see how potentially onomatopoeic items such as *thunder* are represented .

Morphemic word webs

This activity is aimed at raising children's awareness of word structure, spelling patterns and relationships between words. Take a root word which is related to a current class topic or story and show the children how you can generate related words by adding morphemes to form a web of words. When you have started the web, ask the children to extend it further with their own suggestions.

Semantic fields

Take any basic concept (such as food or money) and get the children to tell you as many words and phrases that they know for that concept. This might include 'slang' terms, regional and national variants in English, and words used for the concept in other languages. Display the results as a word web, which can then be used as a focus for discussion.

Free sorting of randomly selected words

Take a random collection of between ten and 20 words, for example, you might use the answers to a crossword, or open a novel at different pages and select the first word that meets your eye. Put the words on cards. Ask the children, in pairs, to sort the words out in any way that seems sensible. When this has been done, the children can explain the rationale for their sorting and compare it with that of other pairs of children. The range of responses to this simple task can be fascinating.

Names

These activities are based on the special role played by names in children's vocabulary development. You need to bear in mind that, for some families, personal names may be inappropriate.

Name origins

Prepare a poster or big book displaying information on the origins of the first names of all the children in your class. Explain to the children that every personal name has a story behind it, and illustrate this with some examples. Children can be encouraged to discuss their own first names and to speculate on their meanings before you turn to the big book to compare their ideas with the 'official' derivation.

Place names

Maps and atlases provide rich opportunities for the study of name origins and name structures. Start with local maps including A–Z-type street atlases and Ordnance Survey material. Ask the children to collect place names and to think of categories into which they might be sorted. These could include names of towns, villages, parks, woods, rivers, farms, streets, housing estates and schools. In covering wider geographic areas, names of counties, countries, mountains, rivers and seas might be included. The listing and sorting activity can be followed by discussion of meanings and origins, regularities in the structures of the names (such as the common English elements -don and -caster, the Welsh Llan and the Scottish and Irish Kil-), and investigation into changes of names.

Business names

The *Yellow Pages* or local business directories provide examples of names based on manipulations of spelling sound and meaning. Kwiksave, for example, is a fairly simple spelling manipulation, BlueFlash (a removal firm) borrows its name from a popular metaphor. Children can list examples and sort them into categories before having a go at making up their own.

Investigating and inventing fictional characters' names

Authors often select names for their characters which have a suggestive but immediate impact. A simple starting point for investigating this area would be the *Happy
Families* series by Allan Ahlberg. How did Mrs Wishy Washy get her name? Why
are alliterative names such as Wishy Washy, Tellytubby and Tintin so common in
fiction for younger children? Can you sort out a set of Dickens's or Dahl's characters into heroes and villains just on the basis of their names? If so, what aspects of
language are the authors exploiting here? Compare this with a list of hero and
villain names from television, comics and computer games. Children can be
encouraged to create their own characters and to give them appropriate names.

Examining and inventing metaphorical compounds

Many folk names for plants and animals take the form of descriptive or metaphori-
cal compounds (for example, sunflower, foxglove and daisy). Analysing such
compounds can help children to coin new descriptive compounds themselves. This
can be related to the historical use of such compounds, or kennings, in early English
poetry; for example the sea could be referred to as the 'whale path', or the human
body as a 'bone house'.

Onomatopoeia

Onomatopoeic words – those that imitate physical sounds such as *crash*, *gobble* and
screech – are amongst the first that children acquire in their speech.

Collecting and sorting onomatopoeic words

Cartoons, advertising slogans and nursery rhymes are all good sources of
onomatopoeic words. They can be collected and sorted into such categories as
animal noises, loud and soft noises, human noises, and so on. The words can then
be regrouped across categories according to patterns of alliteration and rhyme.
Children can be asked to extend the categories with their own examples, and to use
these words to make up rhymes, songs and slogans.

Investigating sounds

Ask the children to list as many words as they can beginning with 'sl' and to look
up their meanings. Is there any significance in the fact that many of these words
have negative meanings (*slime, sly, sleazy, sloppy,* and so on)? What patterns of
meaning can be found in words beginning with' st-', or ending in '-ump'?

Inventing words

A good way of helping children to understand how the components of words are organised is to let them make up their own. For example, a child invented *schlerpph* to describe the sound made by a marble dropping into a jelly.

Onset and rime

From a simple table of onsets and rimes, children can construct a set of 'words' that cannot be found in any dictionary (for example, the onset 'gl-' with the rimes '-ont', '-ard' and '-eng'). Children can be encouraged to think about possible meanings for such words. This could lead to a discussion of what parts of speech categories the new words belong to, and how they would work in sentences.

Morphoshuffle

A useful teaching tool is a set of cards in which word components are set out in three colours: red for prefixes, blue for roots, and yellow for suffixes, perhaps. By shuffling the cards and setting them out in a fixed red-blue-yellow order, children can generate both real words and new words. (Remember that spelling modifications are sometimes necessary when adding affixes.) Familiarity with the meanings of the word parts will enable children to create meanings and to compose definitions for new words.

From word to text

Although playing with words and word families can be fascinating, it is necessary that children have lots of opportunities to see how words operate in whole texts. Many valuable activities are available for starting with texts and investigating the words within them. For example, children can share lists of favourite words (chosen for their sound as well as their meaning) and arrange them into poetic patterns. They can generate stories from sequences of words which act as prompts for a plot; they can create thematic ABCs with alliterative captions; they can create mini-dictionaries giving definitions for some of the words that they have invented; they can compose concordances around words with multiple meanings.

Words are fascinating objects, and the study of their structure, origins and meanings can be very fruitful for children, but it is only when they start to combine words thoughtfully that they put to use the knowledge they have gained.

References

Adams, M. J. (1990) *Beginning to Read*. Cambridge, MA: MIT Press.

Anglin, J. (1993) *Vocabulary Development: a Morphological Analysis*. Chicago: University of Chicago Press.

Beck, I., Perfetti, A. and Omanson, R. (1987) 'The effects and uses of diverse vocabulary instructional techniques', in *The Nature of Vocabulary Acquisition* M. McKeown, and M. Curtis, (eds). Hillsdale, NJ: Lawrence Earlbaum Associates, p.157.

Crystal, D. (1986) *Listen to Your Child*. London: Penguin Books.

Hughes, M. (1994) 'The oral language of young children', in D. Wray and J. Medwell (eds) *Teaching Primary English*. London: Routledge, pp. 7–21.

McKeown, M. (1993) 'Creating effective definitions for young word learners.' *Reading Research Quarterly*, 28, 17–31.

McKeown, M. and Curtis, M. (eds) (1987) *The Nature of Vocabulary Acquisition*. Hillsdale, NJ: Lawrence Earlbaum Associates.

Miller, G. (1993) in *Vocabulary Development: A Morphological Analysis*. S. Anglin (ed.). Chicago: University of Chicago Press.

Miller, G. and Gildea, P. (1987) 'How children learn words', *Scientific American*, 257, 3, 94–9.

Nagy, W. E. and Andersen, R. C. (1984) 'How many words are there in printed school English?' *Reading Research Quarterly*, 19, 304–30.

Perera, K. (1979) *The Language Demands of School Learning*, Open University Course PE232, Supplementary Readings 6. Milton Keynes: The Open University.

Shaughnessy, M. (1977) *Errors and Expectations*. New York: Oxford University Press.

Shu, H., Andersen, R.C. and Zhang, H. (1995) 'Incidental learning of word meanings while reading: a Chinese and American cross-cultural study.' *Reading Research Quarterly*, 30, 76–95.

Stanovich, K. (1986) 'Matthew effects in reading: some consequences of individual differences in the acquisition of literacy.' *Reading Research Quarterly*, 21, 360–406.

Young word processors at work

Ruth Wood

Introduction

For the majority of people who use computers, the word processor is invaluable when engaging with the writing process. Some of the clear advantages are the possibility of editing on screen; trying out words and changing the order of sentences. Mistakes no longer mean a complete rewrite as documents can be saved, loaded and edited quickly and efficiently. Multiple copies can be printed, even after some time has elapsed since the document was first created. Handwriting which may otherwise be difficult to read is suddenly transformed into clear and legible print. Furthermore, images, diagrams, graphs and tables can be incorporated within a document to provide further information and enhance the overall content. In 1988, the Kingman Report acknowledged the potential of the word processor and noted that 'its ability to shape, delete and move text around provides the means by which pupils can achieve a satisfactory product' (DfES 1988: 37). This chapter considers how word processing can support children, from nursery and throughout the primary school, as they grapple with the complexities of becoming a writer. Somewhere along the line, learners will shift from *learning* how to use a word processor to actually *using* a word processor proficiently and competently.

A tool to support writing

The process of transferring thoughts and ideas into a written format is not straightforward. Accomplished and experienced writers engage with a sophisticated process of formulating, interpreting and refining their ideas. Consideration needs to be given to the audience, purpose and content of the writing. It is unlikely that, at the first attempt, a writer will successfully transfer ideas into written text. Whether the writer is a child or an adult, the process of reviewing, reshaping and rewriting is necessary to effectively distil and refine thoughts and ideas represented in this manner. The writer may therefore continuously revise his or her ideas and rewrite or edit the work with, perhaps, the final stages being concerned with layout and the publication of the writing for an intended audience (Evans 2001: 12–13).

What can the word processor offer?

Clearly, a word processor may provide increased opportunity for an individual to refine their written work. It is designed to allow changes to be made quickly and efficiently. The cursor can be moved around within the written text in order to add, delete or replace any part of the work. Whole sections may be cut, copied and pasted from one location to another. Text-wrap allows the writer to concentrate on the construction of his or her work rather than the position of the cursor in relation to the side of the page. A myriad of fonts and formats are available which could provide further opportunities to enhance the presentation.

Individuals who are experienced in the use of word processors may take such features for granted and use them automatically. However, inexperienced users such as children, who are just beginning to get to grips with such technology, are often unaware of these facilities. For example, they can be observed watching the cursor carefully as it approaches the right-hand side of the page in order to press the enter key before their writing encounters the boundaries of the on-screen page. They may delete whole tracts of text by using the backspace key in order to arrive at a mistake some distance away or rely upon the computer for spelling and grammar without necessarily understanding either.

The transition from the physical to the digital is not automatic and writers not only need to engage with the process of constructing their written text but they also need to recognise the limitations and the advantages of the word processor in facilitating such activity.

When discussing the use of the word processor with a group of six ten-year-old children who were using the relatively sophisticated program Word, they identified a range of features which they felt assisted them when constructing their written work. Most highlighted the ability to replace text by deleting and inserting words or letters. All referred to the spellchecker but only one mentioned the use of the grammar checker as assisting them when writing. Presentation was most frequently mentioned with all children indicating that the word-processed documents looked more attractive than their own handwritten work. For example, one child stated that 'the writing on this looks better than mine' whilst another pointed out that, 'it doesn't make a mess when I make changes.' It was clear from the discussion with the children that the features which facilitated the secretarial aspects of writing, such as accuracy in spelling, punctuation and grammar alongside legibility and presentation, were valued most.

Spellcheckers

One of the children who explained that it was 'easy to change wrong spellings to right spellings' was observed responding to the visual indicators associated with the identification of incorrect spellings. As soon as the red underlining appeared beneath a word which the computer had recognised as incorrect, the child stopped and repeatedly attempted a new spelling. In this instance, it could be argued that it is advantageous to the child's learning as this encourages the child to apply spelling strategies. However, the writing process was once again interrupted and the flow of ideas became secondary to the visual prompts issued by the program. By changing the options with regard to the spellchecking facility, the program would cease to identify any errors whilst text is entered and therefore remove the possible distractions which may exist during the process of writing. This may be beneficial in more than one respect as spellcheckers are not altogether reliable. The words contained in the dictionary database are the words which are recognised as correct. If they are not in the dictionary, the program assumes they are incorrectly spelt. As pointed out by Loveless (2003: 59), this can lead to some rather amusing or misleading instances when the program offers alternative words to replace the 'incorrect' spelling. The child can, of course, choose to add the word to the program's dictionary. However, this assumes that the child is both confident and knowledgeable enough to recognise that the computer can be mistaken. Further difficulties arise when homophones enter the scene. One of the most common errors made by children in the course of written work is the incorrect use of 'there' 'their' and 'they're'. These remain undetected by the spellchecking facility as they are all correct spellings but the meaning may be incorrectly situated within a sentence.

Grammar checkers

In addition to spellchecking facilities, programs such as Word may perform grammar checks. This is potentially a useful tool but often the writer requires a good understanding of grammar in order to recognise why the program has highlighted specific sections and how the suggested revisions relate to the text. For an inexperienced writer this could be confusing. Nulty (in Evans 2001: 85–6) describes the way in which a child utilised the spellchecking and grammar checking facilities effectively by assessing the relevance of the 'errors' in the context of his work. Where decisions had been made to write a word in capitals and add a number of exclamation marks to create impact, he chose to ignore the advice offered.

By activating the autocorrect, occasional typographical and keyboard errors, such as the omission of a capital letter at the beginning of a sentence and accidental keystrokes, may be automatically rectified. This effectively allows writers to continue to develop their ideas rather than concern themselves with corrections.

Unfortunately, it could also give a false representation of a child's understanding. For assessment purposes, it is often useful to witness the true form of a child's composition to identify how they may best move forward. Saving the work as separate documents at various stages can provide useful information regarding the development of a child's written work, whilst printouts provide opportunities for reflecting and proofreading away from the computer with or without teacher intervention.

In the following example, Terry-Ann, a seven-year-old, used Word to write a description of how she felt about her hobby, horse riding. The order in which word-processing tools were used was recorded and interventions from the teaching assistant were also noted. At this age, children are becoming quite familiar with the various tools which support the writer in terms of accuracy and presentation. Capitalisation and font size has been selected for impact and the use of print preview seems to indicate that the link between the digital version (what you see is what you get, or WYSIWYG) and the physical printout has been understood.

> I LIKE HORSES BECAUSE
> They are fast and they have very very soft nose. I like horses because thay are sometimes funny. I go horse riding every
> satarday. My fravroit horses are Blossom and
> Blackey and Charle and Pompom.
>
> Terry-Ann

The spellchecker did provide additional support with spelling errors such as 'thay' and 'satarday' which were promptly corrected. Alternative words to replace Blackey were rejected which indicated that the child had sufficient confidence to reject the suggestions offered by the spellchecking facility. The word 'fravroit' did provide some discussion as the list of suggestions did not include the intended word 'favourite'. Some editing occurred with a second and third attempt at the spelling. Finally, after entering 'fravoroit', one of the suggestions corresponded to the word required. Spellcheckers are not always able to identify what the intended word may be if the spelling is too dissimilar. This can encourage the child to attempt a more accurate version. However, it also assumes that the child may recognise what the intended word is and be able to distinguish it from a variety of words vaguely related by component letters.

Commas were problematic and, although explanation was offered by the teaching assistant, the child remained unsure regarding their use. The deletion of 'very' was rejected by the child as she felt it changed the meaning of the sentence.

> I LIKE HORSES BECAUSE
> They are fast and they have a very very soft nose. I like horses because they are sometimes funny. I go horse riding every Saturday. My favourite horses are Blossom,
> Blackey, Charlie and Pompom.
>
> Terry-Ann

Generally, Terry-Ann was beginning to demonstrate a developing awareness of how the word-processing software could support her, but more importantly perhaps, how it did not meet her needs. In this way, she began to take control of the computer rather than the computer taking control of her. Some of the tools may be helpful if there is sufficient understanding regarding the role they play. However, here the grammar checker was playing no active part in supporting the young writer but instead appeared to be highlighting aspects of the work which she was, as yet, unable to understand. The sequence of the process was:

1 Highlighted title and centred it.

2 ABC and grammar checked. The teaching assistant provided an explanation regarding commas as the computer had no suggestions, only informing her that she should 'delete repeated word' and, for the last sentence 'fragment, consider revising.'

3 Print preview.

4 Altered the margin to place the writing where she wanted it to print on the paper.

5 Print.

6 Used the toolbar, view, to return to normal screen.

7 Saved.

Consideration needs to be given to the role of the word-processing program in the writing process. Many of the features described can effectively be switched on or off, allowing the writer to make decisions as to when these are selected during the course of their work. Children need to develop an awareness of the many features available to them and learn how to control the computer as opposed to the computer controlling the child.

Legibility

For those children who experience difficulty in spelling and handwriting, the word processor may offer opportunities to raise self-esteem and increase confidence. (Washtell in Graham and Kelly 2003: 44) Continued revisions and corrections of handwritten work can result in a tangled mess of marks on the page. However, revisions made on the screen do not interfere with the legibility. The writer is free to experiment and alter the composition at will without fear of having to continually rewrite to regain clarity. A variety of fonts is available for experimentation. This can also be a drawback, however, as in the case of one child who was observed spending some time selecting a font, entering a few words before deleting them and repeating the process. Consequently, the transfer of thought to print was rather slow, with the child concentrating less upon the content and process of his writing than on the presentation.

It may also be argued that children who are competent in handwriting may not be inclined to use a word processor as it could effectively slow them down. The QWERTY keyboard appears firmly embedded in the design of the computer and yet its relevance adheres to the typewriter, a technology which has clearly been superseded. Children are required to hunt for the relevant letters which are scattered in what appears to be a random pattern across the keyboard. Upper case letters on keys may be confusing to young children who hunt for lower case letters. This can be alleviated through the introduction of keyboards with lower case letters instead of upper case, or stickers which may be placed over the conventional upper case keys. Those of us who are not touch typists take some time to locate and select the appropriate letters in the correct order to construct words and sentences. However, the possibility of such challenges discouraging children who are perceived as competent in writing from using the word processor is challenged by Nulty (in Evans 2001: 87) who highlights the way in which a group of children, classed as able writers, expressed a preference for the word processor as it provided assistance in editing and presentation. In this instance, the children recognised the advantages the word processor offered them in facilitating the construction of written work and clearly felt that these outweighed the potential limitations.

Where spelling is concerned, cursive handwriting may be favourable as 'strings of letters can be seen as a whole unit and handwriting practice can be used to reinforce such strings' (Kelly in Graham and Kelly 2003: 118). Effectively, the movement of the hand from one letter to another may provide a kinaesthetic aide mémoire to the construction of words. Some individuals, when attempting to spell a more challenging word, may resort to a handwritten attempt, engaging with the 'look and feel' of a word. In this way, the word processor may be viewed as an addition, not a replacement, to handwriting with opportunities to support those who find handwriting and spelling a barrier to communicating in written format. For young writers, something as simple as the space between words may prove to be problematic. As pointed out by Smith (1999: 101), when writing a string of words by hand, the child does not need to physically create a space but when using a word processor, this is a necessity.

Although the QWERTY keyboard and sophisticated word-processing packages may provide challenges to the young or inexperienced writer, there is a variety of technologies which may, to a greater or lesser extent, provide some resolution and facilitate the transition from *learner* to *proficient user.*

The choice of word-processing packages

Young children are unlikely to need powerful and sophisticated software such as Word when taking their first steps into the world of word processing. At the foundation stage, they are just beginning to recognise how they can create on-screen text. As such, a 'limited palette' of icons would be beneficial to reduce any difficulties arising from accidental mouse clicks. 2Publish, created by 2Simple, is one such example of software designed to minimise potential frustrations whilst introducing young children to the potential of technology.

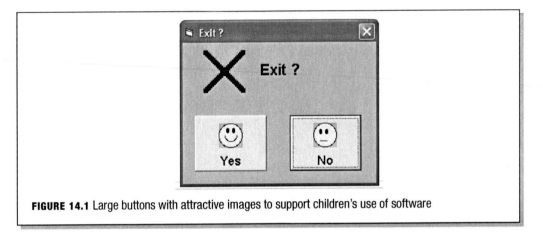

FIGURE 14.1 Large buttons with attractive images to support children's use of software

The screen is uncluttered and contains images of felt tip pens down the left-hand side which represent the range of colours available for selection when painting in the top part of the screen. Thin and fat felt pens indicate the size selected and the active colour is signified by one pen being uncapped. Because the number of icons is limited, there are fewer to choose from and to be confused by. The size of pens and icons increases the possibility of children who are developing fine motor coordination actually selecting these active areas. If, however, the exit button is accidentally selected, the children are required to confirm their choice with visual indicators assisting the child in his or her decision (see Figure 14.1). Underneath the image is a space for written text. However, alternative layouts may be selected from the 'new page' menu (see Figure 14.2), providing further flexibility.

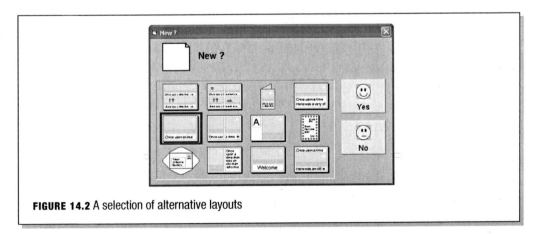

FIGURE 14.2 A selection of alternative layouts

Clicker4 (Figure 14.3) is much more sophisticated than 2Publish and includes features such as a speaking word processor, opportunities to program a grid comprised of cells and more options with regard to icons and drop-down menus. Each cell may be programmed to do something specific upon left and right mouse clicks.

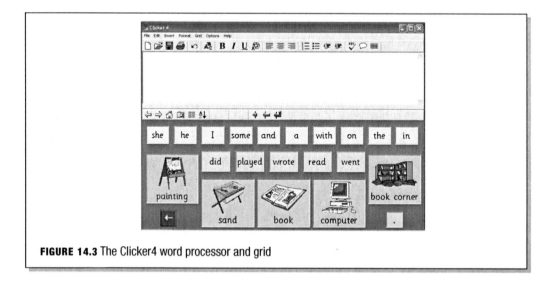

FIGURE 14.3 The Clicker4 word processor and grid

For example, the left mouse click on the word 'wrote' could enter the same text in the word-processing part of the program residing at the top of the screen whilst electronic speech pronounces the word. Right clicking on the same word could prompt a sound file to be played which had previously been recorded through utilities available within Clicker itself. Grids may be linked together and cells resized, moved or deleted whilst background and font colour are selected to enhance the visual aspects of the grid. The program can offer a great deal more, however. It can be seen that much consideration by the teacher may be invested in the design of a Clicker grid in order to help support the writing process.

Speech facilities such as those offered by Clicker4 can be found on a number of word processors designed for the educational market. By utilising speech feedback, children may be able to listen to the pronunciation of words prior to their selection from a word bank (Tyldesley in Monteith 2002: 57). Additionally, when activated within the word-processing program, speech feedback may further support children in their proofreading. As the computer will only read what is entered as text, any errors in construction or spelling may be highlighted when the speech facility attempts to read exactly what is written. In the same way that spellcheckers require some tuition with regard to words which do not appear in the associated dictionary, speech facilities may also need to be developed and refined.

Looking to the future

The technologies described here are already in existence and will, no doubt, make an appearance within primary educational contexts in the not too distant future. Of the two technological developments described, both seek to provide alternative methods of entering the text into a digital format rather than relying upon the use of a keyboard and mouse. Speech recognition software has already been available for some years but it has never really crossed the divide into the type of software common to workplace and home. Effectively, speech recognition software is designed to translate what is spoken into a written format and allow the individual to operate the software using voice commands. This does seem to be an excellent idea and appears to remove the frustrations many of us face when contemplating the hunt for letters on the QWERTY keyboard. However, it takes some time to 'teach' the program to recognise your voice and, even then, it is not always accurate. On a website dedicated to the use of speech recognition software, individuals have begun to create a list of amusing misrecognitions such as this:

'Dictated: RAF helicopters have gone to the aid of a P and O ferry drifting without power off the coast at Great Yarmouth.

'Interpreted: RAF helicopters have gone to the aid of a piano fairy drifting without power off the coast at Great Yarmouth.' (www.out-loud.com)

Whilst some individuals seem to find speech recognition invaluable, others are rather sceptical and critical. Speech tools are now becoming more commonplace and are increasing opportunities for accessibility. Mobile phones, amongst many other gadgets, can be voice operated. It may be just a matter of time before this software becomes more reliable and finds itself commonplace within the school system.

Handwriting recognition appears to have a similar history in terms of misrecognition. Styles of handwriting can be so diverse that it is difficult for software developers to create a reliable product. The tablet PC has entered the educational market in a rather confident manner of late. Using multimodal inputs such as stylus, on-screen keyboard or voice, the individual can enter data. The stylus is used directly on the screen of the PC and, in the case of handwritten text; there is the option of converting this into print. Another development has been that of digital ink. Programs such as Microsoft's Journal allow you to write freely across an electronic on-screen page with opportunities to maintain integrity of the document by allowing the text and images to reflow after alterations have been made. It is possible that technology could be adapting to the ways in which we have traditionally worked when developing our writing. Now, however, the power of technology has been applied and handwriting which has been somewhat permanent after construction may be revised and altered without clarity being compromised. Clearly, one method will not be suitable for all individuals and it is the diversity of writing tools, alongside careful teacher intervention, which will support and enhance the process of writing for children.

References

Adams, A. (1990) 'The potential of information technology within the English curriculum.' *Journal of Assisted Learning*, 6, pp. 232–8.

Department for Education and Science (DfES) (1988) *Report of the Committee of Enquiry into the Teaching of English Language*, Kingman Report, London: HMSO.

Evans, J. (ed.) (2001) *The Writing Classroom: Aspects of Writing and the Primary Child 3–11*. London: David Fulton Publishers.

Graham, J. and Kelly, A. (2003) *Writing Under Control*, 2nd edn., London: David Fulton Publishers.

Loveless, A. (2003) *The Role of ICT*. London: Continuum.

Monteith, M. (2002) *Teaching Primary Literacy with ICT*, Buckingham: Open University Press.

Smith, H. (1999) *Opportunities for Information and Communication Technology in the Primary School*. Stoke on Trent: Trentham Books.

Web links and software

Computing Out Loud http://www.out-loud.com (accessed January 2005)

2Simple Video Toolkit, version 2.0.1, by 2Simple Software, www.2simple.com, London (accessed January 2005)

Clicker4 version 4.1 by Crick Software Ltd, www.cricksoft.com, Northampton (accessed January 2005)

Working with pupils with English as an additional language

Liz Laycock

Introduction

The most recent statistics from the Teacher Training Agency reveal that a very small proportion of newly qualified teachers felt that their courses had prepared them well to teach pupils who have English as an Additional Language (EAL). Similarly, many established teachers feel unsure how to support those pupils new to English. The National Literacy strategy (NLS) materials, initially, gave some guidance (in Section 4 of the *NLS Framework for Teaching* (1998)) about specific strategies to ensure the inclusion of pupils with EAL, but such guidance was not often incorporated into literacy hour planning. Fuller training guidance, which includes video exemplification of approaches to planning and teaching, followed in 2002 with the revised edition of *The National Literacy Strategy. Supporting Pupils Learning English as an Additional Language*. These materials are intended 'to support schools with the development of strategies to promote inclusive teaching and to raise the attainment of pupils learning EAL'.

This chapter considers what is known about how mainstream class teachers can support children's acquisition of English as an additional language. Recent research and further reading are indicated. It considers appropriate pedagogy, focusing particularly on supportive activities in storytelling and the use of picture books in literacy.

Multilingual classrooms

In most urban, and some rural, areas of Britain, classrooms include children for whom English is not their first language. If we are to be truly 'inclusive' as the National Curriculum requires, we need to be well-informed about these pupils and knowledgeable about how the new language is likely to develop. The statement on inclusion in the *National Curriculum Handbook for Primary Teachers in England* (1999: 37. 7–8) states that 'Planning should take account of such factors as the pupil's age, length of time in this country, previous educational experience and skills in other languages' and 'Teachers should take specific action to help pupils who are learning English as an additional language by:

a developing their spoken and written English

b ensuring access to the curriculum and assessment.'

The writers go on to provide clear exemplification of the ways in which teachers can 'develop spoken and written English' and 'ensure access to the curriculum'. All of these examples reflect practice which is appropriate for all pupils whether or not they are new to English.

To begin with, teachers need to find out as much as possible about each child's linguistic and educational background. Children arriving at the foundation stage will have developed oral skills in the language(s) of the home and the community; they are likely to be aware of literacy practices in these languages (from newspapers, notices, letters, religious practices, and so on – see Minns (1990) and Whitehead (2002)). Older children will have well-developed oral skills and may already have literacy skills in another language. For many, their previous education will have enabled them to develop knowledge and concepts in many areas, so we need to find ways of giving them access to the full curriculum in this new context. In order to provide appropriate support, teachers need to acknowledge and draw on the children's experiences, as well as have some understanding of the way in which a new language develops.

In order to build a profile of a child's linguistic and educational experiences, the following aide mémoire, though not exhaustive, may be useful when a child arrives in a school or class. Whenever possible, arrange to meet parents/carers before the child arrives in the classroom, or very soon afterwards, in order to find out:

■ Mother's/father's/child's names and how to pronounce them correctly

■ Languages used at home – by mother/father/siblings/grandparents

■ Languages understood/spoken by child

■ Whether the child can read/write languages other than English

■ Whether the child is learning to read/write languages other than English (for example, at community school)

■ Date of arrival in Britain (if not British born) and where the family have come from

■ Schooling: length of time in school(s) abroad; language medium of school

■ Religion: festivals observed/language involved

In finding out about the family's language(s), try to be accurate; find out about dialect forms which are not written (for example, Sylheti), the script, directionality, and so on. In due course, try to obtain examples of the script and a few basic words ('welcome', 'yes', 'no', 'thank you', 'hello', 'goodbye', numbers) which can be used in the classroom. Some schools and boroughs (for example, Ealing) have compiled 'language gazetteers' which gather basic information about their pupils' languages (as does *The Other Languages: A Guide to Multilingual Classrooms* (Edwards 1996)). Monolingual teachers can demonstrate their interest in and respect for children's other languages by making the effort to use a few words. If children perceive that their language is welcomed in the classroom, through displays which incorporate the language, in the presence of books in the language, and a teacher who tries to use the language, their willingness to become involved with the classroom community will be much greater. The message that it is perfectly acceptable to speak and/or write in the language they know is also reinforced by its visible presence. If there are other speakers of the same language in the class, they should be encouraged to help the new arrival, talking in their shared language. If not, a sensitive native English-speaking 'buddy' could be assigned to help; children make excellent teachers and can often make things clearer than a teacher can.

Arrival in a British, English-speaking classroom, presents challenges not only in relation to the English language but also in learning the cultural expectations of 'school'. Even if they have been to school in another country, children will have to learn the different routines and customs in their new school. It has been suggested (Edwards 1996: 37–41) that a basic phrase book/survival kit can help a newcomer make sense of new routines, especially if phonetic versions of vocabulary are provided to help teachers pronounce words from the child's language when he/she cannot read. An essential resource for children who *can* read, which is surprisingly infrequently provided in classrooms, is an English/other language dictionary.

The main factor, though, which will enable teachers to support children new to English is their awareness of how the language is acquired and developed. There is now much research which sheds light on this. We know that, ideally, the learner needs to experience conditions similar to those they had when acquiring the first language.

- A long listening time is needed before the language is produced.
- Language is learnt through interaction with other language users.
- The learner is surrounded by models of the language in use.
- There is active visual paralinguistic support (for example, gesture/facial expression).
- The motivation is the need to communicate.
- There is expectation of success and no fear of making mistakes.

- Listeners respond to the intended meaning rather than focus on correctness.
- There is little explicit correction; correct forms are constantly indirectly reinforced. (for example, Child: 'I wented to the park'. Adult: 'You went to the park, did you?')

There are, however, differences because older learners new to English will already have learnt to use another language and thus have greater understanding of how language works (an 'underlying proficiency', Cummins 1984). Many concepts will be understood in the first language and do not have to be relearned, but transferred from one language to the other. Equally, the age of the learner and the context will be factors in learning. An infant acquiring his/her first language is normally in a stress-free environment, surrounded by people who respond lovingly and enthusiastically to every little development, not a classroom with 30 others competing for adult attention. We can do much to reduce stress and create class-room environments which are positive and supportive, but we cannot recreate the context in which an infant learns!

We need to appreciate, too, that, given a welcoming context where resources and teaching are geared to the needs of learners of English as an additional language, where there is much emphasis on developing oral skills and positive interactions between children, much progress can be made in a couple of years. It is at this point that we may feel that a child has become reasonably fluent and can cope in English without the additional support we have provided. But it is important, at this stage, to consider a further strand of the research into language development.

BICS and CALP

Cummins (1979) makes an important distinction between two levels of language competence. Cummins's research, and later research by Collier and Thomas (1987 and 1997), show that a learner achieves 'communicative competence' (also termed Basic Interpersonal Communicative skills – BICS) in the new language in about two years, but that it takes five to seven years for 'academic language' (also termed Cognitive/Academic Language Proficiency – CALP) to develop. It is also suggested that more explicit teaching is needed as the learner moves beyond communicative competence and has to deal with more demanding language structures, vocabulary and concepts in English. The learner continues to need support in accessing the school curriculum; even though he or she appears to be quite fluent, the English knowledge is still superficial and not able to deal with more demanding cognitive activity without support. This language development continuum has been developed and forms the basis of a framework for planning approaches to teaching and assessment as shown in Figure 15.1 (Cline and Frederickson (1994); Hall (1995)).

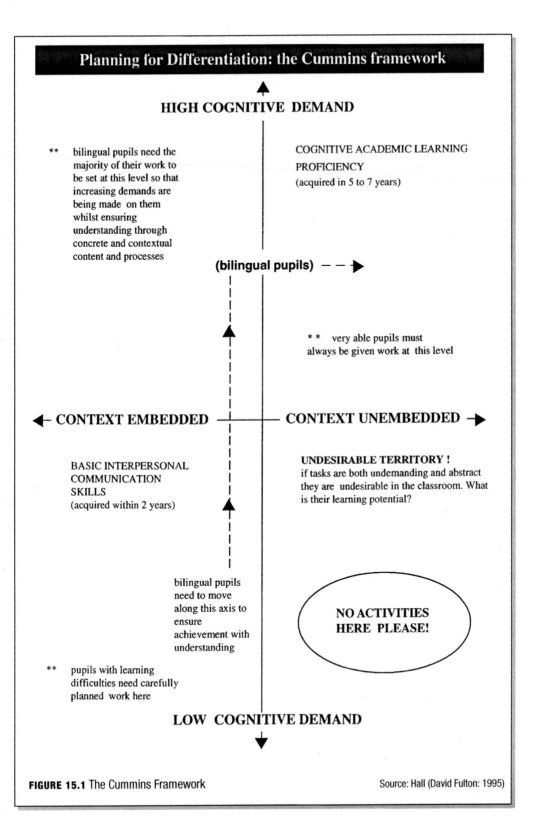

FIGURE 15.1 The Cummins Framework   Source: Hall (David Fulton: 1995)

We need to consider both the context of tasks and the cognitive demands. Hall (1995) suggests that no tasks for pupils with EAL should be cognitively undemanding and lacking a context. Little learning will take place if pupils are merely repeating the utterances of others or mindlessly copying from the board or a book. When learners are at the stage of having 'communicative competence', tasks need to be placed in an understood context and have some cognitive demand. Work at this level can include transferring information from one medium to another (for example, data to a grid), applying known procedures, retelling narratives or describing actions, sequencing, matching. As English learning progresses, activities still need to be embedded in a clear context but can make greater cognitive demands. Pupils should now engage in summarising, planning, comparing and contrasting, classifying, generalising and seeking solutions to problems. It is not until more 'academic language' has been attained that pupils are able to work without the contextualisation with a greater level of abstraction. Now they can be expected, alongside native English speakers, to argue a case, justify an opinion, evaluate critically, interpret evidence and make deductions, hypothesise, predict and apply knowledge to a different situation. Hall provides helpful examples of work planned using the Cummins framework, for KS1 science and KS2 geography.

In order to provide real learning opportunities and to make the content of the curriculum accessible to children with EAL, we need to look carefully at the ways in which we teach and the tasks we ask children to undertake. Tasks for all children are generally devised with an understanding of the cognitive demands; for pupils with EAL we need also to consider the language demands (sentence structures, unusual vocabulary) and plan for support to be given. Where classroom support for pupils with EAL is available, the planning should be done collaboratively (see Bourne and McPake (1991); NLS video (2002)). Attention needs to be given to ways of including and supporting all pupils. In planning for literacy sessions which include pupils with EAL, this may include:

- Consideration of pupils' prior experience
- Careful selection of texts (for example, which include particular English language structures/usage/vocabulary; which allow pupils to become familiar with the sounds, patterns and rhythms of English; which are accessible and encourage interaction)
- Preparing additional resources, props, visual support, word banks
- Planning for pre-teaching of elements of a text (to clarify the context/introduce new vocabulary)
- Deciding on how to involve children who are less confident in English (targeted questions; planned opportunities for them to offer contributions)
- Planning to model and scaffold tasks so that expectations are clear

- Opportunities for feedback, observation and assessment
- Deciding which teacher will lead different parts of the lesson.

The importance of talk

Initially, the most important strand of the English curriculum for those children new to English is speaking and listening. Classrooms where there are opportunities for children to talk (in all their languages), work collaboratively, discuss and present to others, will provide the greatest support for children with EAL who need to hear many models of fluent English and to be encouraged to participate. As the National Association for Language Development in the Curriculum (NALDIC) (2000) states:

> The active use of language provides opportunities for learners to be more conscious of their language use and to process language at a deeper level. It also brings home to both learner and teacher those aspects of language which will require attention. (p.15)

Drama, role play and storytelling are excellent contexts for talk. A year 6 teacher, looking for ways to encourage talk in his classroom, set up a storytelling project with the intention also of making links with the reception class in a neighbouring school. He began by discussing, with children in his class, stories they had heard at home, and some children volunteered to tell and record their stories either in English or in their first language. With the help of bilingual assistants, the non-English versions were accompanied by an English translation and the tapes sent to the reception class. Here the children listened avidly to the tapes and embarked upon their own storytelling. In the year 6 class, utilising the skills of the bilingual EAL support teacher and the classroom assistant, with whom the class teacher planned carefully, the project developed. Storytelling props (for example, model animals, cut out pictures, fruit and soft toys) were provided and three stories 'Hungry tiger and the clever monkey', 'The Zoo' and 'The Monkeys and the Hat-maker' were told and retold; the children told to each other and to all the adults. Eventually the stories were recorded in English and Panjabi (the home language of the majority of children in the class), written down and made into dual language books, illustrated by the children. The reception children, having themselves worked on 'The Monkeys and the Hat-maker' then visited the year 6 class and collaboratively told the story to them, using the props.

Evaluating the project, the class teacher said,' Probably the most positive part of the project was the increased status of talk in the classroom. The children were keen to talk about the stories to adults and to each other. They supported each other in telling the stories accurately, not leaving out any parts of the plot. Another positive aspect of the work was the collaboration between adults working in the classroom.

This partnership approach led to joint planning, small group activities and positive feedback. Equally the opportunity to work with a colleague from a neighbouring school provided a real context for the children's work. The fact that the tapes and the books were made in two languages raised the status of the children's home language and led to them sometimes choosing to tell a story in that language.'

The power of picture books

Written stories, especially picture books, can provide another powerful context for developing English. One of the richest sources of information about the English language and culture for pupils with EAL is the wealth of picture books available. There is a place for picture books which introduce aspects of British culture, the culture of the school and the traditional story heritage. In the realm of daily life in Britain author/illustrators like Shirley Hughes and Janet and Allan Ahlberg have a great deal to offer. The series of 'Alfie' stories (Hughes), for example, deal with universals of family life in a closely observed setting of domestic detail, while *Starting School* (Ahlbergs) shows the routines of the day in a realistic, multicultural classroom. A survey of the class's picture books will uncover many others with settings in domestic and community life which provide a rich source of information for children who are new to it. Equally, the many versions of traditional fairy stories should be a part of the classroom provision. This is not usually a problem in foundation stage and key stage 1 classrooms, but they are seen less frequently in key stage 2. It would be important to include them at this stage when there are older children, newly arrived in Britain. Versions of traditional stories from other cultures are often similar to the ones we know and if these are available (perhaps in languages in which children are already literate) it helps newcomers to draw parallels and make sense of the new versions they encounter.

We also need to include as wide a variety as possible of picture books with text in the languages known to the children. Even when children are not literate in another language, they are likely to have seen examples of writing in their community languages in homes and in the wider environment. Sometimes they will be familiar with other written scripts which have different conventions from English. It is important to recognise this experience and to demonstrate that the school values the linguistic diversity which is part of the children's experience. For those who are able to read already in another language it is essential to make provision for them to continue to read in that language while they are becoming fluent in English. Many literacy skills will be transferable and will continue to be developed in the first languages. It is not always easy to locate picture books in all the languages represented in schools, and there continues to be discussion about whether we should be seeking 'dual-text' books or 'parallel text' versions of the same book, where the text is translated and published as a separate book. *The Multilingual Resources for Children Project, Building Bridges* (1995) includes a very interesting discussion of many of the issues. Some dual-text books have been produced where the minority language seemed to be given lower status than English, but there are now many high quality ones where this is not so. Some books published by Mantra show clearly what is possible. For example, *All the Colours of the Earth* (Sheila Hamanaka) has a lyrical text and richly coloured illustrations and is available in a range of languages, with English. Another of their titles is *Savitri; A Tale of Ancient India* (Aaron Shepard and Vera Rosenberry), which tells the traditional story from the Mahabharata, with delicate illustration perfectly matched to the Indian setting. This is available in all the Indian languages, with English. Hardback picture books of this quality can be enjoyed by children's families in their heritage language and, even if family members do not read English, the story can be talked about when it is shared at home.

One of the most important contributions made by picture books to developing knowledge of English, as well as literacy skills, is the real linguistic support they give to those new to English and new to literacy. Here we should be seeking books with settings all children will recognise, with language which is memorable and which uses the real linguistic structures of English, rather than controlled vocabulary (whether that be 'key words' or phonically regular words) which can often be stilted and artificial. *We're Going on a Bear Hunt* (Rosen and Oxenbury) is an example of a picture book with rhythmic, repetitive text and sound effects to describe the different kinds of movement. Helen Oxenbury's wonderful illustrations capture the movements, both fast and slow, the excitement and apprehension of the bear hunters, again providing visual support for the words of the text. Whilst the readers are enjoying the story, the text provides chunks of understandable language which have a natural structure – 'What a beautiful day.' 'We're not scared.' 'We can't go over it. We can't go under it. Oh no! We've got to go through it.' By the time the story has been read and re-read several times, these structures will have become internalised. *Peace at Last* (Murphy) has the same memorable language structures. Mr Bear's 'Oh no! I can't stand this' became a much used exclamation in one multilingual reception classroom, whenever children were frustrated, bored, or unwilling to tidy up! It was used equally accurately by children who were monolingual and children using English as an additional language. The language lessons provided by books like these are incidental in the process of learning to read.

Many picture books are most suitable for older children. These are not simple books for the very young; though the actual text in many is very straightforward, the ideas, themes and topics are appropriate for older readers. The idea that 'picture books are for babies' – a comment often made by children in key stage 2 – is one which teachers will need to demonstrate is untrue. There are many picture books in which there are subjects to challenge older readers but with text which a beginner in English would be able to read; these are a valuable resource for the less fluent monolingual reader as well as for those with English as an additional language, for whom they should be available at the end of key stage 2 and beyond. Some authors and illustrators have created particularly appropriate books for this stage. Look, for example, at all the work of Anthony Browne, the comic strip formats of Philippe Dupasquier, the work of Michael Foreman, the illustration of Charles Keeping for many quite demanding texts, the complex and thought-provoking issues tackled by Maurice Sendak, the unusual narrative structures used by John Burningham. (For a fuller discussion of picture books for children learning English as an Additional Language, see Laycock (1998).)

Conclusion

The needs of children with English as an additional language will always be a major concern in teaching the English curriculum, but we need to be aware of these and the support needed in all areas. Although teaching about the English language is most likely to be located in literacy sessions, we still need to be aware of the language demands in the rest of the curriculum. The National Association for Language Development in the Curriculum (NALDIC) proposes an excellent set of principles which underpin good practice for pupils learning EAL:

- Activating prior knowledge; prior knowledge of content and language plays a major role in helping to make second language input comprehensible.
- The provision of a rich contextual background to make the input comprehensible.
- Actively encouraging comprehensible output.
- Drawing the learner's attention to the relationship between form and function; making key grammatical elements explicit.
- Developing learner independence – through the selection of planned activities.

These principles are fully explained and developed in NALDIC's Working Paper 5; *The Distinctiveness of EAL: A Cross Curriculum Discipline* (2000) and form a sound foundation for working with children with EAL in every literate classroom.

References

Ahlberg, J. and Ahlberg, A. (1988) *Starting School.* London: Viking/Kestrel.

Bourne, J. and McPake, J. (1991) *Partnership Teaching.* London: NFER/DES.

Cline, T. and Frederickson, N. (1994) *Progress in Curriculum Related Assessment for Bilingual Pupils.* Clevedon: Multilingual Matters.

Collier, V. (1987) 'Age and rate of acquisition of second language for academic purposes.' *TESOL Quarterly*, 21, 617–41.

Collier, V. and Thomas, W. (1997) 'School effectiveness for language minority students.' Paper presented at the Symposium of the Intercultural Project. London May 1997.

Cummins, J. (1979) 'Cognitive/academic language proficiency, linguistic interdependence, the optimum age question and some other matters.' Working Papers on Bilingualism, No 19, 121–9.

Cummins, J. (1984) *Bilingualism and Special Education: Issues in Assessment and Pedagogy.* Clevedon: Multilingual Matters.

DfES (1999) *National Curriculum Handbook for Primary Teachers in England and Wales.* London: Qualifications and Curriculum Authority (QCA).

DfES (1998) *The National Literacy Strategy Framework for Teaching.* London: DfES.

DfES (2002 revised edition) *The National Literacy Strategy. Supporting Pupils Learning English as an Additional Language.* London: DfES.

Edwards, V. (1996) *The Other Languages. A Guide to Multilingual Classrooms.* Reading: Reading and Language Information Centre.

Edwards,V. (1998) *The Power of Babel. Teaching and Learning in Multilingual Classrooms.* Stoke on Trent: Trentham Books.

Hall, D. (1995) *Assessing the Needs of Bilingual Pupils. Living in Two Languages.* London: David Fulton.

Hamanaka, H. (1996) (Yoruba/English text) *All the Colours of the Earth.* London: Mantra.

Laycock, L. (1998) 'A Way into a new language and culture' in *What's in the Picture?* J. Evans (ed.) London: Paul Chapman.

Minns, H. (1990) *Read It To Me Now.* London: Virago.

Multilingual Resources for Children Project (1995) *Building Bridges; Multilingual Resources for Children.* Clevedon: Multilingual Matters.

Murphy, J. (1980) *Peace At Last.* London: Macmillan.

NALDIC (2000) Working paper 5, *The Distinctiveness of EAL: A Cross Curriculum Discipline.* Watford: NALDIC.

Rosen, M. and Oxenbury, H. (1989) *We're Going on a Bear Hunt.* London: Walker Books.

Shepard, A. and Rosenberry, V. (1997) (Panjabi/English text) *Savitri: A Tale of Ancient India.* London: Mantra.

Whitehead, M. (2002) (2nd edn) *Developing Language and Literacy with Young Children.* London: Paul Chapman.

The role of drama in the literate classroom

Suzi Clipson-Boyles

Introduction

The standards of children's reading and writing have always been high on the agendas of schools and governments. Most parents also automatically expect their children to become literate. In the past, these concerns have been predominantly concerned with acquisition, achievement and literature (Street 1994) and have ignored the fact that literacy practices in our society reach far beyond the reading and writing of fiction. To a certain extent, the National Literacy Strategy (DfEE 1998) addressed this through the extensive inclusion of a range of non-fiction texts as well as ensuring a variety of fiction genres. Likewise, more recently, the importance of speaking and listening has been revisited and reintroduced more prominently into the curriculum (DfES 2003a). The importance of early oracy activities, particularly for boys, and their influence on later reading development, is well documented (for example, Wragg *et al.* 1998; CCEA 1999; Clipson-Boyles 2000). Not only are speaking and listening an integral part of thinking and learning, they also feed, and are fed by, the processes of reading and writing.

The literate classroom should aim to reflect relevant literacies from the outside world, so that children have opportunities to encounter, use and create the printed word in different ways for a wide range of purposes and audiences. Just consider the countless examples and variety of the written word out there! A journey on the underground, a visit to the shops, a tour around a farmyard, TV programmes, food in our kitchens – all will reveal vast varieties of print on instructions, labels, logos, advertisements, packaging, and so on. It is also important to acknowledge children's own literacies, and those of their cultures and communities. This helps to develop their own experiences into wider realms (Heath 1993) so that their existing deeper levels of knowledge, skills and identities are extended and developed rather than ignored.

Recognising this vast prominence of print and other semiotic systems is an important step towards creating an effective language environment in the primary school. Likewise, providing opportunities for speaking and listening within carefully planned contexts can enrich children's learning and understanding of reading and writing. Children need a variety of interactive learning experiences through which they can develop their knowledge, skills and understanding, and make well-informed choices and decisions. This approach is more likely to lead to high achievement in literacy than decontextualised exercises and narrow models of 'knowledge transmission' in which children are expected to adopt imposed practices that are totally alien to themselves and their world.

Drama is an ideal means of providing experiences that contribute towards meaningful models of language development and learning. It can be used in many ways to offer encounters with a wide range of language systems and genres, as well as the obvious speaking and listening. These can provide opportunities to learn skills, to provide contexts within which those skills can be practised, and to empower children as decision makers and users of language and literacy. However, before examining actual examples of how this might happen, let us look more generally, first of all, at the background of drama in the primary curriculum.

Drama in the primary curriculum

The twentieth century's two most significant education acts have each had a powerful impact upon drama in primary education. The first, in 1944, set in motion a postwar enthusiasm for self-expression that was harnessed in the 1950s and continued to develop into an experiential approach to learning during the 1960s and 1970s. The second, in 1988, introduced a National Curriculum that resulted in virtually eliminating drama from primary schools.

However, in the mid-1990s, drama was embedded firmly into the revised order for English (DfEE 1995) and became the focus for scrutiny by Ofsted inspections. This led to a slow but steady revival after a decade of virtual extinction. As with most spiral changes, it emerged in a newly adapted form that aimed to resolve past conflicts between those who have seen drama as a purely experiential child-centred activity, never repeated or rehearsed, and those who insist that theatre arts and performance should be included as a distinct curriculum subject in the education of young children (Clipson-Boyles 1997). Such contrasting views have not always been helpful to the cause of primary drama, often being perceived as opposite, and usually irreconcilable, points on a spectrum as illustrated below.

The primary drama spectrum

Educational drama was about providing experiences for children through which they could develop ideas and understanding of themselves and their worlds, both real

Educational drama ←——————————————————————→ Performance drama

child centred   audience centred

spontaneous   planned

unrepeated   rehearsed

process oriented   product orientated

FIGURE 16.1 The primary drama spectrum

and imagined. The process was the all-important feature. Performance drama, on the other hand was seen as the development of theatre skills for the presentation of an end product and was centred exclusively within the performing arts (see Figure 16.1).

Rather than continuing to regard these features as two extremes, the 1990s' approach identified them as complementary, and sometimes interwoven, features of a drama curriculum. Just as experiential drama could sometimes feed into performance activities (for example, an improvisation might be developed into a scripted scene to show to an audience of parents in assembly), so could perform-ance skills and knowledge of theatre arts contribute towards children's experiential learning (for example, sustaining a role during hotseating). In this way, the true richness and diversity of primary drama became recognised and employed for its potential impact upon children's learning and development – but only by a small minority of brave teachers! The demands of an over-packed curriculum meant that 'luxury subjects' such as drama remained marginalised.

However, currently yet another sea-change is taking place. The introduction of a comprehensive national approach to speaking and listening mentioned earlier (DfES 2003a), alongside a call for more creative approaches to the primary curriculum (DfES 2003b), means that drama is now being recognised as far more than a luxury! Teachers are beginning to see for themselves that drama can have a powerful impact on children's learning across the curriculum, not least in developing their literacy skills.

Drama is becoming a vital tool in the literate classroom. But there is no single assumed way of teaching drama. Instead there are many different ways of working, so let us now take a look at the choices of drama modes available to teachers when planning for a literate classroom.

Modes of drama

Drama need not always happen with the whole class at the same time, and it does not always require a large space. A five-minute improvised interview situation with six children in pairs as preparation for writing an imaginary report is just as much a part of the drama curriculum as a full-scale presentation of scenes from 1940s Britain. Drama can happen using:

- Different group sizes
- Different group compositions
- Different time spans
- Different spaces
- Different planned outcomes
- Different levels of teacher input
- Different styles of teaching

Clearly it is beyond the scope of this chapter to provide a fully comprehensive guide to planning drama. This can be found in more detailed specialist drama books (see Clipson-Boyles 1998). However, it is important that you begin to develop an awareness of the main drama modes available to your teaching repertoire. Table 16.1 summarises the most commonly used teaching approaches with examples of how these might be used in the development of literacy.

TABLE 16.1 Commonly used teaching approaches in developing literacy through drama

Approach	Description	Example for the literate classroom
Role play areas	Designated area of the classroom with props, costumes, etc, to encourage role play	Using telephone directories and catalogues, form filling and phone messages
Dynamic duos	Improvisations of interviews, telephone conversations and other work in pairs	Interviewing a character from a story
Hotseating	Character in role (either teacher or child) to be questioned by class	Children research a history topic and prepare questions for a 'time traveller' (possibly teacher in role)
Writer in role	Writing activity taking place in an imagined situation, writing from the perspective of another person	Writing as a politician to explain the plans for a local park
Reader in role	Reading activity taking place in an imagined situation, writing from the perspective of another person	Spontaneous improvisation of response to a letter that the teacher provides (eg news of a competition prize)
Guided action	Children improvise to teacher running commentary	Exploring a desert island after a shipwreck that may lead to writing a message in a bottle
Spontaneous improvisation	Exploring a situation without any forward planning	Discovering that the house has been burgled: make lists of stolen items, write a statement

TABLE 16.1 Continued

Approach	Description	Example for the literate classroom
Reconstructed improvisation	Revisiting a spontaneous improvisation to reshape it for presentation to others	An alternative ending to a particular chapter from a story
Simulation	Creating a pretend experience within which the children will role play and improvise, often discussed extensively beforehand	Recreating an event after research in non-fiction, CD ROMs, etc.
Script work	Writing scripts after improvisation or from stories	Reading a newspaper story, then writing a script to present certain events from the story
Teacher in role	Can be used in different situations, eg to answer questions from the children, to share a problem for them to help solve, to participate in guided action, improvisation, simulation, etc	Teacher in role as parent of a character from a story, asking the children for advice about how to deal with the character's situation
Tableau	Create a still scene of characters	Presenting three scenes that sum up the action or atmospheres from a story or poem
Mime	Representing through movement and expression, but no speech	Creating a nursery rhyme for others to watch and guess
Radio	A range of programmes can be explored, helping children focus on expression and fluency	Rewrite news items from the paper to be read aloud, interviews and language, comments about the report
Video	Using models from film and television to create videoed presentations	Making an advertisement for an invented product
Freeze frame	Still scene that can happen in the middle of action (to be discussed) or that comes to life after a countdown to action	A scene from fiction that comes to life as the characters
Puppets	A vast range, from sticks with a cardboard face to string puppets, can be used to retell stories and create new ones	Puppet characters from known books
Masks	Helps the less confident to take on another character	Used especially for retelling the Greek myths, etc
Dance drama	Movement with sound presenting story or poetry	Composing sounds based on the moods of a piece of writing
Performance	Preparing drama for an audience	Exploring a play, eg *A Midsummer Night's Dream*, improvising scenes, using contemporary language with some of the original vocabulary, presenting a rehearsed summary version of the play

Drama offers contexts for learning that could not normally be part of an everyday classroom environment. It can transport children through time, across seas, into space and into the worlds of fantasy. This is a wonderful resource for teachers to have at their fingertips! In addition, drama can offer much to the shaping and development of collaborative and social skills. High motivation, longer periods on task, and the more effective retention of learning are also positive outcomes of working with drama.

Despite the temptation to expand on all these wonderful advantages of drama in the primary curriculum, we are looking specifically in this chapter at the role of drama in relation to language and literacy. Therefore, we shall now go on to examine how drama can provide multiple purposes for reading, writing, speaking and listening. We shall also consider briefly the place of theatre arts and drama within the agendas of the literate classroom.

Teaching language and literacy through drama

The National Literacy Strategy (NLS) states that drama has an important role to play in developing outcomes from its reading objectives and many of the literacy activities required by the NLS can be supported and enhanced by drama (DfEE 1998).

Drama has three main parts to play in the development of language and literacy:

- To provide frameworks for learning about, using and discussing language as required by the curriculum for English and the NLS
- To provide language learning contexts in other subject areas
- To develop communication and performance and critical appreciation skills, within theatre arts.

Each of these should encompass an integrated approach to language learning, where speaking, listening, reading and writing are interlinked in useful and meaningful ways. Here are some examples.

- Experiences as stimuli for writing and/or reading, for example, improvised interviews between reporter and victim of a burglary, leading to report writing
- Play contexts for practising skills in role, for example, travel agent's role play area, reading brochures and completing forms
- Simulation of situations requiring reading and/or writing, for example, research from non-fiction before preparing an air-raid experience
- Developing spoken language as a starting point for writing, for example, improvisations of a scene to be developed into a script for others
- Providing a context for reading and/or performing aloud, for example, reading a poem while others mime

- Reading and interpreting play scripts, for example, time-limited task to interpret stage directions and then a 'perform' workshop session, reading from the text, to the rest of the class, with movement
- Comparing language in different situations, for example, presenting a short soap opera extract in a different genre

Drama and literature

The place of literature in the foundation stage and primary education is not just about teaching children to read stories and poetry independently. It should also involve discussion, critical listening and a range of reading and writing experiences. The exploration and analysis of literature and poetry can be assisted enormously by drama. Interactive and experiential activities can offer real opportunities for burrowing beneath the surface features of texts and beyond. Not only does this help children to develop as active and critical readers, but also it deepens their knowledge of the workings of texts and their authors that they can, in turn, bring to their own writing. Here are three examples.

Foundation stage: 'Goldilocks and the Three Bears'

There are many ways to help the children become familiar with a story. Reading from a book includes pictures, but telling in your own words can more readily include mime and actions. Adding artefacts to your home corner (redesigned for a fortnight as the three bears' cottage) can take the story into new contexts. For example, Goldilocks may leave gifts or notes for the bears to 'find'. She may leave instructions for tasks ('It is my birthday tomorrow. Please can we have a party?'). New characters could be introduced into the play such as Goldilocks's mother, sister, father, a zoo keeper hunting for bears, and so on! Another wonderful way to extend children's skills of inference and critical analysis is through hotseating. For instance, if you role play Goldilocks, they can ask you questions about your experience.

Key stage 1: *The Snow Maze* by Jan Mark (1993)

Having read the first three chapters and discussed the rhyming taunts of the children ('Joe's mad. Joe's sad. Joe's bad. Mazy, crazy, lazy Joe.', and so on), possibly writing these on to a flip chart and asking children to change the onsets, the activity then turns to an examination of character motivation. Explain to the children that you will pretend to be Joe and they should be kind children, helping him to solve his problem with the unpleasant children in the story. Stress that you want them to ask Joe as many questions as possible and then to try to help him to solve his problem. Using a prop or costume to differentiate between in role and out of role (for example, a baseball cap or an anorak), leave the area and return in role (see hotseating, in the previous section). Remember that you can redirect the questioning if it is not sufficiently deep, for example, 'How do you think I felt when I hid under the table?' 'What do you think I should do with the magic key?' When the hotseating has reached a conclusion, return to normal and discuss the outcomes.

Key stage 2: *The Iron Man* by Ted Hughes (1986)

Read Chapter 1 of *The Iron Man* to the whole class. Discuss the author's use of language, are in particular the atmosphere of the scene and the implied threat that is created by the actions of the Iron Man. Also discuss why the author might have chosen to include the interactions with the gulls (rather than humans) at this point in the book. Next, divide the class into six groups and give each a different role and information relating to that role. Examples might include Ministry of Defence workers who wish to destroy the Iron Man, scientists, local residents, and so on. Having set up the classroom as a meeting room (probably all the children on chairs in a square around the edges of the room), establish signals for in role and out of role, and let the meeting commence to discuss what should be done about the Iron Man. You will also need to select an appropriate child to chair the meeting. You will be in role of Hogarth, using the opening paragraphs of Chapter 2 of *The Iron Man* to guide you about your sighting of the Iron Man. After the role play, ask the children for their views on what events they think would take the story forward in an interesting way.

Drama, theatre arts and the literate classroom

It is perfectly appropriate to include a theatre arts strand within the English curriculum for the following reasons:

- Performance activities can include relevant oracy skills.
- Performance appraisal can include relevant critical skills.
- Reading and writing scripts are valuable language activities that should be placed in a practical drama context.
- Reading and watching the work of professional playwrights are important parts of the literature curriculum.
- Theatres also offer a range of other texts (for example, programmes, posters, reviews) that can be used in the classroom.

Providing children with opportunities to watch and critically appraise the performances of others can offer models of language that they can emulate in their own work. Likewise, theatre visits are also valuable tools for developing the boundaries of critical response.

Drama, non-fiction and real world texts

Fiction, poetry and drama texts are an important part of the cultural and multicultural past and present. However, these represent only a proportion of texts with which adults engage in their daily lives. It is important that the literate classroom reflects this, both in the range of texts available to the children and in the variety of genres within which they are expected to write. Drama offers contexts for learning by creating situations to give their writing a real purpose. The NLS prescribes a broad range of genres in addition to fiction and poetry. Table 16.2 shows some examples of how such texts might be integrated into work beyond the literacy hour using drama.

TABLE 16.2 Drama and the use of non-fiction

Year	Term	Text	Drama activity
Foundation		Recipe	Show them a recipe in book. Mime actions: getting things out of cupboards, measuring, weighing, beating etc
R		Simple recounts	Visit to the moon (whole class in hall) followed by recording together on white board of events chronologically
1	1	Signs, lists, labels	Children creating an office in role play area
2	1	Explanations	Whole-class guided action of an event; write an explanation of each section on a frame chart using *because* as the main conjunction
3	1	Non-chronological reports	Five-minute dynamic duos as parents and teachers discussing pupils; follow-up writing of report writing about their best friend
4	1	Instructions	Role play as safety officers in a supermarket; brainstorming the dangers; designing safety posters for staff and customers
5	1	News reports	Groups of five to create special report television news feature on selected event (improvise, reshape, script, perform or video)
6	1	Diary	Follow-up writing to an improvisation such as the evacuation of a village in the path of a volcano

As with all good teaching, it is important to plan areas of focus when using drama. The teaching points and intended learning outcomes should be made explicit in prepared plans and should be clear to the children as well as the teacher!

Multiple literacies and drama

The wide variety of uses for print in our society, mentioned briefly at the start of this chapter, can differ in five essential ways:

1 Purpose or function

2 Intended audience

3 Text format (outer framework)

4 Vocabulary and construction (inner content)

5 Contexts in which they are used

In order to consider the importance of extending literacy and language so that the multiple literacies of society are included, it can be helpful to look more closely at texts and contexts that are not always featured in the traditional curricula for teaching English:

- Community languages: scenes with translations and/or discussions about language
- Comics: freeze-frame strip cartoons followed by writing speech bubbles
- Television programmes: exploring dialects in soap operas
- Shops: role play corners with associated writing activities
- Cartoons: using as model for personifying different animals
- Advertising: look at examples, then design and sell a product
- Home life: home corner with reading and writing opportunities
- Work places: improvisations and role play with real texts and writing tasks
- Street language: thematic rap as part of performance

Drama across and beyond the curriculum

Such planning should also take place in other subject areas. The teaching of language and literacy is not limited to the curriculum for English, and the literate classroom is one in which the teacher does not merely build on chance language encounters but proactively plans language and literacy learning into other curriculum areas. Cross-curricular issues such as gender, multiculturalism, citizenship and health education can also generate useful contexts for language and literacy through drama.

Conclusion

Literacy encompasses more than mere technical approaches to deciphering and creating codes. Literacy consists of a complex set of practices that have social and cultural implications. This includes a vast range of genres, purposes and audiences, and is inextricably linked to speaking and listening. Acknowledging this rich and diverse nature of literacy, and the complex nature of communication, can assist teachers in providing effective contexts for learning in which children not only develop strong skills and high levels of achievement but also become discerning and confident users of multiple literacy practices.

Drama is an excellent way of providing such contexts. It offers a variety of approaches that can be adapted according to the teaching and learning required. It is a pedagogy that should be part of every primary teacher's repertoire, and the high levels of motivation from children observed during drama activities can only serve to confirm this! If a classroom is to be truly literate, drama should be an integral part of its total curriculum.

References

CCEA (1999) *Focus on Boys*. Belfast: Council for Curriculum, Examinations and Assessment.

Clipson-Boyles, S. (1997) 'Drama', in *Implementing the Primary Curriculum. A Teacher's Guide*, Ashcroft and Palacio (eds). London: Falmer Press.

Clipson-Boyles, S. (1998) *Drama in Primary English Teaching*. London: David Fulton.

Clipson-Boyles, S. (2000) 'Level 1 readers in year 3'. Oxford Brookes University: doctoral thesis, page 144.

DfEE (1995) *Programmes of Study for English*. London: HMSO.

DfEE (1998) *The National Literacy Strategy*. London: HMSO.

DfES (2003a) *Speaking, Listening, Learning: Working With Children in Key Stages 1 and 2*. London, DfES.

DfES (2003b) *Excellence and Enjoyment. A Strategy for Primary Schools*. London: DfES.

Heath, S. B. (1993) 'The madness of reading and writing ethnography'. *Anthropology and Education Quarterly*, 24, 3, 256–68.

Hughes, T. (1986) *The Iron Man*. London: Faber and Faber.

Mark, J. (1993) *The Snow Maze*. London: Walker Books.

Street, B. (1994) 'What is meant by social literacies?' *Language and Education*, 8, 1–2, 9–17.

Wragg, T. *et al.* (1998) *Improving Literacy in the Primary School*. London: Routledge.

Opening the wardrobe of voices: standard English and language variation at key stage 2

Michael Lockwood

Introduction

I can still remember the baffled amusement with which my first teaching group heard me call them my 'class', ask them not to go on the 'grass' at break time and tell them that our topic was going to be 'castles'. They were pupils in a middle school in the south of England. I was a new teacher born and educated, a first-generation grammar school boy, in West Yorkshire. University and training in the south had modified my Yorkshire accent, but the tell-tale vowel sounds still resounded in these words and others such as 'mud', 'blood' and 'bath'! Embarrassment and amusement soon turned to fascination with the phenomenon of language variety for all of us. This chapter is about ways that I have devised of sharing that continuing fascination with the diversity of language with key stage 2 children, in the light of national developments in this area of the English curriculum over the past 20 years. I begin by briefly reviewing some of these developments before moving on to describe and evaluate a particular language project I carried out with year 5 children.

Background

The revival of interest in what the National Curriculum (NC) calls 'language study' probably began with an HMI discussion paper *Curriculum Matters 1* (Department of Education and Science [DES] 1984), which proposed objectives for children's 'learning about language' at 11 and 16. The heated debate amongst teachers initiated by this document, expressed in *Responses to Curriculum Matters* (DES 1986), led to an enquiry into the teaching of English language which produced the Kingman Report (DES 1988). In this report the phrase 'knowledge about language' (KAL) was first used and a broad model of language proposed to 'inform professional discussion', part of which was concerned with language variety in terms of place, time, social grouping and context.

The Cox Report (DES 1989: paras. 6.16–6.21) incorporated Kingman's recommendations into the NC, defining KAL as including the areas of 'language variation according to situation, purpose, language mode, regional or social group... [and] language variation across time'. Like the Kingman Report, it paid particular attention to the subject of standard English and how to teach it. The ill-fated Language in the National Curriculum (LINC) project took as its main concern this 'language variation' strand and produced valuable professional development materials at both local and national level. These materials, however, were never made available to classroom teachers, although some have since been published commercially (see, for example, Bain *et al.* (1992)). My own research at the time suggested that primary teachers remained unsure of what KAL was and urgently needed training and support in its classroom applications (Lockwood 1995).

The change in the political climate that led to the suppression of the LINC materials resulted in the first revision of the NC orders in 1995, and the replacement of KAL with 'Standard English and Language Study'. The authors of this 'slimmed down' NC had wanted to use the title 'Language Study and Standard English' for this section of the programmes of study and protested at these and other editorial interventions that gave prominence to standard English (Blackburne 1994). The dispute over wording can be seen as part of a wider debate: should the use and understanding of standard English be set within the critical and reflective context of language study, including the wider study of language variety, or should the purpose of language study be to increase and improve children's use of standard English in speech and writing? The activities described below were designed and taught with the former view strongly in mind: that increasing children's awareness of the phenomenon of language variation, in terms of register, accent, dialect and standard English, was the most effective way of developing their own repertoire of spoken and written varieties.

In the current version of the NC, as revised for a second time in 1999, the headings 'standard English', 'language variation' and 'language structure' are used throughout the document for the paragraphs which are intended to 'provide a coherent basis for language study'. The paragraphs on standard English are again placed before those on language variation, even though the latter also include variation 'between standard and dialect forms' (Department for Education and Employment [DfEE] 1999: 51). The National Literacy Strategy [NLS] (DfEE 1998) introduces the terms 'standard English' and 'dialect' only in years 5 and 6, and in the context of written language. However, it does provide clear definitions of these terms, which are lacking in the NC. In the NLS glossary, standard English is defined as: 'the variety of English used in public communication, particularly in writing...the form taught in schools and used by educated speakers. It is not limited to a particular region and can be spoken with any accent.' Dialect is defined as: 'a variety of language used in a particular area and which is distinguished by certain features of grammar and vocabulary', and accent, which is in the glossary but not mentioned anywhere in the NLS objectives, is described as: 'features of pronunciation which vary according to the speaker's regional and social origin'.

The project

The project described here meets the requirement in the present NC, under the heading of 'language variation' at KS2, that 'pupils should be taught about how language varies: according to context and purpose, between standard and dialect forms, between spoken and written forms' (DfEE 1999: 51). It could also be used to meet year 5 NLS sentence level objectives such as:

- Term 1, sentence level 2: to understand the basic conventions of standard English and consider when and why standard English is used
- Term 2, sentence level 6: to be aware of the differences between spoken and written language
- Term 3, word level 9: to understand how words vary across dialects
- Term 3, word level 13: to compile your own class/group dictionary using personally written definitions, for example, of slang, technical terms

The activities were carried out with mixed ability groups of pupils, with an equal number of boys and girls, drawn from two parallel year 5 classes (9–10-year-olds) in a junior school. The school had an English language programme based on the use of commercial schemes, including *Mind Your Language* (Palmer and Brinton 1988) and *Exploring Language* (Lutrario 1993). The school policy document acknowledged that:

> ...recent research indicates that 'active processing' is the most effective way of learning – opportunities for discussing, investigating and purposefully manipulating language should be provided. Using language knowledge in real situations will help to consolidate concepts introduced...

Accent, dialect and standard English

I began by sharing with the group poems that highlighted features of accent and dialect. We read the anonymous poem (Palmer 1994) beginning:

> A muvver was barfin' 'er biby one night,
> The youngest of ten and a tiny young mite

and discussed the Cockney pronunciation suggested by the spelling. The discussion widened to include the children's experience of other accents. Working in pairs, the children took a few lines each from the poem and 'translated' them into conventional spelling or 'normal writing'. There were few difficulties with this (apart from the occasional misspelling) and the only non-standard feature not 'translated' was the one element of dialect grammar in the poem which was retained as: 'Your baby has fell down the plug-hole'. The group then re-read the poem using the conventional spellings in their own accents and we discussed the differences. I followed this with a slightly exaggerated reading of the poem in Received Pronunciation, or 'a posh accent' as the group described it, and we talked about how this affected the humour of the poem. The discussion moved on to consider the concept of standard English as a variety of language used in almost all writing, except where the writer wanted to suggest a particular accent, as in the poem.

I made a point of establishing that standard English could actually be spoken in any accent, not just Received Pronunciation, but that, when we used it, we normally modified our local accent, made it less 'broad', as with my own original Yorkshire accent.

The second poem read was 'English cousin comes to Scotland' by Jackie Kay (1992):

> I got skelped, because I screamed when a skelf
> went into my pinky finger: OUCH, loud.
> And ma ma dropped her best bit of china.
> It wis sore, so it wis, so it wis.

The group initially found the dialect words present this time, in addition to accent features, difficult to grasp. However, investigation of our own experiences of dialect words (for example, for 'little finger', 'mother', 'splinter' and 'smacked') resolved this and these dialect words became a feature of the work the children recalled frequently (especially 'pinky'!). The use of regional dialect words was related in discussion to the concept of a standard variety, which in speech and writing used only words understood nationally. We talked about the reasons for regional variations and the value that they had. The poems were read aloud in a variety of ways and recorded on to audio tape. Other poems used in a similar way to raise awareness and generate discussion of accent, dialect and standard English were 'Footy Poem' (McGough and Rosen 1979) and 'Wha Me Mudder Do' (Nichols 1988).

Register

From using poetry texts to investigate language variety, I moved on to exploring the children's own linguistic repertoires. We began by considering register, the way that we talk slightly differently to different people at different times about different things. After some initial role playing using a toy mobile phone, when the group had to guess to whom I was speaking, I asked the children as a group to brainstorm on to a large sheet of card all the occasions during a typical week when they were aware of using 'different voices'. With a little prompting, they came up with a spectrum of situations ranging from 'speaking to the head teacher' to 'talking to my friends in the playground'. Some of the situations were briefly role played, as far as time allowed, and we discussed how and why we changed the way that we spoke at different times. The concept of register was related in discussion to the forms of language variation explored earlier, accent, dialect and standard English.

I then introduced the metaphor of 'a wardrobe of voices' to provide the children with an accessible analogy for their experience of linguistic variation. I explained that we all wear different clothes to suit different occasions. Some people have larger wardrobes than others, but we all have a range of clothing from casual to formal. Similarly with language, we all have different varieties which we use at different times and our range changes as we develop, some varieties being added and some lost. There are fashions in words just as in dress!

Next I asked the children to make a plan of their wardrobe, either actual or imaginary. I provided a design of an empty wardrobe with a rail, on which, at one end, they could draw old clothes for playing in with friends, then casual clothes for everyday use, then towards the other end, smart outfits for parties and perhaps some 'best clothes' for special occasions. I asked them to decide where school uniform might be fitted in. Any other kinds of clothes that children wanted to include (for example, football tops) could be fitted somewhere on the rail too. When the wardrobes were completed – in some detail! – the children improvised situations where they might wear the different styles of clothing (I was careful to point out that it was the situations, and not usually the actual clothes themselves, which triggered our selection of language styles).

We moved on next to consider explicitly the idea of each of us having a wardrobe of voices as well as of clothing: casual ways of speaking when we are with close friends, more formal ways on special occasions, and a mixture in between. We related this repertoire to the use of regional accents, dialects and spoken standard English mentioned previously, and discussed the additional linguistic range of bilingual speakers. The children then introduced a range of different voices into their wardrobes, as in this example, and later role-played 'wearing' them (Figure 17.1).

Slang

In the final part of the project, we looked at the informal end of the linguistic wardrobe and explored slang. This was described as a variety of spoken language which uses special words like a dialect but changes quickly over time and is

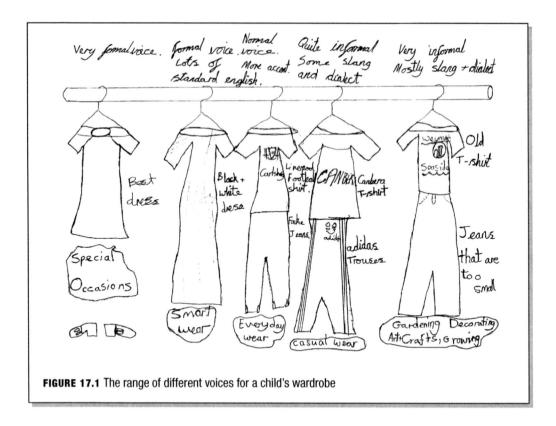

Very formal voice. Formal voice. Normal voice. Quite informal Some slang and dialect. Very informal Mostly slang + dialect

Lots of standard english. More accent.

Best dress

Black + white dress

Carlsberg

Liverpool Football shirt.

CFMBK Canberra T-shirt

Fake Jeans

adidas

adidas Trousers

Weymouth Seaside Old T-shirt

Jeans that are too small

Special Occasions

Smart wear

Everyday wear

Casual wear

Gardening Decorating Art+Crafts, Growing

FIGURE 17.1 The range of different voices for a child's wardrobe

associated less with places than with particular social groups, especially young people. Again we began with poetry, an appropriate choice since slang has been described (by G.K. Chesterton) as: 'The stream of poetry which is continually flowing'. First we shared Michael Rosen's poem (Rosen 1974: 22–3) about a new boy trying to join in with an unfamiliar playground game, beginning:

> If one is one
> if two is two
> I'm Jack Straw
> what are you?

We discussed how playground games, chants and dips could all vary significantly between local schools, as well as ones in other parts of the country. Then we read and discussed the playground language in part of Allan Ahlberg's *Heard it in the Playground* (1989: 98):

> Heard it in the playground
> Quality, quality
> Heard it in the playground
> Skill, skill, skill
> Ace, nice, neat.

I asked the children to brainstorm any words, phrases or sayings that they had heard in their playground, either connected with games or not. The children worked in smaller groups of boys and girls, to see whether there were any differences in their choices (the biggest difference was in quantity, the girls' group providing far more examples!). Swear words were explicitly excluded, as being a separate category from playground slang. Working from the amalgamated brainstorm sheets, the children then worked individually to draft dictionary entries for words that they could define, having first looked at classroom dictionaries for a model to follow. Some entries new to me were the following:

- Crocodile (noun) a person who is chasing after people.
- Durbrain (noun) a person who is a bit stupid.
- Fantastico (noun) a person who is nice or brainy; also fantastico (adjective): for example, 'You're fantastico.'
- Limo (noun) a fast ball game of skill.
- Posthanger (noun) a cheater in the game of 40,40; also posthang (verb): for example, 'He's posthanging!'
- Radical (adjective) totally cool (see Well cool).
- Well cool (adjective) really, really decent.

The drafts were revised and finally 'published', using word processing, in the form of a guide for new pupils.

Evaluation

As part of the assessment of the children's work during the project, I asked them to write a short description of what they thought that they had learnt. Figure 17.2 shows the description given by one girl.

At the end of the activities, I also gave the groups who had worked with me a diagnostic sheet to complete. I hoped that this would give me some additional insight into both their implicit awareness of standard English and their explicit knowledge of terminology, although it was not intended to measure all the learning outcomes of the activities. The sheet, partly adapted from Palmer (1994), is shown in Figure 17.3.

I also asked the remainder of the children in the two parallel classes, who had not worked on the project, to complete the diagnostic sheet. Comparison of the two groups of pupils revealed a slightly increased score by the project group in the first part of the diagnostic sheet, consisting of seven sentences dealing with implicit awareness of standard English (an average score of 37 per cent recognition of non-standard features, compared with 32 per cent). This, of course, could be accounted

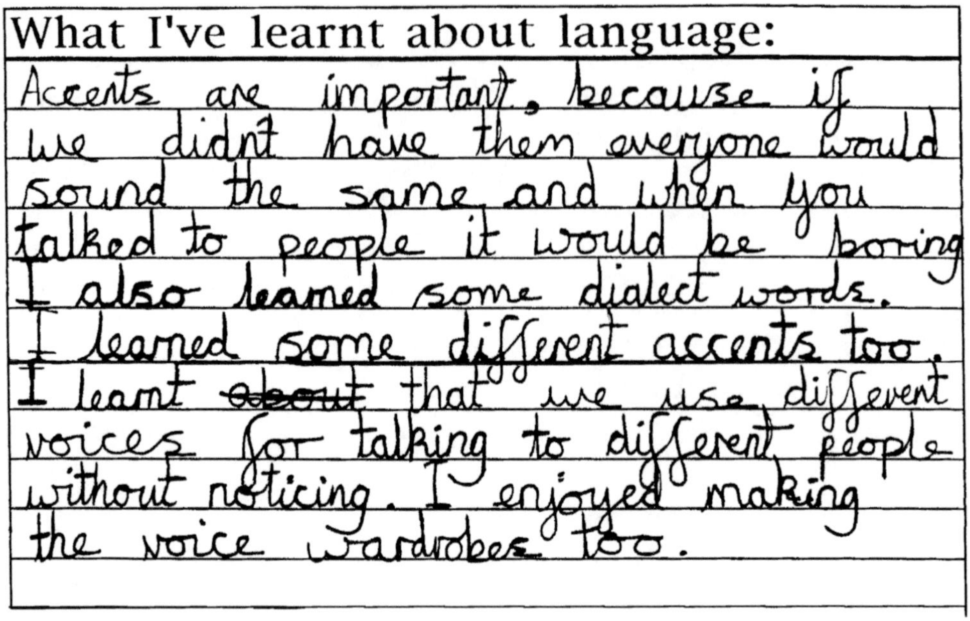

What I've learnt about language:

Accents are important, because if we didn't have them everyone would sound the same and when you talked to people it would be boring. I also learned some dialect words. I learned some different accents too. I learnt about that we use different voices for talking to different people without noticing. I enjoyed making the voice wardrobes too.

FIGURE 17.2 A short description of what one girl thought that she had learnt

Name: Age:

Are there any words in these sentences which don't sound right to you? If there are, please circle the words and write different ones underneath. If you think a sentence is OK, give it a tick at the side.

1. The stories what the children made up was all good.
2. I were that hungry I could of ate a bowl of cold rice pudding!
3. He were the handsomest of the two men.
4. The girls didn't know nothing about geography.
5. I couldn't of got here no quicker.
6. The boy done all his homework so we were wore out.
7. Me and my brother seen a flying saucer.

Do you know what these words mean? Have a guess if you're not sure.

ACCCENT   DIALECT   STANDARD ENGLISH

FIGURE 17.3 A diagnostic sheet

for by differences in the ability range in the two groupings. A clearer difference was observable in the responses to the second part of the diagnostic sheet, where, as expected, the project group showed much better understanding of the metalanguage. The children who had not taken part in the project, although they were following language schemes which dealt with these areas, were successful only in describing accent (59 per cent were able to define this term at least partly). There were no satisfactory responses to dialect; guesses included 'someone who shoots animals' and 'something to do with a phone'! Similarly, none of the non-project children demonstrated understanding of the term 'standard English'. There was a frequent tendency in the guesses recorded here to equate it with a 'high' standard and with assessment: 'a very good standard of English', 'hard English or original English or the best standard of English' and 'English up to your standard' were some examples.

The NC level descriptions do not mention pupils' knowledge or understanding of language, only their skills in using it in terms of speaking and listening and in writing. However, the project described certainly gave the participants the opportunity to demonstrate an observable development in their awareness of standard English, along the lines of the progression outlined in the NC for key stage 2:

- Level 2. They are beginning to be aware that in some situations a more formal vocabulary and tone of voice are used.

- Level 3. They are beginning to be aware of standard English and when it is used.

- Level 4. They use appropriately some of the features of standard English vocabulary and grammar.

- Level 5. They begin to use standard English in formal situations.

- Level 6. They are usually fluent in their use of standard English in formal situations.

More detailed profiles of pupils would, of course, be needed to set children's awareness and use of standard English in the context of wider knowledge about language, as revealed during a project such as that described above.

The project could certainly have been expanded and continued in order to develop language study further in the context of reading and writing, in addition to spoken language, which was the focus for most of the activities. Poetry of the kind used here would be an ideal vehicle for investigating and creating written texts which explore language use. (Further practical activities of this sort and suggestions for other rewarding texts and resources to use can be found in *Practical Ways to Teach Standard English and Language Study* (Lockwood 1998).)

Conclusion

Since this project was originally carried out, some of the constraints of the literacy hour in terms of its closely prescribed structure have been relaxed. It is now much more feasible for teachers to include extended language investigations in their dedicated literacy time. For example, *Grammar for Writing* (DfEE 2000), published as guidance on teaching sentence level NLS objectives, suggests practical whole-class activities through which standard English, dialect and also accent can be explored within the literacy hour (pp. 102–3 and pp. 148–9). *Grammar for Writing* is also clearer than the current NC in its guidance on how to talk about differences between standard English and dialects with children: 'in discussing these differences, the words 'standard' and 'non-standard' should be used, rather than 'correct/incorrect' or 'right/wrong', as the non-standard forms are 'correct' in casual speech' (p.102).

The use of ICT has also become much more widespread in primary schools in the past five years and this technology has great potential for use in the study of language structure and variation, as I suggested in my chapter 'Checking on the checker: using computers to talk about spelling and grammar' in the companion volume to this one, *The Articulate Classroom* (Goodwin 2001: 133–42). For example, it is now quite possible to investigate both language structure and language variation by accessing and searching an electronic corpus, or stored database of language samples, using concordancing software. Alison Sealey and Paul Thompson of the University of Reading, along with Mike Scott of the University of Liverpool, have recently researched the use of this approach to language study with KS2 pupils (an investigation into corpus-based learning about language in the primary school' can be found at www.rdg.ac.uk/slals/sst.htm).

The Primary National Strategy (PNS), successor to the NLS, has recently published *Speaking, Listening, Learning: Working with children in Key Stages 1 and 2* (DfES 2003), a much-needed document which shows how new objectives for speaking and listening can be integrated into activities in the literacy hour as well as other curriculum areas. Explicit links are made between the oral activities recommended and the existing NLS objectives for reading and writing. The suggested PNS speaking and listening objectives fit in well with the approach suggested in this chapter, for example in year 6, term 3: 'to listen for language variation in formal and informal contexts' and 'to identify the ways spoken language varies according to differences in context and purpose of use' (DfES 2003: 15, 17).

Another recent PNS publication, *Excellence and Enjoyment* (DfES 2003), has promoted innovation and creativity in schools, stating that: 'As well as giving them the essential tools for learning, primary education is about children experiencing the joy of discovery, solving problems, being creative...' (p.4). Investigating aspects of language in the ways suggested in this chapter will certainly involve problem-solving, discovery and an awareness of how the creativity of our language resides in its ever-fascinating diversity. It is no coincidence that poetry offers one of the best ways into the study of language, since good poems use the full range and variety of language structure and vocabulary. Alongside the essential development of children's skills in using language as a 'tool' should go a continuing exploration of language in all its variety as an expression of personal, social and cultural identity. And as *Excellence and Enjoyment*, uniquely amongst all the documents mentioned here, makes clear (p.4), children can also have fun doing this – it's now official!

References

Ahlberg, A. (1989) *Heard It In the Playground*. London: Viking Kestrel.

Bain, R., Fitzgerald, B. and Taylor, M. (1992) *Looking into Language*. London: Hodder and Stoughton.

Blackburne, L. (1994) 'English advisers in revolt', *Times Educational Supplement* 13 May.

Haynes, J. (1992) *A Sense of Words*. London: Hodder and Stoughton.

Department for Education and Employment (1998) *The National Literacy Strategy: Framework for Teaching*. London: DfEE.

Department for Education and Employment (1999) *The National Curriculum: Handbook for Primary Teachers in England*. London: DfEE.

Department for Education and Employment (2000) *Grammar for Writing*. London: DfEE.

Department of Education and Science (1984) *English from 5 to 16: Curriculum Matters 1*. London: HMSO.

Department of Education and Science (1986) *Responses to Curriculum Matters 1*. London: HMSO.

Department of Education and Science (1988) *Report of the Committee of Inquiry into the Teaching of the English Language* (The Kingman Report). London: HMSO.

Department of Education and Science (1989) *National Curriculum English for Ages 5–16* (The Cox Report). London: HMSO.

Department for Education and Skills (2003) *Speaking, Listening, Learning: Working with Children in Key Stages 1 and 2. Teaching Objectives and Classroom Activities*. London: DfES.

Department for Education and Skills (2003) *Excellence and Enjoyment*. London: DfES.

Goodwin, P. (ed.) (2001) *The Articulate Classroom*. London: David Fulton.

Kay, J. (1992) *Two's Company*. London: Blackie.

Lockwood, M. (1995) 'What's happening to knowledge about language in the primary years?' in *Developing Language and Literacy* B. Raban-Bisby (ed.). Stoke-on-Trent: Trentham Books.

Lockwood, M. (1998) *Practical Ways to Teach Standard English and Language Study*. Reading: Reading and Language Information Centre, The University of Reading.

Lutrario, C. (1993) *Exploring Language*. Aylesbury: Ginn.

McGough, R. and Rosen, M. (1979) *You Tell Me*. London: Kestrel.

Nichols, G. (1988) *Come on into My Tropical Garden*. London: A. and C. Black.

Palmer, S. and Brinton, P. (1988) *Mind Your Language*. Harlow: Oliver and Boyd.

Palmer, S. (1994) *The Longman Book Project: Language Books*. Harlow: Longman.

Rosen, M. (1974) *Mind Your Own Business*. London: Andre Deutsch.

Sealey, A., Thompson, P. and Scott, M. (2004) 'An investigation into corpus-based learning about language in the primary school' www.rdg.ac.uk/slals/sst.htm

18

'Hey, poetry!'

Chris Powling, with Sean O'Flynn

Introduction

In this article, children's author (and ex-primary teacher) Chris Powling celebrates and shares the work of a young London teacher, Sean O'Flynn, whose class of seven-year-olds, during the course of year, learnt to love poetry. By the end of their time together, regularly reading, learning by heart and writing poetry had provided the children with a strong foundation in the powerful use of words and the enjoyment of listening to the work of many and varied poetic voices. Powling is strongly committed to children having access to all kinds of writing, from the received classic repertoire (such as William Blake and Tennyson) through to the more child-orientated work of current writers (such as Michael Rosen and Grace Nichols) and a variety of voices (such as Valerie Bloom and Benjamin Zephaniah). This chapter encourages teachers to:

- Find and share a wide range of poetry that can be appreciated for different qualities: poems to make us laugh, cry, wonder and empathise
- Regularly share poems and promote learning poetry by heart
- Use poetry as a model for the children's own writing; to help them express their own ideas through crafted writing using their own figurative language

Above all, Chris Powling's message is that poetry should first and foremost be enjoyed. Sean O'Flynn's success with poetry in his classroom is a fine example of how the teacher's genuine enthusiasm for literature will inspire children beyond expectation.

'The Red Thing'

Let us begin with the perfect endorsement of a teacher's work. It is written inside the front cover of *Poetry Please!* (Causley 1996), a selection of poems from the popular BBC Radio 4 programme (Figure 18.1).

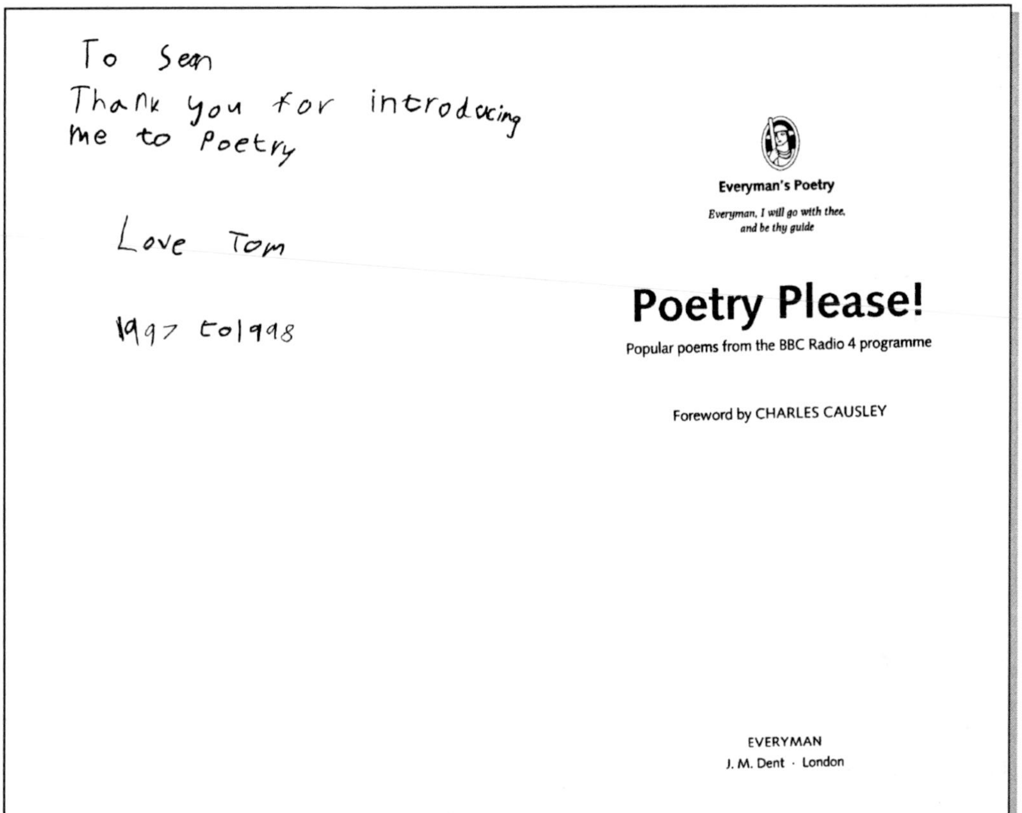

To Sean
Thank you for introducing
me to Poetry

Love Tom

1997 to 1998

Everyman's Poetry

*Everyman, I will go with thee,
and be thy guide*

Poetry Please!

Popular poems from the BBC Radio 4 programme

Foreword by CHARLES CAUSLEY

EVERYMAN
J. M. Dent · London

FIGURE 18.1 A perfect endorsement of a teacher's work

The inscription comes from Tom, aged 7, a pupil in an inner-city primary school. Sean O'Flynn is his teacher. At the end of their school year together, *Poetry Please!* was Tom's farewell present to Sean.

In its own modest way, it seems to me to represent something of a bullseye for Sean. No doubt he was not entirely surprised when it arrived. After all, Tom's enthusiasm for poetry must have been evident for some time – not least in his own writing:

'The red thing' by Tom

It looks like a
Hot man with leaves on top.
It is the red world.
It looks like they are green nits.
It is a red fat finger.
It's a soft cloud.
It feels bumpy.
It feels like hairs.
It smells like a sweet apple with angels.

It smells like a new book.
It is sweet like an orange.
It tastes like all the juices in the world.
It tastes like the juice in a orange
It sounds like it is saying 'Hey strawberry'.

For Tom, clearly, a poem is not just a red thing. It is a written thing, too (and with Sean as a teacher I bet he would spot the joke).

From the outset, then, Tom's encounters with poetry embrace both the consuming and the producing of it. His writing will reinforce and extend his reading...and his reading will do the same for his writing. To Tom, quite rightly, poets are not superior beings with a gift beyond any that he can lay claim to but simply people like himself who happen to have lived, read and written a little longer than he has. At this stage in his education, should anyone wish it otherwise?

In all that follows, then, the focus on how we can best create readers of verse among children of primary school age must not be taken as a downgrading of our complementary obligation to help them to become writers of verse as well. On the contrary, the two go together with a neat classroom-proof handiness that prose simply cannot match.

Back to reading, however – just how was Tom introduced to poetry as a year 2 pupil? Here, I shall hand over to Sean himself:

"You find a poem. You like it. But what can you do about it? Adrian Mitchell (1993) has some ideas in 'What to do when you find a poem you like':

Read it again
And write it
Learn it by heart
Recite it

What appeals to me about this view is its appreciation of poetry as a 'messy' activity. You can be as involved in a poem as in an experiment, a painting or a football match. The poem does not have to stay on the page, pristine and awaiting dissection. Learning it by heart, for example, can be a memorising task (and many children love doing that) but it may also come about as a consequence of having responded to the poem through dance or art or drama. Getting involved with the words in a creative way almost always results in 'knowing' the poem even better than sitting down and learning it by rote.

However, learning poetry by heart was at the core of poetry activities in my classroom. Every week the children were introduced to a 'poem of the week' which they would try to learn. The poem would be blown up on the photocopier and displayed in a frame next to the book from which it came. A handful of photocopies would be mounted on card, laminated and placed in the reading corner – an increasingly bulky area as the year went on.

I would read the poem aloud once or twice before letting the children see it. If I did not do this, the children were distracted from listening by trying to read the text as fast as they were hearing it. Then we might briefly discuss anything that the children noticed about the poem – rhyme, unusual vocabulary, and so on. We read the poem again – this time with the children able to see it. The children joined in if they could remember it, or read it, or both.

Those who felt confident enough would have a go at reciting the poem there and then; others would wait until they had taken their copy home to learn. As the week went on, more and more of the class would 'have' the poem by heart, the less confident being supported by the variety of recitations from teacher and classmates.

When reciting, all efforts were applauded, but precision was also required in order to show a respect to the poet. We discussed how hard poets had worked to select just those words we saw and considered how carefully the choice of word was made in order to mean exactly what was wanted.

Interspersed between recitals would be readings of many other poems, and lots of talk: Do you like this word? Why do you like that part? What can you say about the way that it sounds or looks? None of these questions is earth-shatteringly original. More important is the time allowed for consideration of them and of the children's responses. The more seriously their responses were taken, the more thoughtful they became.

Poetry appreciation and response are difficult to assess in a measurable way. In some ways children's appreciation relies on a teacher's confidence in this area, especially if they have not studied English themselves. However, what I observed more than justified my approach, in particular the welling-up of enthusiasm about poetry that never ebbed. Children often asked for copies of poems other than the poem of the week to take home and learn. Snatches of poetry were often heard being shouted out in the playground. 'Yes!' became the response to being told, 'We're going to look at some poems.' The classroom atmosphere, dictated by the poem, was joyous, silly, awestruck and solemn, but always committed.

This willingness to make poems their own by learning them, questioning them, reciting them, writing their own versions, and so on, grew markedly as the year went on. The children seemed to share Charles Causley's view of poems as 'a living organism . . . of which we make something new every day'."

A rich and varied diet

Sean's approach is as good a start as any, I would say. It is, of course, every teacher's duty to ensure that we encourage youngsters to read as wide a range as possible of the best verse that's available – and that is not exclusively limited to 'classics'. Being prescriptive about the poetry that children experience at school can only be counter-productive. Understandably, there is resistance from some colleagues to the 'snot-and-bogey-pie' variety of verse. A little of this goes a very long way with me, too. However, many excellent poets write in the voices of childhood, about topics of immediate concern to children and appeal to immature senses of humour. When children are introduced to a wide and varied range of poetry, it is most likely that they will appreciate the more taxing reads more, not less. The suggestion that children left free to make their own choices will invariably settle for 'smut' strikes me as little short of libellous – on the children themselves as well as on James Berry, Jackie Kay, Roger McGough, Grace Nicholls, Brian Patten and umpteen other writers who have done so much to make poetry a form that is as accessible and compelling today as any picture book or story. Their achievement has included some adjustment of the familiar poetic repertoire to incorporate new preoccupations, new modes of address and even new ways of 'reading' – on tape, on video or through public performance, for instance. An introduction to different voices, accents, dialects – languages even – can only enhance an appreciation of poetry. I would recommend introducing all children to the work of John Agard (1997), for example, as a matter of urgency.

> explain yuself
> wha yu mean
> when you say half-caste
> yu mean when light an shadow
> mix in de sky
> is a half-caste weather
> well in dat case
> England weather
> nearly always half-caste
> in fact some o dem cloud
> half-caste till dem overcast...

The more traditional anthologies will continue to offer old favourites and 'classics' to which all children should be introduced. 'Stopping by woods on a snowy evening' will always be a good idea, but we also need to be aware that the transforming power of poetry can operate much closer to home in, for example, the work of poets such as Peter Dixon:

> She's at the window again!
> Bug-eyed,
> Dressing gowned, and grey.
> 'See her!'
> squeal the Brownie pack returning from St Johns.
> 'See her!'
> chorus the boys returning from nowheremuch.
> And there she stares –

Tall
and gaunt
and hair unpinned . . . staring
   staring
   staring
staring beyond the silver slates
   of Stanley Street
   of Wilmer Way
and distant Arnos Grove.

Everything is welcome: Miss Hubbard, staring at the moon, or Michael Rosen's (1985) 'Babah and Zaida' or Kit Wright's (1981) 'Useful person' . . . or, indeed, all of the entirely successful attempts by recent children's poets to counteract Adrian Mitchell's (1993) famous pronouncement that the reason that most people ignore most poetry is because most poetry ignores most people.

Meanwhile, what about Sean Flynn's class? These days, with so much material to choose from, and so many literacy constituencies to satisfy, it is not easy to devise a programme of poems for youngsters such as Tom. Sean O'Flynn explains:

"My choice of poems for the class was guided by the simple principle: would they enjoy them? Of course, enjoyment should be part of all learning. However, I was also motivated by my own experiences of poetry at school where any potential for delight in words had been pushed aside by the pressure to analyse.

In the early part of the year it was vital for the children to experience success in learning poems by heart. At the beginning, many of the poems of the week were short, rhyming poems. Their first poem was by Michael Rosen:

Down behind the dustbin
I met a dog called Jim
He didn't know me
And I didn't know him

This is memorised almost as soon as it is heard. A very few repetitions and it is securely known. That was the point. The children became aware that they could deliberately and consciously learn a poem. This produced an excited buzz which was exactly the sort of association with poetry that I wanted them to have.

The poem which they memorised had also made them laugh – a very obvious indication of enjoyment. It might have been tempting to limit the range to humorous poetry; at least this would have guaranteed enjoyment, and this would not have been as limiting as it might sound. There is a huge range of 'funny' poems, from the vernacular humour of Michael Rosen (1981), through the word play of Ogden Nash, to the whimsicality of Eleanor Farjeon, and so on. All these poems are capable of serious consideration by children.

But, of course, children would be missing much of what poetry can do if they thought it could only be funny. So, from the start of the year I occasionally read them more serious poetry that I thought they could enjoy, such as 'The Charge of the Light Brigade'. I would often read these without probing for response. I am convinced that the expectation of enjoyment that had been built up around poetry in my class helped enormously when I did ask for a response to these more 'weighty' poems. This expectation made it easier for the children to concentrate on the parts that they liked, rather than get frustrated and distracted by the parts that they did not understand. They might not have got near to fully comprehending the poem, but they did understand that finding a poem difficult is not the end of the world, nor a reason to give up thinking about it. They learnt that it is legitimate to like parts of the poem, even if you are not sure what those sounds that you find so enticing actually mean."

Here is a selection of the poems shared by Sean and his class:

John Agard	'Where does laughter begin?'
Allan Ahlberg	'Please, Mrs Butler'
William Blake	'The tyger'
Valerie Bloom	'Duppy Jamboree'
Charles Causley	'Early in the morning'
Emily Dickinson	'A slash of blue'
Richard Edwards	'Keep well back'
Max Fatchen	'Isn't it amazing?'
Eleanor Farjeon	'Cats'
Robert Frost	'Stopping by woods on a snowy evening'
Julie Holder	'Chips'
Gerard Manley Hopkins	'Pied beauty'
Wes Magee	'What is the sun?'
John Masefield	'A ballad of John Silver'
Beverly McLoughland	'Lemon moon'
Spike Milligan	'On the Ning Nang Nong'
A. A. Milne	'When I was one'
Adrian Mitchell	'What to do when you find a poem you like'
Ogden Nash	'The duck'
Judith Nicholls	'Riddle'
Brian Patten	'Schoolitis'
Jack Prelutsky	'Black cat'
James Reeves	'Grim and gloomy'
Michael Rosen	'The Michael Rosen rap'
Christina Rossetti	'What is pink?
Willie Russell	'Sammy'
William Shakespeare	'Full fathom five...'

William Shakespeare	'The witches' song' (Macbeth)
Shel Silverstein	'Magical eraser'
Alfred, Lord Tennyson	'The eagle'
William Makepeace Thackeray	'A tragic story'
Kit Wright	'Acorn haiku'

No selection of poems will satisfy everyone, of course. Nor should we ignore the customised aspect of Sean's. His choices are directed at particular children in a particular situation as appraised by a particular classroom teacher. As such, outside commentators should know their place. It seems to have worked for Tom, however, and it is not hard to see why. The predominant tone is light hearted but there is considerable variety in style, tone and mood – including a smattering of non-contemporary verse.

The question of tone of voice arises here – always problematic for adult writers intending a child readership. In fact, the sort of adjustments and modulations that a children's poet makes are no less complex, subtle and necessary than those of a children's novelist... and we have Barbara Wall's (1991) study *The Narrator's Voice* to demonstrate that far more is required of the latter than the mere refusal to 'condescend'. So let us give the children a variety of voices to experiment with, reminding ourselves that poetry's capacity to be numinous, and spine tingling, is only one tool in its kit. It can be mad, bad and dangerous as well. Also, it can cope with reality, however harsh:

I have just discovered
a hole in the floor of my car.
I say 'my' car.
It was my mother's.
She died...

This is from Michael Rosen's superb low-key meditation on his mother's cancer in a poem called 'Bodywork'.

However, I would not suggest that Tom should read this yet. At some stage, nevertheless, he will realise the truth of Wallace Stevens's comment that poetry is 'a response to the daily necessity of getting the world right', a definition which is splendidly agnostic about the what and the how of doing this.

The emphasis on present-day poets lets the children know from the start that poetry is a living medium; also it provides up-to-date models for their own verse writing which are neither too formidable nor too bland. Also, real poetry takes risks. It involves the sort of playing that is a serious business. Tom found this out by getting to verbal grips with his strawberry.

Models – not templates

Sean gives this report on the writing of 'The red thing'.

"We started by looking at a Wes Magee poem which vividly describes the sun: 'The sun is an orange dinghy sailing across a calm sea' (from 'What is the sun?'). In discussing the poem, it felt natural to explain what metaphors and similes were. The best explanation I could provide was that they both made 'pictures with words'. We attempted a class composition about the moon in this style. The children found the idea very difficult at first but, after much discussion, eventually many interesting images emerged, including the following: 'The full moon is a capital O.' 'The moon is a light bulb in the sky.' 'It is a white boomerang thrown into the sky.'

In a later session, wanting to introduce imagery in another context, I asked the children to choose a classmate and to 'make pictures with words' about them. Many of the poems focused on physical appearance:

> Claire's hair is as soft as a rabbit's fur.
> Allan's ears are as round as a ball.
> When Jeffrey
> runs he
> is like
> a rhino.

Other examples used imagery to give a very perceptive view of their classmates' characteristics:

> Jack is a waterfall fastly falling off rocks.
> Elvin is a big black rock.

Jack was rather a blur at times. Elvin did have a rock-like calmness to his nature.

Some children took the idea of envisaging a friend as something else and really flew with it. This was written by a child with English as an additional language:

> Martin is calm as a sun
> He is floating in the sky…
> He has not got no hair
> He's got a yellow face.
> He has no body.
> He's boiling down at us.
> What's the matter with him?

When I introduced the strawberries as objects to write 'pictures in words' about, the children understood immediately. They still needed lots of opportunities to discuss ways of doing this, however. I want to emphasise the role of talk in the success of all these activities. Thinking, discussing and questioning together provided individuals with the confidence to value their own ideas. This had gone on all year, helping them to define what they had read, what they wanted to write, and what they had written.

The children were asked to think of at least three pictures of what the strawberry looked like, smelt like, felt like, sounded like (if they thought it made a sound), and finally – for obvious practical reasons – what it tasted like. At this stage it was important for the children to work on their own, in silence, interrupted only by my sharing with them examples of good work. Paired and group writing are vital, but so is the opportunity for children to work alone, not least to demonstrate to themselves what they are capable of. Silence allowed the children to concentrate intently on creating their own strawberry, seen afresh in different ways:

> It looks like a star
> with a beanstalk
> It is a
> face with freckles
> It feels like
> a dog's nose

The quality of the children's writing was vastly improved by their increasing grasp of redrafting skills. When their first draft was complete they worked in mixed-ability pairs. I asked them to listen to their partner's poem, to say something positive about it and to try to suggest something that could be changed. This could involve adding words, taking some away or switching some around. They then negotiated where slashes were needed to indicate line breaks. All these ideas were being regularly modelled for the children when we redrafted our class poems and in my conferences with individuals.

Tom was thrilled with the quality of his poem – as were all the children – and the class book that we made was a very popular read. Their poems show what children can do when given the time to look and think. I shall never look at a strawberry in the same way again."

Now we have come full circle. What, for me, is most pleasing about the response of Tom Hayes, aged seven, apprentice reader and writer in a school in Rotherhithe, is the likelihood that he has been inoculated already from the sort of anxiety about verse displayed by Dickens's Tony Weller in *The Pickwick Papers*. Charles Causley quotes this in his introduction to *Poetry Please!*

'Tain't in poetry, is it?'
'No, no,' replied Sam.
'Wery glad to hear it,' said Mr Weller. 'Poetry's unnat'ral; no man ever talked poetry 'cept a beadle on boxin' day, or Warren's blackin', or Rowland's oil, or some o' them low fellows; never you let yourself down to talk poetry, my boy.'

This is an opinion that Tom would not share. As for his future, who can tell? With luck, it will include Addlestrop and Arnos Grove, Omar Khayyam and Miss Hubbard, dads with gurgling stomachs and, yes, daffodils – together with more and more verse of his own. Tom is out of Sean's hands now. He has got a long reading and writing road ahead of him. Surely, however, he has made a wonderful start, in that it sounds like he is saying, 'Hey, poetry!'

References

Agard, J. (1997) *Get Back Pimple*. London: Puffin Books.

Causley, C. (1996) *Poetry Please!* London: J. M. Dent.

Dixon, P. (1988) *Grow Your Own Poems*. Basingstoke: Macmillan Education.

Mitchell, A. (1993) *Thirteen Secrets of Poetry*. London: Simon and Schuster.

Rosen, M. (1981) *Wouldn't You Like to Know*. London: Puffin Books.

Rosen, M. (1985) *Quick, Let's Get Out of Here*. London: Puffin Books.

Stevenson, R.L. (1995) *A Child's Garden of Verses*. London: Penguin Children's Books.

Wall, B. (1991) *The Narrator's Voice*. London: Macmillan.

Wright, K. (1981) *Hot Dog and Other Poems*. London: Puffin Books.

Index

accent 189–93, 197–8
Agard, John 204
Ahlberg, Allan 154, 174, 194
Ahlberg, Janet 174
analogies 118, 126
'and then' syndrome 107
Anglin, J. 149, 151
antisemitism 61–2
'autocorrect' facilities 159–60
autonomy 85, 130

Barrs, Myra xv, 31, 81
basic interpersonal
    communicative skills
    (BICS) 170
Bawden, Nina 59, 63–4, 68
Beck, J. 149–50
Belloc, Hilaire 49
Bereiter, C. 111
Bernstein, B. 130
Berry, James 204
bilingualism 140, 193
Blake, Quentin 25
Blake, William 200
'blank page' problem 106
Bloom, Valerie 200
Boden, M. 84
book share sessions 67–8
Browne, Anthony 176
Bruner, J. 14
Buchignani, Walter 58
Bullock Report (1975) xii

Burningham, John 7, 176

Cambourne, Brian 98
Campbell, R. 51
Carrie's War 59, 63–4
Causley, Charles 200,
    203, 209
Chambers, Aidan 6–7, 66–9
Chesterton, G.K. 194
Clark, M.M. 13
Clay, M.M. 13
Clicker4 software 164
cognitive/academic language
    proficiency (CALP) 170
cognitive psychology 91–2
Coles, M. 54
collaborative reading and
    writing 13–14, 122
Collier, V. 170
commas, use of 160
communicative competence
    170, 172
composition, process of
    18, 81–4, 88
comprehension 21, 39–41, 84
computers, use of 123–4,
    157–66, 198
Cork, V. xv, 81
Cox Report (1989) 129, 190
creativity xv, 66, 80–4, 88, 99
Cummins, J. 170–2
Curriculum Matters 189–90

'days-of-the-week' text
    structure 102
de Jong, Meindert 58
demonstrations of reading
    and writing 14, 17
dialect 190–3, 197–8
Dickens, Charles 209
dictionaries 150–1, 169
display of children's work 8
Dixon, Peter 204–5
drama 45, 82–3, 88, 173,
    179–88
Dupasquier, Philippe 176

Edwards, V. 169
Egan, Roland 19
English as an additional
    language (EAL), teaching
    of 167–76
enjoyment of reading 25–32,
    37–8, 55, 198–200, 205–6
enlarged texts 13–15
Entwistle, J. 51, 54
Essex Writing Project 84
Exeter Extending Literacy
    (EXEL) project 90, 106, 108
experiential learning 180, 184
'explanation' genre 109
explicit teaching 84, 99,
    141, 170

Farjeon, Eleanor 205